A Fly-Fisher's Guide to

Saltwater Naturals

and their Imitation

George V. Roberts Jr.

Illustrations by Arolina K̶̶̶̶

Ragged Mountain Press

Camden, Maine

FOR MY FATHER

Ragged Mountain Press

A Division of The McGraw·Hill Companies

10 9 8 7 6 5 4 3 2 1

Copyright © 1994, 2000 Ragged Mountain Press, an imprint of McGraw-Hill, Inc.

All rights reserved. The publisher takes no responsibility for the use
of any of the materials or methods described in this book, nor for the
products thereof. The name "Ragged Mountain Press" and the
Ragged Mountain Press logo are trademarks of McGraw-Hill, Inc.
Printed in the United States of America.

The Library of Congress has cataloged the hardcover edition as follows:

Library of Congress Cataloging-in-Publication Data
Roberts, George V., Jr.
    A fly-fisher's guide to saltwater naturals and their imitation /
George V. Roberts, Jr. ; illustrations by Arolina Kehoe.
    Includes bibliographical references (p. 156) and index.
    ISBN 0-07-053166-8
    1. Saltwater fly fishing. 2. Flies, Artificial. 3. Marine
fishes. 4. Marine invertebrates. I. Title.
    SH456.2.R63 1994
799. 1'6—dc20   94-13952
                                          CIP

The ISBN for the paperback edition is 0-07-135325-9

Questions regarding the content of this book should be addressed to
Ragged Mountain Press
P.O. Box 220
Camden, ME 04843

Questions regarding the ordering of this book should be addressed to
The McGraw-Hill Companies
Customer Service Department
P.O. Box 547
Blacklick, OH 43004
Retail Customers: 1-800-262-4729
Bookstores: 1-800-722-4726

✪ *A Fly-Fisher's Guide to Saltwater Naturals and Their Imitation*
is printed on recycled paper containing a minimum of 50% total
recycled paper with 10% postconsumer deinked fiber.

Printed by Quebecor Printing, Fairfield PA
Photography by William Thuss
Design and production by Dan Kirchoff
Edited by J. R. Babb, Kathy Newman, and Thomas McCarthy

CONTENTS

Part Three: Directory of Fly Patterns............101

LIST OF PLATES

Note: page numbers refer to the text description. Plates 1-8 run after page 52. Plates 9-24 run after page 116.

vii

FOREWORD

George Roberts impressed me the first time we spoke. He was determined, methodical, and relentless in his quest to ferret out and verify obscure facts concerning color vision in gamefish. George wanted to know almost unrecallable details about the research I did over a quarter century ago in preparing my manuscript for *Through the Fish's Eye*. That book (long out of print) was the first to correlate scientific facts about fish behavior to recreational angling.

A Fly-Fisher's Guide to Saltwater Naturals and Their Imitation takes the reader light years beyond where we left off. This book is the culmination of a laborious effort to pull together the essentials on a vital subject. The clocks seem to stand still when one wades through thousands of pages of scientific literature (dull reading at best) followed by countless interviews and conversations.

The route may have been tedious, but the results burst with exciting discoveries. Through the pages of this book you'll understand gamefish behavior, gain insight into the prey on which these predators survive, and become familiar with the fly patterns that imitate the essential food sources. Armed with this critical information, every day on the water will become more meaningful, and you'll begin to comprehend the subtleties that govern a fish's life cycle.

Library shelves are filled with books that discuss the diets of trout and salmon, and the fly patterns that counterfeit these natural foods. Until George Roberts set his keenly analytical mind and innate curiosity to this monumental task, no one had done for the saltwater fly-fisher what countless others have done for our freshwater counterparts. This is the definitive work, and it will stand unchallenged well into the future. For anyone and everyone who picks up a flyrod and with hunks of hair and hackle wound on a hook wages war against marine denizens, it is an absolute essential.

A Fly-Fisher's Guide to Saltwater Naturals and Their Imitation looms as a classic, the standard reference on the subject. It is not a volume to be read once and buried in the bookcase. This is a working tool to be used repeatedly and frequently. Reading it only once has already expanded my understanding of fish behavior, prey species, and fly patterns. I know it will do the same for you.

Mark Sosin

ACKNOWLEDGMENTS

No work such as this can be written from one person's experience. I therefore must acknowledge the contributions of the many people without whose efforts this book never would have been possible.

All the researchers, both named and unnamed, whose important works—a number of lifetimes, cumulatively—make up the scientific content of this material, and all the anglers, both present and past, on whose writings I've drawn.

My dear friend Paula Welch, whose keen eye and feel for the language were invaluable during manuscript preparation.

Dr. Milton Love, Associate Research Biologist at the Marine Science Institute, University of California in Santa Barbara, who offered much valuable criticism on Part One of the manuscript, answered many questions, and supplied much valuable information, and who also collected most of the West Coast specimens from which the artwork of this book was painted.

David Nelson of the National Oceanic and Atmospheric Administration, and Steven Stone, formerly of that organization, who supplied much important information, both published and in-preparation, on estuarine species.

Dr. William McFarland, Director of the Wrigley Marine Science Center in Pasadena, California, who answered a number of questions on fish vision.

Shirley Zeiba of the interlibrary-loan office at Bridgewater State College, who obtained for me many valuable materials not on the shelves.

Dave Vatter of Atlantic Marine Supply in Miami, who collected many of the Florida and Gulf Coast species.

My brother Rick, who helped me collect some of the Northeast species.

Al Werthen, who gave me free rein with his FAX machine.

All the anglers who contributed generously in fly patterns and information, with whom it was my honor to have spoken and corresponded.

Special thanks to Carl Richards, who supplied much valuable information and materials on Southeastern and Gulf Coast species, and to Bill Peabody, who dressed many fly patterns to specification. Thanks also to Debra Brehm at *Fly Fisherman*, who helped me locate many of these people.

Jim Babb, my editor, Tom McCarthy, Dan Kirchoff, and the rest of the staff at Ragged Mountain Press.

INTRODUCTION

At this writing, there are a handful of tactical saltwater fly-fishing books on the market, and a countless number of books on fly-dressing—to the best of which I have little to add. There remains, however, a large gap in this literature. Compared with the vast amount that has been written about the foods upon which freshwater gamefishes feed, information on saltwater forage species is virtually nonexistent.

This book is an attempt to narrow that gap.

All gamefishes, from striped bass to sharks, have their preferred or primary prey, and all gamefishes undergo periods of selective feeding. If you've never experienced this, it's because you haven't put in the time. Flail the salt long enough and you'll meet with feeding fish that are indifferent to your offerings; or, more frustrating, your fly that took several fish five minutes ago no longer gets a look. During such times, a knowledge of selective feeding at its various levels of specificity and a knowledge of the fish's desired prey could be critical to your success.

This book was written for those times.

The text is divided into three parts. Part One is an overview of fish predation as it relates to angling with artificials. Although numerous such overviews have been written, I've read none I felt was adequate. Many, I've found, are overly simplistic and often riddled with erroneous observations and unfounded biases. And the best of these overviews failed to go as deeply into some areas of the subject as I would have liked.

To compile this overview, I sifted through a mountain of scientific literature—and picked the brains of a few experts—on every subject from vertebrate vision and perception to fish physiology to ethology (animal behavior) to ecology to neurophysiology. My research turned up a wealth of information of interest to the angler that had been virtually untouched by previous writers in the field. This information allowed me to bring the subject of fish predation as a whole into better perspective, and I hope it does the same for the reader.

Part Two summarizes the life histories of the major forage species (and a few specialty ones)—fishes, squids, crustaceans, and annelid worms—found in the Western Hemisphere. It concentrates on information of interest to the angler: distribution and abundance, habitats and habits, migrations and movements, spawning times and areas, physical descriptions, what they eat, and what eats them. These summaries are supplemented with color plates of representative or important species (of great value, I think, to anyone who wishes to dress imitations of them and also for identification in the field).

Part Three, the Directory of Fly Patterns, is a roster of representative work of some of this country's most knowledgeable saltwater fly-fishers and fly-dressers, from the early days of the game through recent innovations in tying styles and materials. For many of the patterns, I've tried to get some background information from their originators that the reader might find of value: how the patterns originally came about; insights into the designs; suggestions on how to fish the flies effectively. A word or two of practical advice can go a long way on the water, and some of the anglers' insights are as valuable as their patterns.

This is not a beginner's book in that it assumes a knowledge of saltwater fly-fishing and fly-dressing. However, this is a beginner's book in that an understanding of fish predation and of the forage upon which your quarry preys should be behind your very first cast.

To learn the prerequisite skills of saltwater fly-fishing and fly-dressing, you'll have to read elsewhere—and put in a lot of time. Lefty Kreh's *Fly Fishing in Salt Water* and Lou Tabory's *Inshore Fly Fishing* delve as deeply into the tactical aspects of the sport as any books in print today. Tom McNally's *Complete Book of Fly Fishing* is an excellent all-around text, and is perhaps the first book you should read if you've never fly-fished. There are also a few specialty books in print, such as Randall Kaufmann's *Bonefishing with a Fly*, and a number of specialty books in the works.

To learn how to tie flies for salt water, you'll find any of the fly-dressing books listed in the bibliography a good place to start; all are well worth reading. My own first book of fly-tying was the A.S. Barnes edition of J. Edson Leonard's *Flies* (now published by Lyons & Burford). That this book is still in print after more than forty years is testament to its enduring relevance. Also, Frank Wentink's *Saltwater Fly Tying* is a good instructional introduction to various techniques used for a broad range of saltwater fly styles. No book, however, can teach you everything you need to know. True innovators read the books, and then throw them away. Carrie Stevens, it is said, never read a book on fly-tying. But none of us is Carrie Stevens; read whatever you can get your hands on and take from it what you will.

The intent of this book is not to found a religion of specific imitation for salt water. No book will ever do that, just as none has done it for fresh water. Twenty years have passed since the publication of Ernest Schwiebert's *Nymphs*—nearly forty since his *Matching the Hatch*—yet the Woolly Worm and the Royal Coachman in all their variations are alive and well, and still catching fish. No matter which flies you use for salt water, knowledge of fish predation and gamefish forage is important. That is what this book is about.

The most exhaustive work on any subject in nature is still only an introduction, and this book is no different. But if you take away only a tenth as much from reading it as I did from researching and writing it, I think you'll consider it well worth your investment of time and money.

Some Notes on the Text

Throughout my research I have come across a number of discrepancies regarding various prey species. These discrepancies have usually pertained to distribution, color, and maximum sizes, but have occasionally involved such things as spawning times. In all cases, I've tried to get a consensus; failing that, I went with the information that was most up to date or that made the most sense to me. In most cases, the discrepancies were so minute that it is unlikely they would make any difference for our purposes.

Latin binomials and trinomials are used for identification not because I have a penchant for Latin, but because it is the only sure way we have, when discussing various species, to speak on the same level. If a common name is too localized, it is impossible to know what is meant; also, some species belonging to different families share common names. To help with identification, I have included all common names of species that I have found.

In Part One, I define all prey features that might elicit predatory behavior in gamefishes as *key stimuli*. In the literature of ethology, key stimuli are more commonly referred to as *sign stimuli*. I chose the former term simply because it sounds better within the context of our subject. These two terms are sometimes used interchangeably in ethological literature with the term *releasers*—though this is not always correct and sometimes creates confusion. By definition, a releaser is a bodily feature or a behavior pattern of an animal that has evolved to elicit specific behavior in another animal, usually one of the same species (for instance, the spawning colors of certain fish or the mating call of a bird). Within the context of predation, key stimuli differ from releasers in that the behavior elicited is not intended. That a particular feature of a prey triggers predatory behavior in its enemy is merely a side effect—the feature (key stimulus) is not intended to signal predators.

Much of the information on estuarine species was drawn from a number of published studies supervised by the National Oceanic and Atmospheric Administration (abbreviated NOAA in the text).

PART I

PREDATION AND IMITATION

Gamefishes are predators. To survive, they must capture and eat other living things. In salt water, these prey species consist primarily of fishes, but also include invertebrates such as squids, worms, and crustaceans. Predators and prey alike have been molded in both body and behavior by millions of years' participation in the fight for survival. The process of evolution has selected for greater hunting efficiency among predators, as well as more effective defense mechanisms and behaviors among prey species. As the angler enters the fish's world (by way of rod and line and feathered steel) in an attempt to induce acts of predation, a knowledge of predation's mechanics is essential to consistent success.

Vision and Perception of Gamefishes

Although gamefishes possess all five senses, they hunt primarily by sight. Given the interference encountered by light traveling through water, however, the quality of underwater images is comparatively poor.

Light is luminous energy existing in waves of various lengths. Light waves visible to humans range in length from $\frac{1}{33,000}$ to $\frac{1}{67,000}$ inch. Wavelengths outside this range, such as ultraviolet or infrared rays, are invisible. Colors are associated with various wavelengths, and white light comprises all wavelengths. This can be demonstrated by passing white light through a prism, which separates the waves into the spectrum of colors. When white light hits an object, some of its waves are absorbed into that object. Those that are not absorbed are reflected. What is perceived as the object's color, then, is that part of the spectrum of light that is *not* absorbed. Light-colored objects absorb very little luminous energy, while objects that appear dark absorb much of it. This is why light-colored surfaces such as concrete stay cooler on a bright day than do darker surfaces such as asphalt.

Water, too, absorbs light energy. This is the main reason the upper column of a lake in summer is warmer than its depths. The longer wavelengths, the reds, are the first to be absorbed; even in clear water red light disappears almost completely at a depth of 30 feet. The reds are followed in descending order by the oranges, yellows, and greens. Blue, which exists at the shortest visible wavelength, is the last to be absorbed. At great depths, the ocean takes on a blue-green appearance because those are the only light waves that can penetrate that far.

Color penetration is of little concern to the angler, however. The 12 percent of orange light that remains at a depth of 30 feet is more than adequate for orange-colored objects to be perceived *as* orange, even during the low illumination of twilight. Of greater impediment to underwater visibility are the suspended particles and organisms (silt, detritus, plankton) that catch light and reflect it in all directions. The result of this scattering of light is that even in very clear natural water, visibility is limited to about 40 feet (though in tropical waters, divers regularly report visibility of up to 100 feet). In turbid or muddy water, visibility might be less than 3 feet.

As far as predation is concerned, the function of the fish's eye is to work within these restrictions to collect sufficient light to resolve images into forms, movements, features, and sometimes colors that can be associated with food.

Light entering the fish's eye passes through the *cornea* (the outer covering) and *pupil* (aperture) and is focused by the *lens*. Unlike the eye of higher vertebrates, which focuses the image by flexing the lens, the fish's eye shifts focus by altering the distance between the lens and the *retina* (the cup-shaped posterior of the eye that receives the image produced by the lens). This is similar to the way a camera focuses.

While the projection of a precisely focused image onto the retina is a prerequisite to good vision, it is only the first step. The retina is composed of four interlocking layers of cells. The actual photoreceptor cells of the retina—the *rods* and *cones*—are found at the second layer, called the *receptor layer*. Rod cells are extremely sensitive to light, but produce poorly defined images with almost no detection of color. Cone cells are only about one-thirtieth as sensitive to light as are rod cells, but they detect colors in varying hues (gradations) and give good resolution for detail. Visual acuity, then, is further governed by the concentration of visual cells per unit area of retina. The finer the "grain" of the retina, the better able the fish is to distinguish detail. But grain alone does not signify acuity. One species of eel-pout, for example, has an extremely high concentration of visual cells—approximately 813,400 per square millimeter—but only about 3,400 of these are cones. This tells us that the eel-pout's vision is best suited to conditions of low illumination.

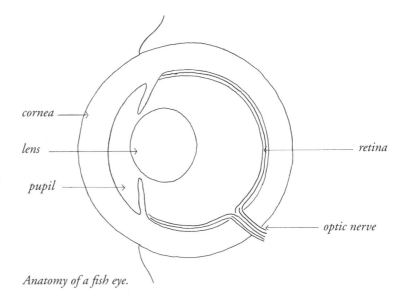

Anatomy of a fish eye.

Retinas having large numbers of cone cells characterize fishes that feed in well-lighted environments and that can distinguish particular food types from a variety. Many herrings, which are generally regarded as filter-feeders, are able to feed selectively from among a mass of plankton.

It has often been written that sharks have no cone cells and therefore do not possess color vision. This is untrue. Color vision is widespread throughout the sharks, including the two most popular game species: the mako (which has a cone-rod ratio of 1:10) and the great white (which has an even higher cone-rod ratio of 1:4).

In humans, most cone cells are densely packed into a pit-like area of the retina called the *fovea*, with all remaining cones close by. Humans move their eyes so that the image of the object they want to examine most clearly is projected onto the foveal area. Few fishes have pit-like foveae, however, and great variations in the distribution of cone cells are found among the species. In some species, the cones are irregularly sprinkled across the retina, while in others there is a high-density area where the cones occur in greater percentage. The retinas of many advanced predatory species are structured in double-cone formations that are evenly distributed and aligned in rows. Decentralization of the cone cells results in a loss of acuity, but it extends sensitivity to prey over a greater portion of the fish's visual field.

The rods and cones are backed up by two layers of ganglion cells—neurons that relay visual information to the brain via the optic nerve. Some ganglia are specialized to respond only to certain types of information (referred to as *feature detectors* in the scientific literature). So we can

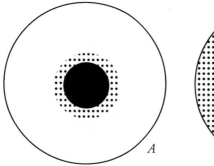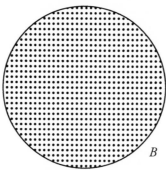

Cone-cell pattern in the human retina (A) and cone-cell pattern in a fish retina (B). Cone cells perceive detailed forms and colors. In humans, most cone cells are densely packed into the center of the retina, allowing for good visual acuity (perception of detail) within a small portion of the visual field. The fish's cone cells are distributed throughout its retina (distribution varies depending on species). Decentralization of cone cells results in a loss of acuity in fishes, but it extends sensitivity to motion and contrast over a greater portion of the fish's visual field, thus making predacious fish highly efficient at detecting prey. (Courtesy of Hierographics, Weymouth, Massachusetts)

see that the numbers and kinds of ganglia supporting the receptor cells are as important to good vision as are the numbers and kinds of receptors. In short, visual acuity is directly proportional to overall retinal complexity.

Few *teleost* fishes (bony fishes: all fishes except sharks and rays) can regulate the amount of light entering the eye. Instead, two adaptations within the teleost retina allow the eyes of many species to function effectively both during the day and at night. First, the rod and cone cells of fishes have the ability to alter their length. For instance, when the sun rises, the rod cells contract, receding from the light, and the cone cells expand forward. During this time, pigment granules move in to surround the supersensitive rods, shielding them from excessive light.

Pigment migration can take up to an hour, while movement of the visual cells is accomplished much more quickly. These mechanisms are not triggered by the rising and setting of the sun, but rather operate on a biological clock, adhering to a regular schedule even if the fish is kept in total darkness for days at a time.

Unlike the eyes of most teleosts, the irises of *elasmobranchs* (cartilaginous fishes: sharks and rays) contract in bright light, producing a reasonably sharp image at any distance.

Sensitivity to light is essentially a chemical reaction. Light hitting the retina causes a chemical decomposition of photosensitive pigments within the rods and cones; this chemical change stimulates the receptor cells, which send out a series of nerve impulses to the brain—the ultimate location of vision.

One reason color vision evolved in fishes was to assist them in detecting prey. To a color-blind animal, even a blue object is difficult to detect against a yellow background if both object and background are of equal light intensity. Color vision enhances the contrast between objects and their backgrounds.

At least three types of cone cells are necessary for trichromatic vision (what is considered normal color vision in humans): one cone type to detect each of the three primary colors. Shallow-water fishes have the full spectrum of light available to them, so it is to their advantage to be able to differentiate among a wide range of colors. Most shallow-water fishes have at least two types of cone cells and some possess all three. Certain fish have demonstrated the ability to distinguish as many as twenty-four color hues, ranging from the red end of the spectrum to the blue, and overall fish can see farther into the violet region than can humans. Despite this, research into the visual pigments of fishes indicates that the primary function of color vision in predacious fishes is to highlight prey against various backgrounds; discerning spectral compositions of prey is secondary. Therefore, precise replication of the colors of prey is perhaps less critical than some anglers contend. We'll explore this further when we discuss selective feeding.

Such is the basic design of the fish's eye, though evolution has produced a multitude of specialized modifications. For instance, the bonefish's adipose eyelid—made of transparent fatty tissue with a pinhole aperture centered over the pupil—protects the eye while the fish is rooting in the sand or mud without obscuring its vision. (Some scientists speculate that the tissue also polarizes light.) A few fast-swimming species such as wahoo have a similar adaptation that serves a different function: The wahoo's adipose eyelid is shaped to lessen water turbulence around the eye, thereby improving vision at high speeds.

Given the diversity of eye structures among various fish species, we can make few generalizations regarding their vision. We can reasonably conclude, however, that the fish's eye is suited primarily to detect motion and contrast; it is deficient in perceiving detail. The major shortcoming of the vertebrate eye is its lack of versatility: sensitivity at the price of acuity, and vice versa. Although we might regard the fish's vision as inferior to our own, it is well suited to its environment. A fish with human vision would be an inept predator under dim light or poor visibility—conditions endemic under water.

Despite our knowledge of the mechanics of vision, we know little of how the brain actually processes and uses visual information. Far from being instruments that receive and project accurate representations of the world, the eye and brain systematically filter out some pieces of visual information while in effect exaggerating others. Which information is retained or omitted depends on the animal species. Each species perceives its environment differently, and in a way that most benefits its survival. Even for humans, perception is a constructive, interpretive process upon which visual information is only one influence (if this were not the case, no human would ever be shot for a deer). Given the design of the fish's visual apparatus coupled with its prereptilian brain, it is impossible for us to know what a fish sees, and it is fundamentally incorrect to liken its vision to our own. Magazine articles on fish vision that include photographs depicting how such and such a fly pattern looks to a fish are misleading. We will never be able to see through a fish's eye as the fish does. Even if it were possible to fit us with a fish's eyes, along with the supporting nerves, we would still not see as the fish does because we lack the fish's brain. Rather, we must look to the fish's behavior and observe how it responds to various stimuli to speculate about what goes on inside its head. And even then we cannot know for certain; our observations can, however, provide us with information useful to our angling.

Secondary Sensory Apparatus

Although the fish's actual attack is ultimately triggered by visual stimuli, its senses of smell and hearing can play crucial roles in leading it to that instance.

As we might expect with such restrictions on their vision, most predacious fishes have a highly developed sense of smell. In most species the olfactory detector is arranged in essentially the same way. The fish's snout has two nostrils, each leading to a separate olfactory chamber lined with primary sensory cells. Water flows into the chamber by the forward movement of the fish, by pumping, or by the action of cilia lining the chamber. Chemical substances dissolved in the water contact the sensory cells, which send impulses to the brain via the olfactory nerves. Most gamefishes have four nostrils—two on each side of the head, placed one behind the other—or an equivalent modification. This arrangement allows water to enter the forward nostrils and exit the rearward ones, creating a fast, continuous flow over the sensory cells.

The olfactory sense in some species is so acute that it can detect single molecules of particular substances. The skin of some fishes contains cells that secrete alarm substances if the skin is damaged, alerting other members of the species. The drawback to such a defense mechanism is that it alerts predators as well. (Which makes you wonder when some enterprising chemist is going to package Fish Terror in an aerosol.)

With such sensitivity, it is no surprise that fish use smell to track food even at considerable distances. Anglers take advantage of this ability by chumming with ground fish, mollusks, and fish oils to lure fish within casting distance.

Although water is a poor conductor of light, it is an excellent conductor of sound. Sound travels five times faster in water than it does in air. The fish makes full use of this with a twofold auditory system consisting of ears and a lateral line—both of which (but more so the latter) the angler can use to advantage.

The fish's ears are buried inside its head, closed off from the water, and lack eardrums. Despite this, the fish is quite sensitive to sound waves contacting its body. In some species, the ears are directly connected to the swim bladder. The membrane of the bladder picks up vibrations from the water, resonates them within the bladder, and transmits them to the ears. The fish's ears can detect far-field sounds, which are created by waves that cause water molecules to vibrate in place. These waves can travel many miles; the fish's ears equip it with long-range hearing. An example of a far-field sound is the humming of a boat's engine heard underwater at a couple of hundred yards.

The detection of near-field sounds (low-frequency waves that cause a displacement of water molecules) falls to the lateral line. Low-frequency waves are of the type created by surface disturbances and underwater movement in general, and have an

The lateral-line system in fishes detects low-frequency waves created by the movements of prey, sometimes at considerable distances. Popping bugs mimic the distress actions of wounded baitfish and can give anglers a chance at fish outside casting range. Bulky streamers that "push" water create subsurface waves better than do slimly dressed flies, and are more effective when visibility is poor.

effective range of about 50 feet. The lateral-line system consists of a row of water-filled channels extending from head to tail along both sides of the fish. Within the channels are groups of hair cells. Sound vibrations and water pressures outside the fish move the water in the channels, which in turn moves the highly sensitive hair cells. The sensory neurons of these hair cells send signals to the brain. The functions of the lateral line include the detection of water currents and the navigation of stationary objects. The lateral line also enables the fish to discern the general direction and approximate size of a moving object at a distance of about 20 feet, or pinpoint its position at about 5 feet. The value of such apparatus to predator and prey alike is obvious, particularly under conditions of poor visibility.

In most cases, it is necessary for an angler to place imitations within the fish's field of vision, yet certain types of imitations are designed to appeal primarily to the fish's auditory senses. The surface disturbance created by popping bugs mimics the distress actions of wounded baitfish and can sometimes give anglers a chance at a fish outside casting range. Subsurface disturbance is increased by bulking up the imitation to displace, or "push," more water. This is often done by adding a heavily wound hackle collar to the pattern. Some commercial popping bugs are equipped with small rattles similar to those used in plastic worms. These rattle poppers emit far-field sounds as well as near-field sounds, and likely can be heard by fish from a greater distance. Similarly, bead-chain flies, which whistle during casting, produce a corresponding sound under water when retrieved, enhancing the pattern's auditory effect.

The fish's two remaining senses, taste and touch, are perhaps the least important to the angler using flies or lures. With taste buds both outside and inside the mouth, fish do have a good sense of taste, and it likely plays a major role in the ingestion of dead bait and the rejection (after the strike) of artificials. The fish's tactile sense, as it pertains to feeding, is less well known, though many anglers argue that a fish will hold on to an artificial longer if it feels soft or natural. Whatever the case, the angler using artificials must set the hook before the fish gets wise.

Prey Recognition

Many anglers believe that if fish could see as well as humans, they would never strike at our imitations—but this belief misrepresents the case. That a fish will strike at a crude minnow imitation or an outlandish attractor pattern says nothing of its visual capabilities; it is wrong to conclude that the fish is unable to perceive any of the details of its prey. On the contrary, many fishes have demonstrated the ability to discriminate well enough to distinguish prey from non-prey species and to exercise specific hungers or prey preferences. That these same fish often strike at a simple hunk of hair lashed to a hook, or at a fly quite unlike anything they have ever seen, presents something of an enigma—one deserving of our scrutiny.

There is good evidence to indicate that predacious fish are instinctively equipped to recognize potential prey by only a few rudimentary aspects. This suggests that the fish does not, at the most elementary level, recognize a specific prey as such, but perhaps recognizes only a category of prey whose forms are similar within that category, such as fishes, worms, or shrimps. Responding to general aspects allows the fish to include a wide variety of prey in its diet—important in a highly competitive environment in which the availability of various prey is in constant flux. Survival depends on adaptability; a fish that fails to exploit opportu-

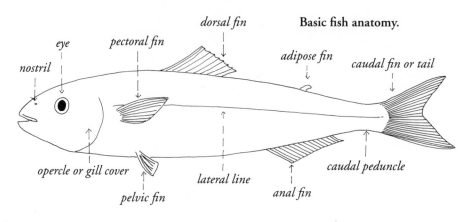

Basic fish anatomy.

nostril · eye · pectoral fin · dorsal fin · adipose fin · caudal fin or tail

opercle or gill cover · pelvic fin · lateral line · anal fin · caudal peduncle

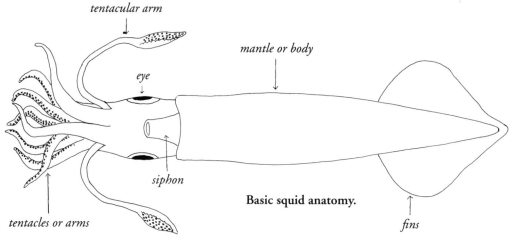

tentacular arm · mantle or body · eye · siphon · tentacles or arms · **Basic squid anatomy.** · fins

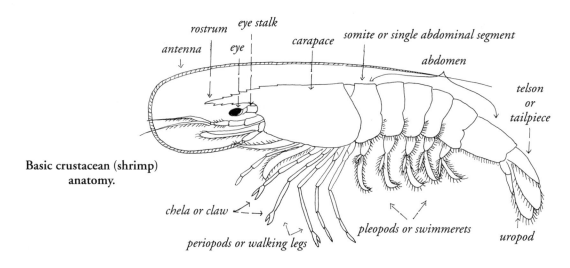

antenna · rostrum · eye stalk · eye · carapace · somite or single abdominal segment · abdomen · telson or tailpiece

Basic crustacean (shrimp) anatomy.

chela or claw · periopods or walking legs · pleopods or swimmerets · uropod

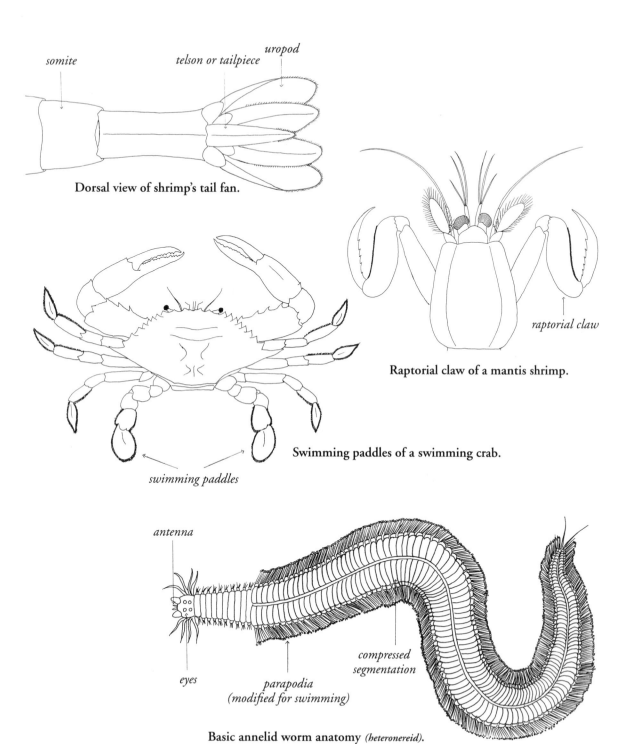

somite

telson or tailpiece

uropod

Dorsal view of shrimp's tail fan.

raptorial claw

Raptorial claw of a mantis shrimp.

Swimming paddles of a swimming crab.

swimming paddles

antenna

eyes

parapodia
(modified for swimming)

compressed
segmentation

Basic annelid worm anatomy *(heteronereid).*

nities probably won't live long. So even after becoming familiar with a number of specific prey, the fish continues to react to general aspects.

Form, however, is only one component of prey recognition. For example, a frog will strike at small moving objects, which for the frog almost always turn out to be insects. Surrounded by freshly killed insects, though, the frog will starve. The frog's visual apparatus and brain are wired in such a way that it perceives and reacts only to features of its environment important to its survival; everything else is blocked out. Motion is an important prey-recognition feature for many predators, including saltwater gamefishes, nearly all of whose prey display *some* motion.

Like the frog that snaps at small moving objects, the fish that strikes at a crude minnow imitation or attractor pattern is not reacting to the entire fly, only to a small portion of it. In the language of ethology, a cue that elicits a certain behavior in an animal is called a *key stimulus* (more commonly called a *sign stimulus*). For instinctive behavior, the response is elicited not by a multitude of cues, but by only a few essential ones. In the case of the crude minnow imitation and the attractor pattern, the visual stimuli of form and motion are the only cues necessary to trigger an attack from the fish. Despite what it might be capable of perceiving, the fish strikes "blindly" at the imitation. We might liken this to a deer hunter who mistakenly shoots at a moving patch of white cloth. In the same way, the angler attempts to get the fish to "misfire."

As with the deer hunter, the fish's willingness to strike at a crude imitation has much to do with its predisposition. A foraging fish expects to see prey just as a deer hunter expects to see a deer. In general, hunger heightens the fish's awareness of forms (objects) that are potential prey, and broadens the range of forms it is willing to regard as prey.

This is as good an explanation as we can offer as to why fish take our nondescript or bizarre-looking artificials, all of which can be broadly categorized by form and many of which display movement.

Sometimes, however, it is important for fish to discern more than rudimentary aspects of their prey—for instance, to discriminate between desirable and less desirable prey when offered a choice. At such times, prey recognition seems to operate at a more refined level. This too we'll explore further when we discuss selective feeding.

However instinctive they might be at the core, prey recognition and feeding behaviors in general are certainly influenced or modified by experience, but to what degree remains disputable. The nature-versus-nurture argument is centuries old, still raging, and too complex to go into at length here. For our purposes, both genetics and environment interact to determine how a fish behaves. Fish might learn to recognize obvious features of various prey, or they might learn to associate various types of prey with certain areas or habitats. They might also learn to associate certain movements with certain types of prey. For instance, fishes such as trout, which feed on both moving and stationary forage, are proficient at associating motion, or lack thereof, with various prey. Therefore, imparting action to a spent-spinner imitation is unlikely to draw a strike from a trout feeding on the natural, just as baitfish imitations are virtually ineffective without motion.[1] Striped bass have been observed rooting in the sand and mud to uncover buried sand lances. This behavior is probably learned, though genetics can-

---

1. Relatively speaking. A streamer hanging in a current is regarded by an observing fish to be moving against the flow. And even dead-drift streamer presentations are usually punctuated by twitches or short darts. An exception to this is a pattern drifted in a chum line of cut or whole dead baits, under which circumstance the fish might become temporarily conditioned to accept only dead-drifting baits and actually reject live ones.

not be ruled out entirely: In order to learn any behavior, an organism must have the innate (genetic) capacity to learn it. Unlike the striped bass, the bonefish seems built for rooting. The bonefish's rooting behavior is probably fundamentally instinctive, though many aspects of it might also be learned.

Defensive Adaptations and Behaviors

Camouflage

Think of the ocean as an around-the-clock restaurant, most of whose diners are liable suddenly to become the entree of another. With this ever-present threat, most marine animals have had to develop ways to increase their chances of survival so that their species is not wiped out entirely. Many species of marine worms have flourished by adapting to life in burrows and crevices, out of reach of most predators. They emerge to feed only at night or during low-light conditions, or, in some cases, to spawn. Free-living organisms have developed other means for their defense.

Conspicuous creatures (those that contrast with their environment, such as a dark eel swimming over white sand) are easily spotted by predators, so a number of adaptations have evolved that make them less noticeable. The most common of these adaptations is camouflage: coloration (and sometimes body structure) that makes a creature difficult to distinguish from its surroundings. For instance, certain crustaceans have at their command several pigments whose display they can regulate according to their backgrounds. Grass shrimps of the genus *Palaemonetes* collected from a patch of eelgrass are tinted green, while those found on a sandy bottom are transparent tan.

Fishes are free-swimming, and because they can be viewed by predators from various angles and against a variety of backgrounds, they have developed an elaborate system of camouflage to minimize the differences between themselves and their surroundings.

Predators perceive prey by two main visual features: silhouette and bulk (the appearance of being rounded and having solidity). These features are most obvious if the prey has a sharp outline, casts strong shadows, or is a different color from its background. Most gamefishes and forage fishes have light-colored bellies and dark-colored backs. This countershading conceals the fish in several ways. Viewed from above, a dark dorsal surface more closely matches a dark background (rock, sand, weedbed, or the darkness of the depths) than would a lighter surface. Likewise, a light ventral surface, viewed from below against a well-lighted sky, is less striking than a darker one would be. Countershading is also instrumental in the suppression of shadows. Lighted from above and viewed horizontally, uniformly colored objects are shaded beneath. Countershaded fish appear uniformly colored and therefore flat, disguising their bulk and minimizing their contrast to background radiance. In addition to countershading, some fishes are also marked with a series of vertical bars along their sides (called a *disruptive pattern*) that breaks up the outline. Some fishes—such as certain species of silversides (family Atherinidae)—have translucent bodies that avoid

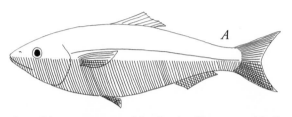

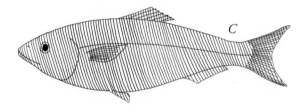

Gamefishes perceive prey fishes first by silhouette and bulk. Countershading helps suppress these features. Lighted from above, a uniformly colored fish (A), when viewed horizontally, would be shaded beneath. The countershaded fish (B), when lighted from above (C), appears uniformly colored and therefore flat, disguising bulk and mimimizing contrast to background radiance.

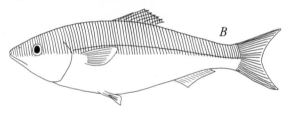

casting strong shadows or presenting distinctive outlines. Most fishes are able, to some degree, to alter their color by means of their nervous systems. This allows the fish to match its surroundings more closely, thereby obscuring its silhouette.

Many fishes are silvery in appearance. This silveriness is a result of decomposing fragments of the protein guanine wedged between the epidermis and the scales. Light striking the fish is reflected by the guanine; the fish's scales act in effect as mirrors. If this seems a detriment—the reflection of sunlight resulting in a flicker that could alert predators—it is so only near the surface. In depths at which sunlight is highly diluted by absorption and scattered by suspended particles, the fish's scales reflect the surrounding light that would have reached the observer's eye if the fish had not been there in the first place. And the flickering of scales in strong surface light is less of a detriment than it might seem. Observed from below, the flickering of scales merges with the glittering of the water's surface, which is present even under relatively calm conditions. Furthermore, as we shall see when we discuss schooling behavior, flickering has other benefits for forage fishes.

A further adaptation found to some degree in most fishes is *lateral compression*. This reduction of the dorsoventral silhouette minimizes the figure contrasted against the bright surface background, making detection from below even more difficult.

The fish's eye—in many cases a large dark pupil centered within a lighter background—is a high-contrast feature; and as with silhouette and bulk, nature has, in many instances, taken steps to make the eye less conspicuous. The fish's eye is often obscured by being incorporated into the dorsal coloration; other times, such as with the freshwater daces, it is covered with a dark stripe. (The least conspicuous eyes are generally found on non-schooling or weakly schooling species.) Many species of fish have eyespots toward or on their tails to draw predators' attentions away from the head.

Schooling

Schooling in fishes is a complex matter, but the scientific community generally agrees it is of primary importance as a defensive behavior—an anti-predator device.

At the simplest level, schooling is advantageous to prey because the less dispersed they are, the less likely they are to encounter predators. And for predators on the hunt, it is harder to approach a school than an individual because the school has not two eyes but many, keeping a continuous, all-around watch. Should an individual sense danger, its excited actions quickly alarm the school.

Experiments with fish show that a single prey specimen placed into a tank with a hungry predator will be quickly devoured, but that increasing the number of prey decreases the predator's success rate. In ethology, the advantage of sheer numbers is known as the *confusion effect* (also referred to as the *effect of mass*). Confronted with a number of prey, the predator might simply have difficulty choosing a single target. Pike have been observed, between attacks on schools of minnows, to continually orient themselves toward fish after fish, apparently unable to decide among them. Apart from simple indecision, the movement of one individual is likely to distract the predator from the movement of another. When attacking a densely populated school, a predacious fish usually has difficulty sticking with one specific target, oftentimes pursuing one after another—and oftentimes missing them all. Similarly, novice bird hunters might fire randomly into a flock, but these shots rarely hit anything. Only shots at individual birds drop game consistently.

Much of the confusion experienced by a predator confronted with a school seems to stem from the identical appearance of its members. The predator's success is dependent on its ability to fixate visually on its target. Experiments show that prey individuals that look different, or behave differently from the rest of the school, are more likely to be singled out. Minnows marked with India ink are more likely to be snatched from a school by pike, just as a black pigeon in a white flock is more likely to be captured by a hawk. Therefore, natural selection shows a

Nature often takes steps to make the fish's eye, a high-contrast feature, less conspicuous to predators. In the case of the eel (A), the eye is greatly reduced and merges with the dorsal coloration. The mackerel's eye (B) is more pronounced, but unlike the eel, the mackerel is a schooling fish and finds its primary defense in the advantage of numbers (confusion effect). The least conspicuous eyes are generally found on non-schooling or weakly schooling species.

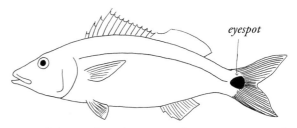

eyespot

Many fishes, such as the tomtate, have eyespots toward their rear ends or on their tails to draw predators' attentions away from the head (fish are more likely to survive an attack to the tail than to the head)—further evidence that the eye is an important prey-recognition feature and aiming point for predators.

definite preference for uniformity of appearance. For instance, if, in a population of green-backed fish, a gene mutation appeared that colored a few of the next generation brown, they would likely be singled out by predators from the predominantly green school and devoured before they could pass their brown genes on to future generations.

In addition to the confusion inherent in numerous identical targets, defensive maneuvers enacted by the school create further confusion for predators. Alarmed by a predator, the school often crowds together or balls up, increasing the number of targets in the predator's field of vision. Frightened fish quicken their movements and continually change position within the school, allowing the sun's rays to reflect off their scales at different angles and creating a flickering effect that makes it difficult for the predator to single out any individual.

For these reasons, it is unlikely that a fish within the school—and behaving in kind—will be captured. When a fish is captured, it is almost always because it has lagged or strayed or in some other way set itself apart from the school. What this amounts to is a higher incidence of predation on the weak, sick, and injured members of a population. Fluttering at the outskirts of a well-defined, well-organized school, our odd-looking, oddly behaving artificial makes a prime target in every sense.

A predacious fish must be able to fixate visually on a target within a school to successfully capture it, so odd-looking or oddly behaving prey, or prey outside the school, are most vulnerable. Artificials—odd-looking and out-of-sync with the rest of the school—make prime targets.

Foraging Strategies

A hungry fish searches for things to excite its prey-recognition system. Remember: Natural selection favors efficient feeders; efficient foraging maximizes energy intake and minimizes energy expenditure. Under laboratory conditions, fish have been able to increase their foraging efficiency over time by avoiding areas of their environment that never contain food—that is, they can *learn* an efficient foraging strategy. So there is good reason to believe that fish in the wild strive to maximize foraging efficiency by avoiding nonproductive areas and concentrating on areas conditionally associated with food. And because the locations and abundance of various prey change throughout the season, predacious fish must modify their behavior accordingly if they are to survive. This makes knowledge of forage habitat and habits of great importance to the angler.

Because the school is generally a safe haven for prey that stay within its bounds, the tactic of the predator is to try to cause disarray within the school, to separate some of the individuals from the mass. In the wild, jacks and groupers have been observed to circle a school of sardines or other fish for hours without making a single attempt to capture one. But should one individual happen to become agitated and flee the school, or behave differently from the rest of the school, then that individual is devoured instantly.

The most opportune time for predators to launch an attack on a school is in the twilight hours. It is during these changeover times between night and day—when various forage schools are moving either offshore or inshore—that the attacking predator is most likely to create confusion within the school's ranks. Also, this is when the forage fishes' protective coloration is least effective. With the rays of sunlight coming in at a strongly horizontal, rather than vertical, angle, the glittering of the water's surface is at a minimum. For a short time, the forms of forage fishes, illuminated from the side, are seen clearly by any predator lurking below.

While schooling behavior lessens the chance that predators will gain access to a school, chances increase when the predators themselves form schools. Relatively few predacious fishes hunt collectively, but those that do (bluefish, for example) enjoy several advantages. First, it is easier for schooling predators to locate prey for the same reason that it is easier for schooling prey to become aware of predators. Multiple predators can cover more territory than can a single one, and just as the prey's excited actions signal danger throughout the school, the behavior of a predator that has spotted food is quickly relayed to its cohorts.

Prey are more easily disoriented and panicked by a number of predators than by a single one. Schooling predators often work in twos and threes to isolate and run down prey.

A school of predators can surround prey and prevent it from escaping. A common tactic in open water is to drive the prey to the surface. Cut off from protective cover, some prey panic. Those that try to escape quickly fall victim. Another strategy is to herd the prey into a closed inlet or to pin it into a corner (such as that formed by a rock jetty and the shoreline).

Competition within a feeding school is fierce. To get sufficient food, a predator must be quick and agile. Therefore, the larger members of any gamefish species tend to hunt alone, or with one or two other fish of equal size. Large striped bass habitually position themselves beneath schools of marauding bluefish and feed lazily on their spoils.

Prey Selection

The fish's diet can be seen in terms of energy foods (carbohydrates, proteins, and fats) and nonenergy foods (vitamins and minerals). Gamefish species vary in their nutritional requirements, just as forage species differ in their nutritional value. While it is accepted that various predators prefer one prey species over another,[2] the patchy distribution of forage makes locating and capturing prey a more pressing problem for gamefishes than is selecting it. The need for food is paramount; choice is only an intermittent luxury. Therefore, diet is often determined by what is available. The general rule of thumb is, the greater the variety of prey available to a predator, the more selective is its diet. The most expansive diets are found in the harshest environments.

Studies show that as the abundance of a particular prey increases, the number of prey

2. It has been demonstrated (in animals other than fish) that prey preference can be an inherited (that is, genetic) trait.

specimens in the fish's diet increases rapidly at first, and then increases at a diminished rate until it finally levels off. Predacious fish have been observed to feed for a time on a particular prey, and then suddenly switch to another, even though the former prey was still available. Such behavior might be nature's way of ensuring a varied (and presumably superior) diet.

According to optimal foraging theory, another way that predators attempt to maximize efficiency is by concentrating on the largest specimens of a given patch of prey (provided their net yield of energy exceeds that of smaller specimens[3]). This, however, is the ideal. In actuality, predacious fish feeding on schools of forage usually take what they can get.

As a fish grows, the average length of its prey decreases proportionally to its own body length. For instance, young fish can consume prey that are 40 to 50 percent their own length, while most prey taken by adults are only 10 to 20 percent as long as themselves. An explanation of this phenomenon might go beyond mere preference, taking into account such factors as the differences in maximum lengths attained by predacious fishes and their prey, comparative abundance of small prey species as opposed to large prey species within a given area, and ease of capture of small prey as opposed to large.

Selective Feeding

Perhaps the most mentioned and least understood phenomenon in angling is that of selective feeding. While predacious fishes are generally considered opportunistic feeders—that is, they eat whatever forage they happen upon and can capture—at times they can be highly discriminating about what they will eat and, more important to the angler, what artificials they will strike. The angler with an insight into selective feeding has a decided edge.

First I'd like to clear up some prevalent misconceptions about selectivity, and then see if I can draw a more utilitarian description of the phenomenon.

I believe the word *selective* is sometimes misused in angling literature to mean *uninterested.* That a fish refuses an artificial is not in itself an indication that it is being selective. A fish might decline to strike for a variety of reasons, the most obvious being that it is simply not feeding. Only fish that are actively foraging can be said to be selective.

Some angling writers have explained selectivity as the result of fishing pressures: Certain trout flies fished repeatedly over a particular piece of water sometimes lose their effectiveness, so new patterns (usually more imitative of the trout's forage) are developed. In ethology, however, the subject of selective feeding deals only with the selection of *prey*. Avoidance of harmful foods is widespread throughout nature. And while it is possible that a fish might learn to recognize and avoid a particular fly pattern that has hooked it before, such a fish cannot be called "selective" in the scientific sense. Rather, the fish is "educated." It has learned to avoid harm the way a once-stung frog refrains from snapping at bees, or the way an educated bird avoids eating the poisonous monarch butterfly (and also its harmless mimic, the viceroy butterfly). Interestingly enough, many distinctive trout patterns, such as the Royal Coachman, remain as popular and effective today as they did a century ago (though catch-and-release, which creates educated fish, has been practiced widely only within the last few decades). A

---

3. Factors governing such a determination include the amount of energy required to capture large prey specimens as opposed to small, and differences in handling time (the amount of time it takes to kill and eat a prey item once it has been captured).

fascinating subject, but one I won't explore, given that the fly-fishing pressure on our oceans cannot be compared to the fishing pressures on our trout waters.

The opportunistic/selective concept of foraging is misleading. It pushes us into an either/or mindset: Either the fish is feeding opportunistically, or it is feeding selectively; either the fish will strike at anything presented to it, or it is being very fussy. Foraging is not so cut-and-dried. First, every fish has various thresholds of attack—that is, for the fish to regard any object (alive or inanimate) as a potential meal, the object must meet some basic criteria. An angler who approaches any species of fish with the idea that he has only to put his line in the water to catch one has already put himself at a disadvantage. Even bluefish (a species whose voracious feeding habits have become legend) that aren't being particularly selective (and they can be very selective) will reject an imitation that has had its fishlike essence chewed from it. All acts of feeding, even those considered opportunistic, are, in some sense, selective. And even a selectively feeding fish must be something of an opportunist.

Selective feeding in its behavioral sense operates at various degrees of specificity (that is, some selectivity is more difficult than others), and is more accurately likened to a tuning knob than to a toggle switch.

In the first and broadest sense, selective feeding limits the fish's foraging efforts to a single category of prey, to the exclusion of other available categories. (Given the aggregative or schooling nature of much marine prey, this often results in the selection of a single species.) The reasons for this behavior are still open to discussion, but two hypotheses prevail: Selective feeding, it has been proposed, is yet another way for the fish to forage efficiently. When one prey becomes abundant, it might be more efficient for the fish to feed on that prey exclusively rather than to spend time and energy searching for other kinds of prey. The other possibility has been stated here previously: The fish's proclivity to suddenly ignore one category of prey and begin feeding on another (even though that category might be less abundant than the former) allows the fish to vary, and therefore balance, its diet.

Neither of these ideas seems incompatible with the other, nor does it seem unreasonable that selective feeding might serve more than one purpose. A further explanation of the phenomenon that is buzzing around angling literature still is that some foods simply taste better than others. While the role of taste in feeding cannot be discounted, there is to my knowledge no good evidence that it is the impetus for selectivity—and such a proposition would be difficult to prove.

In any case, it is less important for the angler to understand *why* selective feeding happens than it is to understand the *way* in which it operates. One explanation of the mechanics of selective feeding can be found in the two closely related concepts of *search image* and *selective attention*.

Examinations of the stomach contents of trout have turned up numbers of non-food objects about the same size and shape as what the trout were feeding on at the time. To some researchers, this and similar phenomena suggest that after a few successive encounters with a particular prey, the predator develops an image in its mind of what it should look for. The animal behaviorist Jakob von Uexküll was the first to conceive of the notion of a searching image, and his idea persists some 60 years later, most notably in the work of Luke Tinbergen. Search images, Tinbergen postulated, increase the predator's ability to detect specific prey, thereby increasing its chances of capturing that prey.[4]

---

4. Tinbergen's experiments with search images involved predators hunting cryptic prey, but the concept is also useful in explaining how predators distinguish among various prey types.

The obvious question that arises is: "How specific is the fish's search image?" or rather, "How closely must the artificial resemble the natural in size, shape, color scheme, detail, and movement, in order to fool selectively feeding fish?" There is no easy answer.

In making the transition from opportunistic to selective feeding, predacious fish seem to undergo a perceptual shift, ceasing to respond to a broad range of visual cues in lieu of more specific ones. This is believed to result from an adjustment in the filtering mechanisms—the retina and central nervous system—that determine which visual information the fish actually utilizes. The specifics of this process are poorly understood, but neurophysiologists liken it to a system of gates that selectively suppress the flow of some pieces of information while admitting others. Simply put, the "gating" of visual stimuli endows the fish with a *selective attention*—a tunnel vision that keys in on specific visual cues of desired prey while blocking out irrelevant stimuli. Once the search image has been set, the predator has difficulty switching attention back and forth between various prey types.[5] Thus, the explanation goes, selectively feeding predators tend to overlook or ignore prey that are different from the prey for which they are searching.[6]

Which visual information is actually utilized for any given instance of selective feeding probably depends on the diagnostic needs of the fish to make decisions regarding selection. Consider a hypothetical situation:

Imagine that one or a few predacious fish are given a choice between sand lances and alewives—two species that are most obviously (to me, anyway) differentiated by their forms. Given the place of fishes at the low end of the vertebrate scale, we know that their capacity for processing a complexity of visual information is far less than our own. We also know that animals in general, unless specifically trained, have difficulty attending to a number of features simultaneously, and that the more they attend to one feature the less they attend to others. Assuming the foraging fish, in selecting between the two prey, are attending primarily to form, then color likely would play little part in eliciting a strike. However, if the foraging fish were given a choice between alewives and blueback herring—two species that are nearly indistinguishable visually except for their dorsal coloration—and decided to select one over the other, then color (or some quality of it, such as shade) might well be a determining factor (that is, become a key stimulus).

While certain visual stimuli might have greater strike-eliciting value than others in a given situation, investigations (in areas other than selective feeding) have shown that key stimuli are most effective when presented in conjunction with other, even less effective stimuli. So rather than complicate matters needlessly with speculation about what the most important stimulus might be for a given situation, the most practical course is to note the obvious visual features of the prey you wish to match and to use imitations that display those features.

A multitude of factors can work to your advantage in overcoming any deficiencies in the accuracy of your imitations. These include the visual restrictions imposed by given water

---

5. Within the entire context of selective feeding, *prey type* can refer to a particular prey category or species, or a particular morph within a category or species.

6. To describe selectively feeding fish as "overlooking" or "ignoring" prey that are different from the prey for which they are searching might not always be accurate. One instance that sticks in my mind is an encounter I had with a large school of bluefish that were feeding actively on 3-inch baitfish. I wanted to test my hot-glue sand lances, which were about twice the length of, and a different color scheme from, what the blues were eating. The result was many follows and subsequent rejections and only a few strikes. My flies weren't ignored, but the result was the same. I can only speculate that the action of my imitation was enough to get their attention, but that (for most of the fish) it lacked the stimuli critical to eliciting a strike.

and light conditions, degree of hunger, rate of feeding, number of predators and the level of competition among them, and the difficulty of prey capture.

The most significant factor determining the necessity of an accurate imitation seems to be *prey density.*[7] In addition to restricting foraging efforts to a single prey category, selective feeding is further refined such that the predator might limit its efforts to certain morphs (individuals that can be differentiated from others of the same category by their appearance, such as color) within that category. Research shows that at high prey densities, odd-looking prey (that is, the less-common morphs) are more readily taken—such as the black pigeon in a white flock or the minnow marked with India ink. This is known as *oddity selection.* At medium prey densities, the commoner morph tends to be preferred; this phenomenon is termed *apostatic selection.* At low prey densities, various morphs are taken indiscriminately. These different types of selectivity are explained thus by some researchers: At high prey densities, where the confusion effect makes it difficult for the predator to single out individuals, odd-looking prey (including those that behave oddly) are most easily targeted. At medium prey densities, where the confusion effect is not a problem, it is more efficient for the predator to concentrate on the commoner individuals rather than shifting attention to uncommon ones; thus, prey that appear different from the majority tend to be overlooked or ignored. (It seems unlikely, though, that a common morph would be rejected in most cases on the basis of odd behavior, unless perhaps the behavior were inordinately odd, such as a moving spent spinner.) At low prey densities, where there is no efficiency advantage in concentrating on any particular morph, all individuals are taken without preference.

Selectivity, then, seems to discriminate first by size. More than once I've watched anglers equipped with surf tackle and large plugs unsuccessfully try nearly every lure in their tackle boxes while I was able to take striped bass consistently on a fly whose only virtue was that it approximated the size of the 5-inch silversides the bass were chasing. Selectivity was in effect, but it was easily overcome.

Some clarification might be needed here concerning oddity selection. Imagine again the predacious fish feeding selectively on alewives. If the alewives occur at a high density, a blueback herring that happens to be mixed in with them is without doubt odd-looking and will likely be attacked immediately (such selection in mixed-species schools has been documented numerous times), whereas at a lower density the blueback might be ignored altogether. To the angler, this means that an imitation that matches the size, but differs significantly in other aspects (such as color) from the actual prey, can be deadly effective in one situation and virtually worthless—when used on the same fish feeding on the same prey—in another.

Don't let these elaborate explanations overwhelm you. Approximating the size and general configuration of what the fish are eating will go a long way toward overcoming most selectivity you will encounter in salt water. Never hesitate to trim a fly, reducing its length or even its bulk to make it more closely resemble the desired prey. More than once this has been the deciding factor for me.

Although matching the size of the desired prey is of primary importance in hooking selectively feeding fish, there will be times when it won't be enough, times when our imitations—patterns that match the prey in size and shape, patterns that have always produced—will move untouched through roiling water. As research suggests, this apostatic selection is

---

7. In a practical sense, prey density should be regarded not simply as the number of prey individuals within an area, but their proximity to each other as well. The ideal high-density situation would be a large school of baitfish that has balled up under siege.

most likely to take place at medium prey densities. Such situations are most obviously discerned when visible feeding activity is spread out over a considerable area, while in high-density situations the activity is more closely confined.

The question remains, however, as to how closely imitations must match the natural to take fish during these periods of stringent selectivity. No one has been able to answer this conclusively, and the subject is hotly debated within the angling community. Given the limits of the visual acuity of fish, coupled with the aforementioned factors of restricted visibility due to water clarity and light conditions—and the fact that most imitations will be moving, denying an opportunity for close examination—many times, simple suggestive patterns will work as well as any in hooking selectively feeding fish. But there will be other times when something more specific is needed.

At any given time, fish utilize only a small portion of the total visual information available, so much of the effort that goes into an excruciatingly detailed imitation is undoubtedly lost on them. Not even during periods of stringent selectivity is an exacting imitation needed to catch fish—the imitation need only display the few features the fish are keying in on. However, an imitation that closely matches the desired prey allows you to cover more bases, to push more of the fish's potential predatory buttons.

Even if one key feature is absent from an imitation, other key features might still evoke a response from a fish, though the response might be weakened—the difference between a tentative strike and a vicious one. In essence, a fish striking an artificial is responding to what is right with the imitation and is overlooking what is wrong with it.

Much has been made by some anglers of the necessity to precisely match the colors of naturals—perhaps too much. Remember that the primary purpose of color vision in predacious fishes is to contrast prey against background. Even selectively feeding fish frequently disregard color when selecting prey, and when fish do key in to colors, they doubtless generalize to some degree as they do for such features as size and shape (perceptually speaking, loss of information implies generalization). If they didn't, we'd never be able to catch them. For given the limitations of the colors of natural and synthetic tying materials available to us, and the ranges of coloration within prey species (its complexities and subtleties), our most exacting imitations are still only approximates. Most of the fly patterns listed in Part Three are at least good suggestions of the forage for which they are named. Detailed descriptions and color plates of forage species appear in this text to help the angler choose and create good suggestive patterns, as well as patterns that will produce under conditions of strong selectivity.

While it is true that predacious fish are able to key in on various patterns of movement (such as the steady undulation of a sand lance), mimicking the specific movements of prey seems to be more important in those quiet periods when many species tend to be less active, usually after dark. I discovered this by accident when, after having fished a particular piece of water for 20 minutes or so (using my usual foot-long strips) with no success, I began reeling in line to move to another spot, and a fish struck. The first time this happened I thought little of it. By the third time, I knew it was more than coincidence. (This always happened after dark with little or no visible feeding activity.) And while it is not always important to closely imitate the specific movements of the natural (that is, the slow, steady movements), at times it can make a difference. This is not usually the case, however, when fishing in the presence of baitfish under siege. Panicked baitfish move quickly and in spurts; wounded baitfish move erratically. Retrieves that suggest such behavior usually work best, though simple foot-long strips often suffice. Obviously, forage such as worms and shrimps have their own peculiar locomotions, and their imitations should be fished accordingly.

That fish are feeding on one food form exclusively, even selectively, doesn't mean they won't take another form. It is possible that what they are feeding on is all that is available, and that a change in diet would be welcome. In his book *Lee Wulff on Flies*, Wulff wrote that he believed trout have certain food preferences that they never lose (this belief has been substantiated to some degree by science), and no matter what the hatch conditions are, they will disrupt their routine for one of their favorites. Wulff called this his "strawberries-and-cream" theory, and despite the informality of the explanation, the practice is sound: If your best imitations fail to hook selectively feeding fish, switch to an imitation that is very different from what the fish are eating and is, ideally, of something they are known to like. Just as the fish must be adaptable to its changing environment if it is to thrive, so must you adapt your tackle and techniques to the fish's capriciousness and be willing to try new approaches if you are to take fish consistently.

Before we finish with this section I should note that many researchers take exception to the idea of search images—and for good reasons. The concept of the search image introduces a host of perceptual problems and raises as many questions as it answers. Ultimately, it boils down to this: We cannot know the subjectivity of fish, whether or not they hold images in their mind as we do. Although laboratory observations of foraging behavior seem to correspond with the notion of search images, the fish's brain might operate nothing like this. But it is impossible for us to conceive of such things as vision and perception apart from our own experiences of them.

This sketch of fish predation, I believe, comprises a good general schema of imitation, and does much to explain why artificials work and why they don't.

Imitations

Examine a variety of specific imitations and you will likely be struck by their dissimilarity to the naturals they are supposed to represent. Fly dressing tends to embrace Impressionism and Expressionism more closely than it does Realism. Imitations have no one-to-one correspondence with the structure of the natural, but rather are a display of its aspects. Some aspects are exaggerated, others merely hinted at, still others are omitted entirely; colors are absent, or colors are present that don't seem to belong—all depending on the whim of the creator. What results when a tyer sits down to the vise is as much a personal statement as it is a statement about nature. Often, imitations resemble the natural in only the vaguest sense, the way one of Picasso's cubist portraits resembles a human. Nevertheless, they are constructed and employed with the hope that they will depict nature at least well enough to cause a fish to strike. And often they do—often enough, anyway, to keep us going back to the water. Given our knowledge of predation, we understand why simple patterns are often as effective as any, and that our imperfect imitations actually have something of an advantage in that they represent members of the forage population most likely to be cropped by predation: the lame, the confused, the oddities of nature. We also understand that while our most imitative patterns will never match the naturals perfectly, the odds are that they will be close enough to produce under most circumstances.

The late Joseph Bates Jr. wrote that he considered the most important elements of streamer design to be action, form, and flash, respectively.[8] Sound advice, for as nature demonstrates, it is these features that betray the prey fish's presence to the predator.

Form should be considered in terms of length and silhouette. Forage fishes show two important silhouettes to the predator: dorsoventral and profile. How the gamefish hunts determines which silhouette is best emphasized in the imitation. For example, dolphin inhabit the upper water column and feed most often within 20 feet of the surface, attacking prey more or less horizontally; in contrast, skipjack tuna hunt from the depths, searching for prey silhouetted against the surface light and striking from beneath. These different modes of attack suggest that patterns used for dolphin should exhibit strong profiles, while skipjack patterns should be dressed thickly to cut light penetration, enhancing the ventral silhouette. Many fly patterns present both silhouettes well. Consider the pattern's form not as it looks in hand, but how it looks as it moves though the water.

Action is both the action imparted to a fly by the angler and the action built into the pattern itself. Some patterns rely primarily on the former, while others—most notably tarpon flies—are dressed with splayed tails and hackle collars (also known as *breather* patterns) that pulsate with the movement of the fly, enhancing its inherent action. Sometimes a pattern is weighted at the head with bead-chain or lead eyes to give it a jigging action suggestive of an injured baitfish. Some materials are better suited to certain conditions than others. For instance, a streamer with a wing of saddle hackle undulates more realistically if left hanging in a current than one winged with stiff bucktail or an equivalent synthetic. Some synthetics (such as nylon), on the other hand, create a more durable fly than do natural materials, which could be a major consideration when fishing for toothy predators.

Flash is added to streamer patterns usually with tinsel or Mylar piping fastened to the hook shank, as well as with strips of Mylar or some other synthetic (such as Krystal Flash or Flashabou) incorporated into the wing. Note, however, that many successful streamer patterns contain no flash material at all.

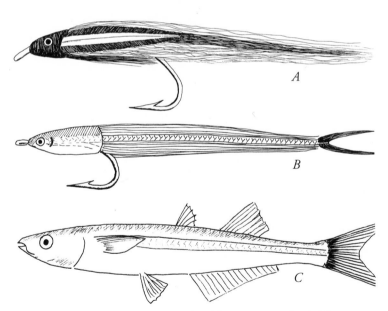

Impressionism and Realism. Harold Gibbs' Striper Bucktail (A) creates a rudimentary impression of the Atlantic silverside, Menidia menidia, *(C), while Bob Popovics' Surf Candy Spearing (B) more accurately depicts the natural's obvious features: eye, silver midlateral band, and color scheme. The feather tail is probably more attractive to the angler than to the fish.*

8. Ranking is a partial inference on my part. Bates' wording implies form is more important than flash in that flash might be helpful in getting a fish's attention, but that action and form are what make it strike.

Color and color combinations, Bates wrote, are important in themselves to streamer design, but not as important as action, form, or flash. Very often this is the case. If it were not, popular colors such as hot pink and fluorescent chartreuse, which do not exist in nature, would not be viable options for artificials. Close replication of the color schemes of naturals is important, if at all, only in the most severe instances of selective feeding, and most likely under conditions of good visibility.

Sometimes fish actually show partiality for colors that have no bearing on their foods. For example, Jimmy Nix ties his Mullet pattern in either green or yellow when fishing for dolphin, convinced such flies produce better than those colored closer to the natural. Whether this is an actual preference by the fish, or simply the result of heightened contrast or visibility, no one has explained to my satisfaction.

Some flies, such as the Streaker Streamer (A) or many of the classic feather-wing streamers, are strong in profile but lacking in ventral silhouette (B). Streamers such as the Catherwood Giant Killers (C) present substantial ventral silhouettes as well as good profiles, which could make a difference when fishing for predators that search for prey silhouetted against the surface rather than from the side (e.g., skipjack tuna).

These, in a nutshell, seem to be the important elements of streamer design; the rest, in most cases, might just be window dressing. One embellishment worth mentioning, however, is eyes. That nature often takes steps to make these high-contrast features less conspicuous suggests that depicting them in imitations can be of value. Most anglers interviewed for this book feel that eyes can increase a baitfish pattern's effectiveness. In a 1993 article for *Fly Fisherman*, Trey Combs wrote that when using a sliding foam head in conjunction with a sailfish fly (for this rig, the head is customarily put several inches in front of the fly), he never puts eyes on the foam head but rather on the sides of the fly. "Once, as an experiment, a friend put ¾-inch doll eyes on a sliding head. The sailfish hit the head so hard that it blasted the Ethafoam sliding popper off the shock tippet. The fish was not hooked." This corroborates Dan Blanton's assertion that predacious fishes are "headhunters." And of those anglers who still believe that the primary purpose of eyes is to *sell* flies, I think even they would concede that eyes detract nothing from a pattern's effectiveness. Izaak Walton put eyes on his cloth minnow imitations, so if nothing else, you are in good company putting them on your own.

Today, some baitfish imitations from the blossoming School of Realism include a tail (usually a hen breast feather or saddle-hackle section cut to shape and attached to a length of monofilament). As nature indicates that the gamefish's attention will be directed primarily toward the prey fish's head, I personally consider the inclusion of a tail superfluous (and so does Bob Popovics, whose Surf Candies popularized them). However, it's a nice aesthetic touch, and it certainly won't detract from the imitation's effectiveness. In short, anything you can do to

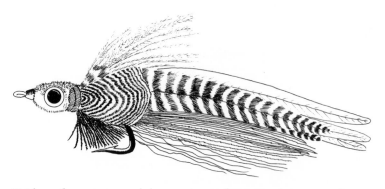

Evidence from nature and the experience of many anglers suggest that eyes on baitfish imitations can increase their effectiveness. The oversized eyes on this Sar-Mul-Mac variation underscore Dan Blanton's assertion that predacious fishes are "headhunters." Given this, never put the eyes too far from the point of the hook.

help the fish associate your fly with its prey can only increase your chances for success.

Most of what we've said about streamer flies applies to patterns used to represent non-piscine forage as well. Approximating the size, shape, movement, and colors of such food items as worms, shrimps, and crabs is often all that is necessary to catch fish that are feeding on these creatures. Chico Fernandez's mantis- and snapping-shrimp patterns approximate the naturals in general shape and color, and are among the most effective of bonefish patterns. Other innovative fly dressers, such as Carl Richards, are working toward developing patterns that more closely imitate specific crustacean species.

The other major component of fly design is function. In general, too little consideration is given to overall performance, particularly in commercially dressed patterns, which rely primarily on aesthetic appeal to sell. A well-designed and well-constructed fly—one that casts easily, seldom fouls, and takes a fair number of fish before it needs replacing—allows you to make the best use of your time. Although there has been some scattered writing on the subject of fly quality, experience is the best instructor. After a few seasons on the water, you will know at a glance how a particular pattern will perform, and if it will endure. Any student of the game will do well to study the techniques of such tyers as Hal Janssen, whose patterns are a brilliant blend of function and aesthetics.

Pattern Selection

There are scores of established saltwater fly patterns, but the selection process need not be difficult. Your main considerations are knowing your quarry's primary prey and what is available to it in a particular area and habitat at a given time of year. The thorough angler also uses any

Simple but effective, the Fernandez-style shrimp fly approximates the general shrimp form well. Variations in size and color scheme of the basic dressing allow the angler to suggest a number of shrimp species.

and all information at hand in determining which pattern to fish: what is swimming in the water, what the birds are feeding on, what is chased up or washes up on the beach during a blitz, the stomach contents of a freshly caught fish (often they'll regurgitate a recent meal), and observation of feeding activity (that is, might the fish be feeding on something other than baitfish, such as worms or shrimps?). Furthermore, many forage species look enough alike to be successfully imitated with a single pattern. For instance, two or three streamer patterns should effectively suggest most forage fishes likely to inhabit any given area. General patterns fished knowledgeably are far more effective than specific ones fished in ignorance.

Other factors can also influence pattern choice. Fish can't see color at night, so obviously color is irrelevant then; light-colored flies will certainly take fish, but many anglers feel a dark or black fly produces the best silhouette against any backlighting from the moon or stars. This text deals with naturals and their imitations, but the fact is that most saltwater flies are attractors, and no angler should ignore the all-around effectiveness of attractor patterns. If the water is very murky, you might do well to forget imitation and choose a brightly colored pattern with a lot of flash. Or you might choose a pattern with a heavily wound hackle collar—such as one of Dan Blanton's Whistler series (a popular choice for muddy-water tarpon, and a fly I am never without when fishing for striped bass), to push water and alert fish by means of pressure waves. Attractor patterns can also be effective on uninterested fish. The fish's strike is not always a feeding impulse, and a fly that appeals to its curiosity (that is, its *exploratory behavior*) might be more effective than one that appeals to its hunger, especially if it is not particularly hungry.

Final Notes

Some of this information is highly theoretical. The so-called laws of nature are mere descriptions; fish are under no obligation to act in accordance with them. You'll doubtless meet with some that behave to the contrary. Fish have a way of confounding our notions, especially as they pertain to angling. Angling axioms should be limited to warnings against such things as dull hooks, poorly tied knots, and frayed leaders.

This sketch of fish predation, however, is the best one I can draw at present, though some of the ideas are likely to become modified or obsolete with time. This information, then, is intended not as the final word on the subject, but as a place to begin.

Key Points

Vision and Perception of Gamefishes

- Gamefishes hunt primarily by sight, and their eyes are sensitive to motion and contrast rather than to detail.
- Saltwater gamefish generally enjoy good color vision, which primarily enhances the contrast between prey and various backgrounds. Fish are devoid of color perception at night.

Secondary Sensory Apparatus

- Most gamefishes can smell prey at considerable distances. Chumming might lure fish within casting distance.
- The lateral-line system of gamefish detects low-frequency waves emitted by moving prey. Use bulky or noisy artificials under conditions of poor visibility, or to alert fish outside casting range.

Prey Recognition

- Fish instinctively recognize prey by only a few aspects: basic form plus motion.
- Hunger heightens the fish's awareness of potential prey and broadens the range of forms it is willing to regard as prey.

Defensive Adaptations and Behaviors

- *Camouflage* makes a creature difficult to distinguish from its surroundings. Fish camouflage consists of *color change* (altering color to better blend with their environment), *countershading* (dark dorsal and light ventral surfaces that make fish less noticeable to predators looking at them from below or above, and also to disguise bulk), and *lateral compression* (reduction of the dorsoventral silhouette that minimizes the figure contrasted against the bright surface background). Camouflage also involves *silveriness* (scales reflecting surrounding light), *translucency* (semitransparent body that avoids casting strong shadows or presenting a distinctive outline), and *eye obscurity* (making the fish's eye, a high-contrast feature, less conspicuous).
- *Schooling:* Defensive behavior of fish that makes it difficult for predators to fixate on individuals. Odd-looking or oddly behaving individuals are most likely to be taken from a school.

Foraging Strategies

- Fish strive to forage efficiently by concentrating on areas conditionally associated with food, which makes knowledge of forage habitat and habits (particularly as they vary throughout the season) of great importance to the angler.
- The foraging predator tries to separate individuals from a school, most often during twilight.
- Predators that hunt in packs can more easily locate prey and isolate individuals from a school. Schooling predators can surround prey and prevent them from escaping, cut them off from protective cover, or herd them into close quarters.
- The larger members of any gamefish species tend to hunt alone or in very small schools of equally sized fish.

Prey Selection

- Predators have preferred or primary prey, but their diets are often determined by what is available or abundant. The most selective diets are found in environments containing a wide variety of prey.

Selective Feeding

- Predacious fishes generally feed opportunistically, though at times they can be highly selective. This makes knowledge of the fish's desired prey of great importance to the angler using artificials.
- Selective feeding is enacted for forage efficiency: It is more efficient to feed exclusively on an abundant prey type; thus, the fish's foraging efforts become temporarily limited to a single category of prey.
- A selectively feeding fish might carry a *search image* in its mind of what it should look for.
- Desirable prey are discriminated from undesirable prey first by size. Usually the artificial need only approximate the length and shape of the desired prey to fool selectively feeding fish.
- Sometimes (most likely at medium prey densities), the artificial might need to display colors or other obvious features (including specific movements or behaviors) of the desired prey.
- The most selective fish generalize when discriminating such things as form and color.
- If your best imitations fail to hook selectively feeding fish, switch to an imitation that is very different from what the fish are eating.

Imitations

- Simple fly patterns are often as effective as any, and imperfect imitations actually have the advantage of representing prey most likely to be cropped: the lame, the confused, the oddities of nature.
- The essential elements of any imitation are *form* (length and silhouette) and *action* (action inherent in the pattern as well as that imparted by the angler).
- Flash materials help get a fish's attention.
- During some periods of selectivity, matching colors of desired prey can be important, but colors generally are not as important as are form and action. Sometimes colors outside nature (chartreuse, for instance) are very effective, perhaps because of heightened contrast or visibility.
- Color is irrelevant at night, though many anglers feel black flies produce the best silhouette.
- Evidence suggests that eyes on baitfish imitations can increase their effectiveness, while such embellishments as realistic tails are essentially aesthetic.
- The main considerations for pattern selection are knowing your quarry's primary prey and what is available to it in a particular area and habitat at a given time of year. Careful observation of such things as prevalent forage and visible feeding activity is sometimes crucial in determining which pattern to fish. Many forage species look enough alike to be successfully imitated with a single pattern. A single fly can effectively suggest a host of forage species.
- No angler should ignore the all-around effectiveness of attractor patterns, especially if the water is murky or if the fish are not particularly hungry.

PART II

SALTWATER FORAGE SPECIES

FISHES

Sand Lances (Family Ammodytidae)

Plate 1

Elongate, somewhat laterally compressed fishes with a long, pointed head and a projecting lower jaw, sand lances (or launces, or sand eels, as they are more commonly known) superficially resemble eels. As schooling fishes, they are a primary food of many marine predators, including salmon and sea-run trout, striped bass, bluefish, mackerel, and bonito.

Sand lances are noted for their ability, when resting or when threatened, to burrow several inches into the sand or mud, where they might remain when the tide recedes, and until it returns. Lances are gathered for bait by raking the sand along the water's edge during a falling tide. Striped bass have been observed rooting around the bottom like bonefish to turn up buried specimens.

Of the three species of sand lances inhabiting North American waters, two are of primary interest to the angler: the American sand lance and the Pacific sand lance.

American Sand Lance *(Ammodytes americanus)*

This species inhabits the inshore waters and estuaries over sandy or muddy bottoms from the Canadian Maritime provinces to Cape Hatteras, North Carolina. Its dorsal coloration varies from olive to brown to bluish green, ranging to olive at its edge; its sides are bright silver, often with a steel-blue iridescence (I have observed some specimens on the island of Martha's Vineyard with a pinkish or pearlescent iridescence); its belly is white. The American sand lance's small eye is yellowish with a black pupil.

Food consists mainly of copepods (tiny crustaceans), but a variety of other organisms are also eaten, including marine worms and fish fry. Feeding takes place around the clock, but studies suggest perhaps more so after dark, contradicting the widely held notion that this species beds down for the entire night. Burrowing is far from cut-and-dried; it is not simply a case of the lances burying themselves whenever they are threatened. Numerous times I've watched striped bass in the shallows at night take sand lances from the surface. Some of the population might have burrowed, but obviously many had not. In any case, sunset often brings the lances closer to shore.

Sand-lance schools are not always well defined. Often, the lances seem to inhabit a general area, or they are strung out loosely along the shore for a considerable distance. One October along Lobsterville Beach on Martha's Vineyard, I watched a yard-wide, seemingly endless convoy of sand lances hug the shoreline as they swam against the current. The best-defined schools I have seen were during the day, and when the lances were being harassed by fish.

Sand lances act nervous when you wade through them at night. Then, even the actions of casting are enough to make them jump spastically from the water. As they can be nearly impossible to see clearly after dark, this nervousness is a good clue to their presence. When you have the opportunity, watch what the terns are diving for during the day. If what they're taking are small and difficult to see, it's a good bet they're taking lances.

Spawning occurs inshore, peaking in either December or January and ending in

February. The species matures in twenty months at a length of about 3⅓ to 3½ inches (8.5 to 9 centimeters), the males maturing at the smaller size. Adult American sand lances can live to twelve years and attain a maximum length of about 7 inches (18 centimeters).

A related species, the northern sand lance (*A. dubius*), which is found strictly offshore from Greenland to Virginia, is so close in appearance to *A. americanus* as to make distinguishing them difficult even for experts.

The American sand lance is a popular bait both live and dead, particularly for striped bass.

AKA: Equille, inshore sand lance, lancon d'Amérique (French), lant.

Pacific Sand Lance *(Ammodytes hexapterus)*

Although this species is found from the Bering Sea to Los Angeles, California, it is rare south of Tomales Bay, California. Studies supervised by NOAA reveal patchy estuarial distributions. Estuarine areas of greatest abundance appear to be Puget Sound to Skagit Bay, Washington, which support year-round populations of juveniles and adults. (Within the study area, this region showed the only significant amount of spawning with the exception of Tomales Bay.) Other estuaries supporting year-round populations are Gray's Harbor and Willapa Bay, Washington; the Columbia River estuary, bordering Oregon; and Humboldt and Tomales bays, California. Common to abundant presence of adults and juveniles has been recorded from about March to October (non-spawning periods) in estuaries from Nehalem to Coos bays, Oregon. *A. hexapterus* is also found in Hudson Bay, Canada.

The Pacific sand lance differs from its East Coast counterpart in several minor ways (for instance, a fold of skin running the length of the belly), the most noticeable being its dorsal coloration, which is a metallic blue or green. Like *A. americanus*, it prefers sandy or soft-bottomed shallows (into which it also burrows when resting or escaping from predators) and feeds primarily on zooplankton.

Pacific sand lances can reach sexual maturity after one to three years, at which time they are approximately 4 inches (10 centimeters) long. The spawning habits of the Pacific species are not well known, but are assumed to be similar to those of *A. americanus*. *A. hexapterus* spawns from November to March in marine waters of varying depths and probably in strong currents.

Maximum length of the Pacific sand lance is about 8 inches (20 centimeters), though few specimens attain this. It can live to be eight years old.

Pacific sand lances are eaten by many West Coast predators, including Pacific halibut, Pacific hake, lingcod, and salmons, for which they are a primary forage in the Strait of Juan de Fuca.

AKA: Arctic sandlance, needlefish, Pacific sandlance, sand eel, sand-lance, sand launce or sandlaunce.

Eels *(Order Anguilliformes)*

The order Anguilliformes comprises the many species of elongate, snakelike fishes having small, narrow gill openings and indistinct tails (most lack scales), known collectively as eels. This large order includes the single family of freshwater eels (Anguillidae).

Eels come in a multitude of sizes and colors and are found in a variety of habitats from inshore to deep sea. Common to all is a transparent, ribbonlike larval stage called a *leptocephalus*. Excepting the members of the family Anguillidae, all eels are marine.

Eels have the highest nutritional value of all forage fishes.

Freshwater Eels *(Family Anguillidae)*

One species of freshwater eel, the American eel, inhabits North American waters; it is absent from the Pacific Coast.

American Eel *(Anguilla rostrata)*

Plate 1

The American eel begins life in the Sargasso Sea area of the Atlantic Ocean. Upon hatching from the egg, the eel takes on the thin, transparent, ribbonlike larval form known as the leptocephalus. Thus begins its migration to coastal waters, which is believed to take a year.

During the winter, as it approaches the coast, the leptocephalus transforms, becoming a transparent eel that is 2⅜ to 2½ inches (6 to 6.5 centimeters) long and known as a *glass eel*. These glass eels (also called *elvers*) enter estuaries as early as March and begin their ascent of coastal rivers, sometimes in huge numbers, in May and June. Ascent up rivers usually occurs at night.

Upon entering fresh water, the elver gradually gains pigmentation, becoming grayish green to nearly black, at which time it is 2½ to 3½ inches (6.5 to 9 centimeters) long. Some elvers remain in brackish water close to the river's mouth, where they reside until their spawning migration; the majority ascend farther upstream, swimming close to the shore.

Males occupy the coastal regions and lower reaches of rivers—ceasing to grow after five years and attaining a maximum length of 19½ inches (50 centimeters). Females continue their upstream trek, some finding their way into silt-bottomed ponds and lakes considerable distances inland, where they might remain nine or more years.

After several years in fresh water, the eels take on a greenish or olive-brown color above (sometimes with bluish overtones), and are yellowish along the belly. They are at this stage referred to as *yellow eels*. (Eels, however, can redistribute pigment to alter skin color within hours.)

When sexually mature, the eels begin their spawning migration back to the sea. At this time they take on a metallic sheen: bronze to black above and light to silvery below. These are referred to as *blank eels*. Blank eels move from the rivers into the sea at night during late summer and fall. The eels now cease feeding; it is presumed that fat stores built up in the body provide the energy necessary for the journey back to the spawning grounds in the Sargasso Sea. Little is known of the movements of adult eels at sea, but studies suggest spawning occurs from February to July, after which the eels presumably die.

Food depends on life stage. Larval eels eat plankton, while juveniles and adults in fresh and brackish water are predacious, feeding mainly at night on invertebrates and small fishes (eel traps are frequently baited with the eggs of horseshoe crabs). Freshwater eels are primarily nocturnal, though a couple of times I have seen good numbers of elvers active during the afternoon in a river just south of Cape Cod. While considered primarily bottom dwellers, eels are quite mobile within the water column, slithering with a locomotion akin to that of a snake; I have watched eels take baitfish from the water's surface at night just as a trout rises to an insect.

The eel's body is elongate, almost cylindrical in cross-section anteriorly, somewhat compressed posteriorly. Its head is elongate, nearly wedge-shaped, its snout pointed, and its mouth large. The eye and gill openings are small.

A. rostrata's territory ranges from Greenland southward into the Gulf of Mexico, thence on to the Guianas. Maximum size reported is about 60 inches (1.5 meters).

While the largest eels are probably prey for only very large predators, smaller eels (particularly elvers) are a favorite prey of both striped bass and bluefish. Eels 10 to 16 inches (25.5 to 40.5 centimeters) long are a popular live bait.

AKA: Anguila (Spanish), anguille (Cajun), anguille d'Amérique (French), Atlantic eel, bellied eel, black eel, bronze eel, common eel, eel, freshwater eel, green eel, silver eel, whip, yellow eel.

Snake Eels *(Family Ophichthidae)*

Members of this marine family are slender and almost entirely round, their tails ending in a horny point (those swallowed by predators sometimes use this tail to bore through the predator's stomach and make their way into the body cavity, where they become mummified). Snake eels are most likely to be found over grass beds and coral reefs. Coloration varies from drab to striking; many are mottled, barred, or spotted. Unlike freshwater eels, many of these eels are active during the day. These eels are eaten by many predacious species, including groupers, snappers, tuna, and barracuda. A.J. McClane reported that in his examinations of the stomach contents of bonefish, snake eels and cusk-eels (see Family Ophidiidae) were more abundant than their natural occurrence would suggest, indicating some selective feeding by the bonefish. There are twenty-eight species of snake eels in North America.

AKA: Shrimp eels, snapper eels, worm eels.

Key Worm Eel *(Ahlia egmontis)*

The key worm eel is found in seagrass beds in bays and mangroves and also around offshore reefs. It occurs from Florida (including the Keys; a few leptocephali have been found as far north as the Scotian Shelf) to Brazil, including the Gulf of Mexico, the Bahamas, and the West Indies. The body of the key worm eel is brownish, covered with many tiny black specks. Its snout is roundish, U-shaped when viewed from above. Maximum length is 15 inches (38 centimeters).

Silversides *(Family Atherinidae)*

Worldwide, silversides number about 240 species, 10 of which inhabit North American oceans. As their name implies, they are characterized (in most cases) by a distinct silvery midlateral band running the length of the body. Typically, silversides are elongate, narrow-bodied, round-bellied fishes, usually light green above and pale below. Some species are translucent—that is, you can actually see through them. Most species are found close to shore, usually at the surface and always in schools. They can often be seen dimpling the surface as they feed, or leaping over floating debris (including a fly line). A delicious foodfish, silversides are often caught commercially and marketed as smelts (though they are not related to the true smelts of the family Osmeridae). Because of their similarity to other species, identification is often difficult, particularly on the East Coast. Silversides are a primary forage of many species of predacious fish.

Atlantic Silverside *(Menidia menidia)*

Plate 1

One of the most abundant of our small East Coast fishes, the Atlantic silverside inhabits the shorelines of the open ocean, brackish-water marshes, and intertidal creeks and estuaries from the southern end of the Gulf of St. Lawrence to northeast Florida. Typical of silversides, its body is long and slender, laterally compressed and with a rounded belly. Dorsal coloration is light olive to light green, and its body is translucent. Abdominal walls are whitish silver, sometimes with pearlescent reflections. The belly is white and the eye large. The silver midlateral band is edged above with a narrow black line. Connecticut angler and author Ed Mitchell has donned mask and flippers to swim among silversides. He reports that the silhouette and, to a lesser degree, the eye are the fish's predominant features under water, where dorsal coloration is muted considerably; the silver stripe is apparent only near the surface, flashing as the fish turns on its side while feeding.

In its coastal habitat, the Atlantic silverside is found in schools—usually composed of like-sized individuals—along sandy or gravelly shores, where it traverses their length with the movements of the tide. (It has been my experience that silverside schools along the open shore are more common toward autumn as the fish prepare to move to deeper waters offshore to winter.) In the estuaries, silversides are equally at home along silty or muddy shores. Schools are not always well defined; the fish can be strung out loosely along the shore for a considerable distance. During high-tide periods, they are often found feeding among the intertidal grasses.

Spawning occurs in abundantly vegetated estuaries from March through August, with regional variation (earlier in the south, later in the north). Spawning takes place in the intertidal zone during daytime high tides near the time of the full and new moons. Life span is twelve to twenty-four months (studies conducted in the Chesapeake Bay region showed that most fish there lived only one year and died soon after spawning). The maximum length is about 6 inches (15 centimeters).

An omnivorous, primarily diurnal feeder, the Atlantic silverside eats a variety of planktonic organisms, as well as shrimp, small squids, and marine worms. Chief predators are striped bass and bluefish, though it is also consumed by a number of other gamefishes, including bonito, false albacore, and weakfish (because of its delicacy, however, it is rarely used as bait). Silversides can often be seen leaping from the water in flight (particularly in the fall, when stripers go on an eating binge for their southward migration). I've seen entire bays glutted with silversides to the point where you couldn't get a fish to see your fly.

AKA: Capelin (incorrectly), capucette (French), green smelt, northern silverside, sand smelt, shiner, spearing, sperling, whitebait.

Inland Silverside *(Menidia beryllina)*

M. beryllina is found in coastal fresh and tidal waters (usually over sand) from Massachusetts to southern Florida and throughout the Gulf to northeastern Mexico. It lives sympatrically with the Atlantic silverside, and hybrids of the two species have been reported in Florida. Elongate, slender, and moderately compressed, it is pale greenish above and pale below (somewhat paler in color and stouter of body than is *M. menidia*). Its midlateral band is silvery, bordered by a black line above. Maximum length is about 4 inches (10 centimeters).

In areas where its range overlaps that of the tidewater silverside (*M. peninsulae*), the inland silverside is found almost exclusively in fresh water.

AKA: Waxen silverside.

Tidewater Silverside *(Menidia peninsulae)*

Very similar to the inland silverside, the tidewater silverside inhabits brackish waters and waters of full salinity (it never occurs in inland waters) from New England to southern Florida and in the northern Gulf of Mexico (except Louisiana and northeast Texas). It grows to 6 inches (15 centimeters).

Key Silverside *(Menidia conchorum)*

Occurring only in the lower Florida Keys, *M. conchorum* inhabits ponded waters of varying salinity. It is similar to the tidewater silverside and is considered a possible subspecies. The key silverside grows to 2 inches (5 centimeters).

Rough Silverside *(Membras martinica)*

The rough silverside occurs along the shore and in bays and inlets from New York to Mexico, including the Gulf of Mexico. As its name implies, it is rough to the touch. It grows to 5 inches (12.5 centimeters).

Hardhead Silverside *(Atherinomorus stipes)*

A pelagic coastal species found from southern Florida to Brazil (including the Bahamas and Panama), *A. stipes* is the most abundant silverside within its range. This species frequently schools with the reef silverside (*H. harringtonensis*). With a head distinctly wider than its body (when viewed dorsoventrally), it has two dusky horizontal stripes on its lower side beneath its silver midlateral band. Its eye is very large. The hardhead silverside grows to 4 inches (10 centimeters).

Reef Silverside *(Hypoatherina harringtonensis)*
(formerly listed as *Allanetta harringtonensis*)

The reef silverside occurs in coastal and offshore waters (particularly around drift lines) from southern Florida to northern South America, including Bermuda and the Bahamas. It is frequently found schooling with the hardhead silverside (*A. stipes*). It is distinguished from all aforementioned species in that its dorsal coloration is separated from its silver midlateral band by an unpigmented area. Dusky in color, the reef silverside grows to 4 inches (10 centimeters).

Plate 1

Topsmelt *(Atherinops affinis)*

The topsmelt is found in schools in the surface waters (occasionally to depths of 30 feet [9 meters; 5 fathoms]) along sandy beaches, in bays, around piers, over reefs, in kelp beds, and occasionally offshore. It ranges from the Gulf of California to Vancouver Island, British Columbia (though it is rare north of Tillamook Bay, Oregon). It is one of the most abundant fishes in many Pacific Coast estuaries, and one of the most commonly caught from California piers. It is often found in waters of high turbidity. Although it is an excellent foodfish, there is little commercial fishing for topsmelt. Those that are caught are usually taken alongside jacksmelt (*A. californiensis*). The topsmelt is an elongate, laterally compressed fish, green above and silvery below, with a bright-silver midlateral band. Unlike some species of silversides (such as the Atlantic silverside [*M. menidia*]), topsmelt are not translucent—that is, you cannot see through them. Presently, five subspecies are recognized.

Although some juveniles and adults occupy the open waters of estuaries and bays all year long, most topsmelt prefer the neritic areas and coastal kelp beds during fall and winter. In spring they are often found at the entrances of bays. During late spring and summer, adults move into the shallows and the mud flats where there is appropriate submerged vegetation in which to spawn. In Newport Bay, California, spawning occurs as early as February, but most occurs during May and June. In San Francisco Bay, spawning lasts from April to October, with peaks in May and June. Most spawning takes place at night. The topsmelt appears to lay its eggs in batches, primarily on eelgrass, spawning more than once during the season. After spawning, adults move to the upper estuarine areas.

The northern varieties of topsmelt grow larger than do the southern. The subspecies found from Monterey to San Diego Bay, *A. affinis littoralis*, reaches maturity in two years at a length of about 4¾ inches (12 centimeters). In Oregon, most topsmelt mature in three years at a length of 8 inches (20 centimeters). Overall, the species can live up to eight years and attain a length of about 14½ inches (37 centimeters).

The topsmelt is omnivorous, consuming plankton, algae, and even insect larvae, though those inhabiting bays and estuaries feed primarily on plant material. Most feeding takes place during the daylight hours. Topsmelt often feed near the surface; in water less than 6½ feet (2 meters; 1 fathom) deep, though, they feed off the bottom.

Topsmelt are an important prey for many predacious fishes, including yellowtail, barracuda (particularly around kelp beds), bonito, halibut, and sandbasses.

AKA: Bay smelt, capron, jack pescadillo, least smelt, little smelt, panzarotti, rainbow smelt (incorrectly).

Jacksmelt *(Atherinopsis californiensis)*

Very similar to the topsmelt, the jacksmelt is found from Yaquina, Oregon (though it is most common south of Coos Bay), to Bahía de Santa Maria, Baja California, Mexico. (It is not commonly found in Anaheim, Alamitos, or Newport bays, California, though topsmelt are abundant in these waters.) Perhaps the only major differences in appearance between the two species are color (the jacksmelt is greenish blue above) and size (the jacksmelt has a maximum length of 17½ inches [44 centimeters]). Like the topsmelt, with which it frequently schools, the jacksmelt is seldom found far from shore, seeming to prefer turbid, murky waters and bays with large freshwater inflows. While the jacksmelt is found from the surface down to 95 feet (29 meters; 16 fathoms), it is most commonly found between depths of 5 and 50 feet (about 1 and 15 meters; about 1 and 8 fathoms).

Spawning takes place in shallow coastal waters and in bays and estuaries over marine vegetation (primarily eelgrass) that allows the eggs to become entangled. Spawning can occur from

October to March, and reportedly year-round in southern California. In San Francisco Bay, spawning occurs from October to early August; in San Pablo Bay, from September to April; in Tomales Bay, from January to March.

In one year the jacksmelt can grow to 5 inches (12.5 centimeters). Some individuals reach maturity by their second year, at which time they are 6 to 8 inches (15 to 20 centimeters). All mature by their third year. Maximum age can reach eleven years.

The jacksmelt is an omnivorous feeder. Primary foods include crustaceans (copepods), algae, and detritus.

The jacksmelt makes up the largest portion of the "smelt" catch in California, and although it is not considered an important fish commercially, it is an important forage species for other fishes, including yellowtail, kelp bass, and sharks.

AKA: Blue smelt, California smelt, horse smelt, peixe rey, pescado del rey, pesce rey.

California Grunion *(Leuresthes tenuis)*

Similar in appearance to the surf smelt (*Hypomesus pretiosus*), the California grunion is found off sandy beaches from just behind the surf line to a depth of about 60 feet (18 meters; 10 fathoms). It occurs from San Francisco to Bahía de San Juanico, Baja California, Mexico, but is most abundant from Point Conception southward.

Grunion are famous for their on-beach spawning and are captured at this time by beach-goers, who by law may use only their hands. A delicious foodfish, grunion are usually fried whole. They are sometimes taken in the live-bait fishery. Grunion are prey for a number of West Coast gamefishes, including sandbasses and striped bass. Halibut have been known to beach themselves while chasing grunion.

Spawning takes place from late February to early September, peaking in late March to early June. Governed by the lunar cycle, spawning occurs on sandy beaches from two to six nights after each full or new moon, and then for only three or four nights. Spawning lasts from one to three hours immediately preceding the high tide. Females spawn from four to eight times per season at about fifteen-day intervals. Spawning occurs most frequently from Morro Bay southward.

Maturity is reached in one year, at which time the grunion is about 5 inches (13 centimeters) long. Some live up to four years and reach a length of 7½ inches (19 centimeters).

Elongate and spindle-shaped, the grunion is greenish above and silvery below with a silver-blue midlateral band. The grunion's body is translucent, and there is a bluish spot on its cheek.

Herrings
(Order Clupeiformes; Family Clupeidae)

This large family of small- to medium-sized fishes not only comprises the most important fishes in the world commercially, but also forms the essential nutritional base for many marine predators. With an average protein and fat content of 18 percent each, the nutritional value of herrings is second only to that of eels. Herrings are also high in minerals, particularly phosphorus and calcium, and contain a number of important vitamins.

Found in schools near shore as well as in the open ocean, herrings are a slender, laterally compressed fish, usually silvery in color. Most species feed selectively on plankton, usually during the day (for most species, nocturnal feeding is restricted to moonlit nights).

There are twenty-seven species of herring in North America.

AKA: Arenque (Spanish).

Alewife *(Alosa pseudoharengus)* Plate 1

Alewives occur in coastal waters and estuaries from Newfoundland and the Gulf of St. Lawrence to Winyah Bay, South Carolina (rare south of Bogue Sound, North Carolina), with some natural landlocked populations (introduced into the upper Great Lakes as forage for other fishes). Many southern estuaries north of New River, North Carolina, support common to abundant year-round populations of juveniles.

Like other species of the genus *Alosa*, marine populations are anadromous, spending their adult lives at sea and returning to fresh water only to spawn. Spawning runs aside, the alewife is captured most often at depths of 185 to 360 feet (56 to 110 meters; 31 to 60 fathoms).

Alewives are vertical migrators, following the upward (night) and downward (day) movements of the zooplankton on which they feed. They have also been known to eat shrimp, small fishes, and fish eggs.

Anadromous populations of alewives spawn annually after reaching sexual maturity. Maturity is reached in three to five years, at which time the fish are 10 to 11 inches (25 to 28 centimeters) long. Spawning takes place in rivers, streams, lakes, and ponds. Apparently, the slower waters of streams are preferred. In southern waters, spawning can begin as early as February and last through May. In the species' northern reaches, spawning usually begins in late April, lasting into June (but sometimes spawning does not begin until June). Spawning in Chesapeake Bay typically begins from early to mid-March and lasts through April. Larger and older fish spawn first.

Immediately after spawning the fish run downstream again, and it's not unusual for spent fish to pass those on their ascent. Fish on their spawning run cease feeding, but once they reach brackish water on their return they begin to feed voraciously and can be hooked on a small artificial fly.

Upon hatching, the young alewives are slightly less than ¼ inch (5 millimeters). Some river-spawned alewives move upstream of their birthplace, but autumn brings about a seaward migration, most having entered salt water by fall at a length of 2 to 4½ inches (5 to 11.5 centimeters). Studies reveal that at this time both juvenile alewives and blueback herring (*A. aestivalis*) tend to concentrate toward the bottom during the day and near the surface at night. However, in Massachusetts I have seen them more than once congregated around river mouths at the surface during the day in September.

The alewife's body is deep, moderately elongate, and strongly compressed. The head is somewhat small and pointed. Color above is grayish green; sides and belly are silvery, iridescent, with shades of green and violet on the sides depending on how the light hits it. Sea-run alewives have a golden or brassy cast. Some adults have lateral stripes above the midline. There is a dusky spot behind the gill cover at eye level. The alewife can grow to 15 inches (40 centimeters), but usually reaches only 12 inches (30 centimeters).

AKA: Branch herring, forerunner herring, freshwater herring, gaspareau (French), gaspereau, glut herring, goggle eye, grayback, kyak, kiack, river herring, sawbelly, spreau.

Blueback Herring *(Alosa aestivalis)*

The blueback herring ranges from the Gulf of St. Lawrence to St. Johns River, Florida, but is more numerous in southern waters (there are also some landlocked populations in the southeastern United States).

Like the alewife, the blueback is anadromous, entering fresh water to spawn, after which it returns to the sea. Because the blueback is so difficult to distinguish from the alewife, both its life at sea and in fresh water are poorly documented.

It has been suggested that bluebacks are found most often at lesser depths—88 to 180 feet (27 to 55 meters; 15 to 30 fathoms)—than are alewives. But like alewives, they show vertical migrations, following the nocturnal and diurnal movements of their planktonic food supply in the water column. Spawning takes place in rivers, streams, lakes, and ponds, usually just above the head of the tide. The blueback's spawning usually begins three to four weeks later than the alewife's where the species coexist, but the runs overlap when the two use the same stream. The spawning runs last two or three months. Most spawning begins in March, but in the Delaware River it occurs between late April and mid-June; in Connecticut it has been observed from late April to mid-September. In Carolina's Cape Fear River estuary, studies indicate spawning might be taking place from January to June; in St. Johns River estuary in Florida, it might be occurring from January to April. When spawning, the blueback does not usually ascend as far into fresh water as does the alewife, and it is more selective about its spawning site, preferring fast water over a hard substrate. Spawning occurs yearly after sexual maturity is reached.

Studies place sexual maturity at three to four years; at three years, the fish is 8 to 9½ inches (20 to 24 centimeters). Maximum length is 15 inches (38 centimeters), but does not usually exceed 12 inches (30 centimeters).

Color above is blue-green to dark blue or bluish gray. There is a series of faint horizontal stripes above the midline. Sides and belly are silvery and iridescent. Some fish exhibit a brassy cast. There is a black spot behind the gill cover at eye level.

Scientifically, little is known on the predation of alewives and bluebacks at sea, though they most certainly sustain heavy losses during both spawning runs and fall seaward emigrations, particularly from such predators as Atlantic salmon, striped bass, bluefish, and weakfish. "Live-lining" alewives and bluebacks at the mouth of a run is a popular spring striped-bass tactic in the northeast.

AKA: Alose d'été (French), black belly, blue herring, blueback, blueback mulhaden, glut herring, kyack, river herring, summer herring.

Plate 2

Atlantic Herring *(Clupea harengus harengus)*

Ranging from northern Labrador to Cape Hatteras, North Carolina (uncommon south of New Jersey; seen occasionally in small numbers in Cape Hatteras in winter), the Atlantic herring was for hundreds of years the most important commercial fish in the northeastern Atlantic. It occurred in such abundance that it was at one time considered inexhaustible. Overharvesting, however, has all but decimated some populations (such as on Georges Bank).

The Atlantic herring is marine, occurring in shallow inshore waters (I've snagged 3- to 6-inch [7.6- to 15.25-centimeter] specimens while fly-casting the Massachusetts salt, both in bays and in the surf), or offshore from the surface to depths up to 650 feet (200 meters; 108 fathoms). It does enter bays and estuaries freely (less abundant in enclosed waters during the warmer months), but has never been reported in water that is considerably fresh. The Atlantic herring forms schools of like-sized individuals. Small schools are a rarity; schools usually number in the hundreds or thousands. Immature fish and fish preparing to spawn can form huge schools. A school at the surface can be detected by a fine rippling of the water (that "nervous water" to which anglers should always be alert). Schooling at the surface during the day is most likely in calm weather; overall, they are more likely to be found at the surface at night. Unlike many fishes (such as menhaden), Atlantic herring are not known to break the surface with their snouts or by "finning." A feeding school tends to be relatively stationary, drifting with the current rather than swimming against it. The Atlantic herring is less frightened by the approach of a boat than are other fishes (such as mackerel), and they do not jump unless frightened. Small herring being pursued by fish such as striped bass is a common sight.

The appearance of the Atlantic herring is sporadic, fluctuating greatly from year to year, week to week, and day to day, even in its established areas of abundance.

Scientists recognize a number of separate populations, each of which seems to have a preferred spawning ground. There are two spawning seasons: spring and summer-autumn. Some populations are restricted to one season, but others spawn at both times. Spring spawning has been reported in the Gulf of Maine (from the west coast of Nova Scotia); other than this, all spring spawning apparently occurs north of that area and is less extensive than is summer-autumn spawning. The mouth of the Bay of Fundy—especially on the shoals southwest of Grand Manan—is an important summer-autumn spawning site, with most spawners showing up in July, August, and September (though the spawning doesn't actually begin until early August). The spawning in this area ends in some years by early October; other years it can continue until late in the fall. Southward along the coast, the spawning season becomes progressively later and shorter. At Mount Desert, Maine, for example, the spawning season lasts from mid-August until October. Spawning grounds south of this throughout Massachusetts Bay—Ipswich Bay, Cape Ann, various areas along Massachusetts Bay, and around Provincetown—play host to breeding herring mainly during October. The Woods Hole, Massachusetts, vicinity sees spawning in late October and early November. Block Island, off Rhode Island, is the species' southern breeding limit. Spawning takes place mainly over rocky, pebbly, or gravelly bottoms in depths from 12 to 180 feet (3.5 to 55 meters; 2 to 30 fathoms), both inshore and over various shoals and ledges that lie within 25 miles (40 kilometers) of the coast.

Growth rates vary with population, but 2 to 2½ inches (5 to 6.5 centimeters) is the predominant size of immature herring found around Provincetown at the end of June. Fry of 2⅛ to 4 inches (5.4 to 10 centimeters) are found on Nantucket Shoals in mid-July. They reach 3½ to almost 5 inches (9 to 12.5 centimeters) by the end of their first year; fish of that size, presumably of the previous autumn's hatch, are abundant in the fall in the Bay of Fundy and at Boothbay, Maine. At Woods Hole, herring hatched in October and early November are 3 to 5 inches (7.6 to 12.5 centimeters) by the following autumn. Herring one to two years old and 4 to 8 inches (10 to 20 centimeters) are abundant throughout the summer east of Penobscot Bay, Maine (especially in the Passamaquoddy Bay region). Herring of 4 to 7 inches (10 to 17.75 centimeters) show up in numbers off the Massachusetts coast sometimes as early as late June, but other times not until July or August.

Plankton is the Atlantic herring's primary food, on which it feeds selectively, or sometimes by filtering. Adults, however, might feed on shrimps, as well as the larvae of sand lances, silversides, and other herrings. Most feeding takes place during the day or at twilight (little or no feeding occurs in complete darkness). The Atlantic herring feeds most actively from September to November.

Sexual maturity is reached in three to five years at a length rarely less than 9½ inches (24 centimeters). Maximum length is 18 inches (45 centimeters)—at which size the fish can weigh 1½ pounds—but usually is no more than 12 inches (30 centimeters). Mature herring are seen in numbers at the surface only briefly before, during, and after spawning, after which they are presumed to depart for deeper water to winter.

The body of the Atlantic herring is elongate, tapering slightly at each end, and is strongly compressed. The head is relatively small and pointed; the lower jaw projects slightly. The eye is moderate. Color above is steel blue or greenish blue with green reflections; sides and belly are silvery and generally iridescent with reflections of blue, green, and violet. The scales are large, rounded at the rear margins, and so loosely affixed that they slip off easily when the fish is handled. Gill covers sometimes have a golden or brassy cast.

The Atlantic herring is sold as kippers—smaller ones are sold as sardines—and also as bait. It is an important food for many predacious fishes, including cod, pollock, striped bass, bluefish, Atlantic salmon, tunas, and mackerel sharks. It is often rigged in "daisy chains" as bait for tunas.

AKA: Bloater (when smoked), brit, digby chick, hareng atlantique (French), Labrador herring, sardine, sea herring, scaidhlin or scaithlin (when salted or smoked), skadlin, sperling (small specimens).

Plate 2

Atlantic Menhaden *(Brevoortia tyrannus)*

The Atlantic menhaden is a schooling marine species—schools number from hundreds to thousands of fish—found in open seas as well as in bays and estuaries from the Gulf of St. Lawrence to Jupiter Inlet, Florida. It is especially abundant in U.S. waters, though its abundance has been known to fluctuate greatly from year to year. Although they can be found offshore, menhaden seldom move far from land and rarely leave shelf waters. Menhaden are often found at the surface—where they will often break the surface with their snouts or by "finning"—especially in the southern part of their range, mainly on warm, calm, sunny days. Schooling by size is a characteristic behavior of the genus.

Spawning takes place mainly at sea and in larger bays of U.S. waters, though the year-round presence of the species in the St. John River, New Brunswick, suggests that it spawns in Canadian waters as well. In the northern part of the Atlantic menhaden's range (Maine to Massachusetts), spawning takes place from May to October. In the southern part of its range, it spawns from October to April offshore of Cape Hatteras and Cape Lookout, North Carolina. Rhode Island's Narragansett Bay has a split spawning period: May through August, and then again in late October (the fall spawning is much more productive). In the northern reaches, spawning occurs farther inshore as the summer progresses, some taking place within the estuaries. The depth at which the Atlantic menhaden spawns is unknown, but its eggs are found in the water column at depths less than 33 feet (10 meters; 5½ fathoms).

Young menhaden are estuarine-dependent, spending about half their first year of life there (May to October). They tend to move into the upper reaches of the estuaries, preferring waters fringed with emergent vegetation (in open water they prefer seagrass beds). Most leave the estuaries in dense schools from August through November, migrating southward to overwinter offshore of the southeastern Atlantic Coast. Adult fish migrate southward as well, returning in the spring (they are present in Narragansett Bay from April to November, most abundantly from June to mid-September). The older, larger fish tend to move farther north.

At a length of about 1½ inches (4 centimeters), the juvenile Atlantic menhaden shows most of the characteristics of the adult, with the exception of its eyes, which are proportionately larger on the juveniles. Most fish are sexually mature by the end of their second year, at which time they are at least 8½ inches (21.5 centimeters) long; all mature by age three. Atlantic menhaden can live to ten years, but fish older than four years are relatively rare. Although some large specimens have been recorded, few exceed 10¾ inches (27.5 centimeters). One of the largest Atlantic menhaden on record measured 16½ inches (41.8 centimeters).

Food consists primarily of phytoplankton, particularly diatoms, but the menhaden also eats zooplankton, annelid worms, and even detritus.

The menhaden's body is elliptical with strong lateral compression. Its head and mouth are large, and its eye is fairly small. Color above is bluish, blue-gray, greenish, blue-green, or brownish, and sometimes bluish brown. Its sides and fins are silvery with a strong yellow or brassy cast. In back of the gill cover is one black or dusky spot, behind which are several smaller spots, irregularly arranged. Larger specimens have many spots.

Menhaden are preyed upon by many species of fish, including bluefish, striped bass (the Atlantic menhaden is one of two dominant prey of striped bass in the Chesapeake Bay during summer and fall, the other being the bay anchovy), bluefin tuna, swordfish, and sharks. An oily fish, the menhaden makes excellent chum, and is a popular live and chunk bait for striped bass and bluefish.

AKA: Alewife (incorrectly), alose tyran (French), bugfish, bugmouth, bunker, fatback, mossbunker, pogy, shad. All menhaden species are collectively referred to as *sardine* by the Cajuns.

Gulf Menhaden *(Brevoortia patronus)*

The Gulf menhaden is similar to the Atlantic menhaden, but with a greenish dorsal coloration, yellowish green fins, and an even larger head. It also differs in that its black shoulder spot is followed by a single row (rarely two rows) of smaller dark spots. *B. patronus* ranges from southern Florida to the northern Gulf of Mexico to southern Texas, in similar habitat as *B. tyrannus*; it supports a sizeable commercial fishery. Spawning takes place offshore in fall and winter, and the young fish move into estuaries soon after hatching, sometimes moving upriver 30 miles (48 kilometers) or more. Overwintering in the estuaries, the young fish move closer to the river mouths as they grow, moving out to sea (at about age one) with the adults in the fall.

The Gulf menhaden grows to 12 inches (30 centimeters), but rarely exceeds 10 inches (25 centimeters).

AKA: Pogy.

Yellowfin Menhaden *(Brevoortia smithi)*

The yellowfin menhaden occurs in similar habitat as the Gulf and Atlantic menhaden: from North Carolina to southern Florida and the eastern Gulf of Mexico (Florida). Its color is greenish or bluish above, silvery on the sides. It has a single dark shoulder spot. Fins are golden yellow. Maximum length is 13 inches (32 centimeters).

The yellowfin menhaden might hybridize with the Atlantic menhaden in southern Florida.

Finescale Menhaden *(Brevoortia gunteria)*

Found from the Chandeleur Islands, Louisiana, to the western Gulf of Mexico (most common off southern Texas), and southward to Yucátan, Mexico, the finescale menhaden shares a number of physical characteristics with the preceding two species, making identification difficult. The finescale can be distinguished from the Gulf menhaden in that it is more silvery and never has more than one spot on its sides. The finescale can be distinguished from the yellowfin in that they occupy different areas: the yellowfin is found in the eastern Gulf; the finescale occurs from the Chandeleur Islands westward and southward. *B. gunteria* grows to 10 inches (25 centimeters) in length.

Plate 2

Atlantic Thread Herring *(Opisthonema oglinum)*

The Atlantic thread herring ranges from Cape Cod to southeastern Brazil, including the Gulf of Mexico and the Bahamas. It is often found in harbors. Although a schooling fish, single individuals have been observed numerous times. The thread herring's lower profile is deeply curved, its head ending nearly in a point. Color above is bluish or greenish with six or seven dark horizontal streaks; sides are silvery. There is a dark spot above the gill cover, and a larger dark spot behind the gill cover. Behind this larger spot is usually a row of dark spots. Lobes of the dorsal fin and tail are dusky to black at the tips. The last ray of the dorsal fin is prolonged, giving the fish its common name. Maximum length is 12 inches (30 centimeters).

AKA: Hairy-back.

Gizzard Shad *(Dorosoma cepedianum)*

The gizzard shad occurs in coastal waters from New York to central Florida, and in the Gulf of Mexico from central Florida to central Mexico. There are also landlocked freshwater populations of gizzard shad that were stocked originally as forage for other fishes, though its rapid growth and size make it unsuitable prey for all but the largest predators.

Marine populations of the gizzard shad prefer brackish waters near river mouths to the open sea. In the spring, the shad move upriver to spawn. The young spend several years in fresh water before moving toward the sea. They mature in two to three years and can live to age ten.

Color above is dark blue or gray, with six to eight dusky horizontal stripes. Sides are silver to brassy, and the belly is white. There is a large dark shoulder spot on young and small adults. The gizzard shad has the deep-curved lower profile and threadlike dorsal fin of *O. oglinum*; unlike it, though, its snout is blunt. An herbivore, the gizzard shad can reach 20 inches (50 centimeters) and weigh 3 pounds, but it does not usually exceed 14 inches (35 centimeters).

Threadfin Shad *(Dorosoma petenense)*

Similar to the gizzard shad and the Atlantic thread herring, but less deep in profile and with no horizontal streaks, the threadfin shad is found from Florida to the northern Gulf of Mexico and southward to Belize. It is found most often in estuaries and coastal freshwater streams within its range, though it sometimes occurs in larger bays and harbors. Spawning occurs in both spring and autumn, with the threadfin (like the gizzard shad) moving upriver into fresh water. In 1953, the threadfin shad was introduced into California and is now occasionally found in coastal waters from California to Oregon.

The threadfin shad is compressed and silvery with an elongated dorsal ray and a rather pointed snout. There is a single dark spot behind the top of its gill cover. The center of its tail is golden yellow. In salt water the threadfin shad grows to 9 inches (23 centimeters).

False Pilchard *(Harengula clupeola)*

The false pilchard occurs in southern Florida, but is rare there; it is found primarily in the Bahamas and from Yucátan, Mexico, to southeastern Brazil. It inhabits coastal waters and shallow bays, especially where sewage is discharged, and is widely used as bait (particularly for snappers and groupers in the West Indies) and as food. It is presumed to occur in mixed schools with the redear sardine (*H. humeralis*). The false pilchard's body is slender, its profile not strongly curved. Its back is a dark greenish, its sides silvery. There is a pale yellow or orange spot at the edge of the gill cover, and a dark spot behind the gill cover. Maximum length exceeds 7 inches (18 centimeters).

Redear Sardine *(Harengula humeralis)*

Found from southern Florida to Brazil—including the Gulf of Mexico, Bermuda, and the Bahamas—the redear sardine is often found in large schools in the same habitat as is the false pilchard (and often mixed in with them), frequently coming close to shore. Like the false pilchard, it is widely used as bait and food.

The body of the redear sardine is slender, its upper and lower profiles evenly curved. Overall appearance is silvery, but it has a considerable amount of orange when alive. Along its upper side are three or four dark (sometimes orangish) broken lateral stripes that have the appearance of dotted lines. There is a diffuse reddish-orange spot at the edge of its gill cover. Also, the jaws and iris are marked with orange. It reaches a length in excess of 8 inches (20 centimeters).

Scaled Sardine *(Harengula jaguana)* Plate 2
(formerly listed as *Harengula pensacolae*)

Found from northeast Florida (rarely as far north as Georgia), throughout the Gulf of Mexico, and southward to the Caribbean and Brazil, the scaled sardine is the most common inshore herring on the Continental Shelf (except off Louisiana, where menhaden are more common). The scaled sardine is a coastal fish, only occasionally entering estuaries (and then only the high-salinity areas). *H. jaguana* is similar in appearance to the redear sardine, but its lateral stripes are often inconspicuous, never orangish, and are seldom broken. Also, there is no orange spot on the gill cover. There is, however, usually a single small dark spot at the upper edge of the gill cover, and sometimes one just behind the gill cover (in line with the eye). The scaled sardine is greenish above, its sides silvery, and its belly deeply curved. Maximum length is 7 inches (18 centimeters).

The scaled sardine is an important baitfish in Florida.

Spanish Sardine *(Sardinella aurita)*
(also listed as *S. anchovia*)

The Spanish sardine occurs from Cape Cod to Brazil, including the Gulf of Mexico, Bermuda, and the Caribbean (but primarily in the tropics). It is rarely found close to shore. More round and slender than are other herrings (not as deep-bodied as the scaled sardine), its color above is reportedly dark blue to bluish gray, sometimes greenish. Carl Richards reports the dorsal coloration of the Spanish sardines in Florida's Ten Thousand Islands area as light green. Its sides are silver to brassy. It grows to 10 inches (25 centimeters).

Orangespot Sardine *(Sardinella brasiliensis)*

Similar to the Spanish sardine, but with a narrow bronzish line along the upper part of its side, the orangespot sardine is found from southeastern Florida throughout the entire Gulf of Mexico. It grows to 10 inches (25 centimeters), but is usually smaller.

Dwarf Herring *(Jenkinsia lamprotaenia)*

Plate 2

Members of the genus *Jenkinsia* are all round-bellied, pallid, and translucent. All have a greenish cast to their backs and a silvery midlateral band. The silvery lining covering the internal organs can be seen through the muscles of the body wall. They are similar in appearance to anchovies (family Engraulidae) and silversides (family Atherinidae). *Jenkinsia* are important forage for many predacious fishes such as jacks and barracuda, and are frequently herded by them.

The dwarf herring occurs in enormous schools in clear-water bays and coastal regions of southern Florida (rare in the northwestern Gulf) to Bermuda and the Bahamas, and throughout the Caribbean to Venezuela. It commonly schools with the shortband herring (*J. stolifera*). The dorsal coloration of *J. lamprotaenia* is greenish, the silvery midlateral band broad throughout. The band is bordered above by a blue-green line, giving the body a bluish flash, and its width is equal to the diameter of the eye. The dwarf herring grows to a length in excess of 3 inches (7.5 centimeters). It is probably the *Jenkinsia* species of herring that are known (along with young-of-the-year anchovies) as *glass minnows*.

Little-Eye Herring *(Jenkinsia majua)*

This herring is found from the Florida Keys to Central America, including the Bahamas, the western Caribbean, and the Gulf of Campeche, Mexico. The little-eye herring is similar to the dwarf herring, but is more slender (its body depth is less than 15 percent of its overall length), and its midlateral stripe is narrower than its eye. It grows to 2½ inches (6.5 centimeters).

AKA: Slender herring.

Shortband Herring *(Jenkinsia stolifera)*

The midlateral stripe of the shortband herring is only half the width of its eye; it is narrowest or absent toward the front. Found from southern Florida to Venezuela, *J. stolifera* grows to 3 inches (7.5 centimeters).

Pacific Herring *(Clupea harengus pallasii)*

The Pacific herring is so similar to the Atlantic herring (*C. harengus harengus*) that it is considered by some researchers to be a West Coast population rather than a separate species. Found from the Gulf of Alaska to northern Baja California, *C. harengus pallasii* is present in most estuaries (though common in bays only during spawning season; sometimes found considerable distances offshore) from Morro Bay northward. It is found primarily north of Point Conception, California, however, and is seasonally one of the most abundant fishes within this region. Some are taken for human consumption, but baitfisheries that harvest juveniles exist in Puget Sound and other estuaries. The Pacific herring is a primary prey of many predacious fishes, including striped bass, white seabass, and salmons (for which they are a popular bait). Salmon boiling on schools of herring is a common sight.

Schooling fishes, Pacific herring are sometimes found at the surface along the open coast (usually when they are driven up), and they have been captured at depths exceeding 1,000 feet (300 meters; 166 fathoms). Distribution of populations and their movements at sea are poorly known, but the Pacific herring does not make extensive coastal migrations. However, schools move onshore and offshore as they spawn and feed.

During winter and early spring, adults move onshore, residing in holding areas before moving to adjacent spawning grounds. There are a number of spawning groups along the coast. San Francisco Bay marks the southernmost major spawning run, though Elkhorn Slough, California, supports a lesser run. San Francisco spawning begins in November; spawning begins later to the north. California spawning peaks around December and January, Puget Sound in February and March, and off British Columbia as late as April. Pacific herring spawn in the same areas every year: protected coastal habitats and bays and estuaries, usually with a substantial freshwater inflow. Most eggs are laid at night in intertidal and subtidal areas on eelgrass, kelp, algae, pilings, and rocks. Spawning occurs annually after the herring reach maturity.

Depending on water temperature, the eggs hatch in about ten days. Juvenile Pacific herring are highly abundant in many estuaries throughout the summer. Growth is rapid (more so to the north), and by fall the juveniles are 3 to 4 inches (7.5 to 10 centimeters) long, at which time they leave the shallows and head out to sea. Some juveniles, however, reside in estuaries the whole winter (such as in southern San Francisco Bay).

The Pacific herring feeds selectively on plankton (although some filter-feeding has been observed); adults eat fish larvae as well. The herring move toward the surface to feed at dawn and dusk.

California stocks mature in two to three years, at which time they are 6½ to 7 inches (16.5 to 17 centimeters). Stocks in Washington and British Columbia mature more slowly (in three to four years), but live longer. Herring off Alaska can live to nineteen years; California specimens have been aged to eleven years. Maximum length is about 18 inches (46 centimeters), usually less for southern stocks.

The body of the Pacific herring is of the same configuration as that of the Atlantic herring. Color above is dark green to bluish green to olive; below is silvery white.

AKA: California herring, ches-pechora herring, eastern herring, herring, kara herring, Pacific Ocean herring, seld, white sea herring.

Flatiron Herring *(Harengula thrissina)*

A nearshore species that is rare north of southern Baja California, the flatiron herring is deep-bodied and compressed, with a large eye and a single dark spot behind the gill cover in line with the top of the eye. Color above is bluish, fading to silvery below. It grows to 7¼ inches (18 centimeters).

Plate 3

Pacific Sardine *(Sardinops sagax)*

Found close to shore as well as hundreds of miles out to sea, the Pacific sardine lives near the surface in schools—often found schooling with the Pacific mackerel (*Scomber japonicus*)—from Alaska to Mexico, though California is about the northern end of its common range. Abundance of this species is of a cyclical nature (probably due to weather patterns; the Pacific sardine is partial to warmer waters). Its decline in the 1940s and 1950s caused its fishery to collapse. Abundant once again, most Pacific sardines caught today are used as bait.

Most spawning takes place inshore, but some can occur as many as 350 miles (563 kilometers) offshore. Recent studies show year-round spawning that peaks from summer to fall. About half reach sexual maturity in two or three years, at which time they are about 7 to 8 inches (18 to 20 centimeters). All are mature at 9½ inches (24 centimeters). Life span is about ten years, and maximum length can reach 16¼ inches (41 centimeters), but is usually less than 12 inches (30 centimeters).

A fast-swimming fish, the Pacific sardine is elongate and moderately compressed. Color above is bluish to dark green; below is silvery. Usually there are several dark spots (number and arrangement vary) along the upper side. The gill cover is striated as on the eulachon smelt (family Osmeridae). The Pacific sardine is an important forage for a number of West Coast gamefishes, including yellowtail, dolphin, white seabass, albacore, bonito, barracuda, halibut, and kelp bass.

AKA: Firecracker (when small), pilchard.

Middling Thread Herring *(Opisthonema medirastre)*

Similar to the other thread herrings, *O. medirastre* is found from Redondo Beach, California, southward, and is common around southern Baja California, occurring in large schools near shore. It is sometimes used as bait for tunas. A deep-bodied, strongly compressed fish, the middling thread herring is silvery blue above and silvery below. It grows to 10¾ inches (27 centimeters).

Round Herrings
(Family Dussumieriidae)

This small family of fishes resembles the herrings of the family Clupeidae, except that they are rounded. There are perhaps two species in North American waters.

Round Herring *(Etrumeus teres)*
(also listed as *E. sadina*)

The poorly known round herring occurs from the Bay of Fundy to southern Florida (rare south of South Carolina, but sometimes found in the northern Gulf of Mexico). It inhabits coastal waters, but is not usually found in bays or shallows. A slender, elongate fish, its belly is rounded in cross-section. Color is olive green above, silvery below. The round herring grows to 10 inches (25 centimeters).

AKA: Shadine (French).

Pacific Round Herring *(Etrumeus acuminatus)*

Considered by some researchers to be of the same species as *E. teres*, the Pacific round herring is found in large schools in coastal waters from Monterey Bay to Chile. Color is bluish above, silvery below, sometimes with a row of specks along its back. It grows to 12 inches (30 centimeters).

Sculpins and Gobies

Representing two families of the order Perciformes, these fishes are grouped because of their similar appearance and habitat.

Sculpins (Family Cottidae)

This large family of small, mostly bottom-dwelling fishes occurs along the East and West coasts (more abundant in colder waters), particularly in shallows and rocky tide pools. There are many freshwater species as well. Sculpins are characterized by a large toadlike head (that is to say, somewhat flat, with the eyes located high or on top) and a body that is rather stout toward the front and tapering toward the rear. The dorsal fin is long, and the anal fin is usually long. All sculpins have large fanlike pectoral fins. The tail is usually round or squared. Most sculpins are drab in color: various shades of greens and browns (ranging to dull red) predominate, usually blotched or mottled. Few species exceed 12 inches (30 centimeters). Sculpins are an important forage for predators in both fresh and salt water.

There are nearly one hundred species of saltwater sculpins in North America, thirteen of which inhabit the Atlantic. Species identification is difficult. For a more comprehensive listing of sculpins and gobies, consult the Peterson Field Guide series.

Grubby *(Myoxocephalus aenaeus)*

The grubby is the smallest of our common East Coast sculpins, and the only species found in very shallow water in southern New England. It ranges from northern Nova Scotia to New Jersey, where it inhabits estuaries as well as the open shore. (In the Bay of Fundy and the Gulf of Maine, it is found more so along the coast than in estuaries, but it is common around the mouths of rivers in these areas.) The grubby is found over a variety of bottoms, but is most abundant among eelgrass.

The body of the grubby is moderately elongate, the head broad, and the caudal peduncle rather slender. Color is variable and dependent on the bottom. Color above ranges from light to dark gray or greenish gray with darker irregular barrings along the sides. The head is mottled light and dark, and there are broken bars along the fins. The belly ranges from pale gray to white. Few specimens exceed 6 inches (15.2 centimeters).

The grubby consumes a variety of foods, including various mollusks and the young of many species of fish. Although there is little scientific data, it doubtless falls prey to a variety of shallow-water gamefishes.

AKA: Crapaud de mer nain (French), little sculpin.

Plate 3

Pacific Staghorn Sculpin *(Leptocottus armatus)*

The Pacific staghorn sculpin commonly occurs inshore, especially in bays and estuaries, and usually in sandy habitats from the Gulf of Alaska to north-central Baja California (Pacific staghorns older than one year are not found in estuarine waters that are appreciably fresh). It is forage for a variety of predacious fishes, including striped bass, halibut, spotted sandbass, barred sandbass, and yellowfin croaker. It is sometimes used as bait.

Spawning occurs from October through March or April, peaking in January and February. Eggs are probably laid in marine waters. The staghorn matures in one year, at which time it is usually 5 inches (12.5 centimeters) long. The species can live as long as three years and grow to 8 inches (20 centimeters). In Washington, it has been known to reach ten years and 9 inches (23 centimeters). Adults feed on fishes and crustaceans.

Color above is tan to greenish brown or grayish, and yellowish to white below. Dorsal, caudal, and pectoral fins are whitish yellow with dark bars. There is a dark spot at the rear of the dorsal fin.

Gobies (Family Gobiidae)

Similar in appearance to the sculpins, but usually somewhat more elongate, gobies are a large family of small to tiny fishes occurring in tropical and temperate salt and brackish waters (more abundant in tropical waters). Primarily bottom dwellers of shallow to moderate depths, gobies prefer sandy or silty areas strewn with shells and debris, and also vegetated areas. Gobies are variably colored—often brightly—and many species are capable of rapid changes in color and pattern. They move in spurts and darts, resting along the bottom in between. There are seventy species in North America, including some freshwater species.

Naked Goby *(Gobiosoma bosci)*

An abundant species from Cape Cod to Campeche, Mexico, the naked goby is found in weedy, sheltered coastal waters and estuaries, particularly around oyster beds. The length of its body is colored with nine to eleven broad, dark vertical bars. It grows to 2½ inches (6 centimeters).

Sharptail Goby *(Gobionellus hastatus)*

Occurring from North Carolina to Campeche, Mexico, the sharptail goby is found near shore over mud bottoms of bays and sounds. It is a slender, elongate fish, brown above with lighter sides; its belly is pale. Each side bears a dark oval spot below the spiny dorsal fin, and there is a small dark spot at the base of the tail. The head is bluntly rounded. The sharptail goby grows to 8 inches (20 centimeters).

Code Goby *(Gobiosoma robustum)*

Plate 3

The code goby ranges from Chesapeake Bay to Florida, throughout the Florida Keys and the Gulf of Mexico to Yucatán, Mexico. It is found in shallow, protected waters of full salinity (uncommon in deeper waters), particularly over seagrass-covered mud flats (especially in Florida and the northern Gulf of Mexico). It is also found over sand and mud-shell bottoms in bays and beach ponds, on oyster reefs, in river sloughs and rocky channels, and among mangrove roots.

The body of the code goby is dark green marked with a chainlike pattern of irregular interconnected bands of dark greenish gray, each having pale spots. Along the code goby's midside is a distinctive series of black dots and dashes (hence its common name). The code goby lives to a maximum of two years and grows to a length of about 2 inches (5 centimeters). It is eaten by a number of flats-dwelling predators, including bonefish, barracuda, and sharks.

Longjaw Mudsucker *(Gillichthys mirabilis)*

The longjaw mudsucker is a common inhabitant of the mud-bottomed shallows, tidal flats, bays, backwaters, estuaries, and coastal sloughs from Tomales Bay, California, to the Gulf of California, Mexico, but most commonly from San Francisco Bay southward. A particularly hardy fish, the mudsucker can tolerate extreme ranges of salinity from nearly fresh water to water with a salt content almost 2½ times that of seawater; it can survive water temperatures as high as 95 degrees F (31.5 degrees C). If kept moist, it can live out of the water as many as 8 days (at low tide on tidal flats, they can often be found hiding in holes in the mud).

Mudsuckers mature in their first year at a length of 2 to 3 inches (5 to 7.5 centimeters). Spawning occurs—in nests built by the males in mud banks—from December through July, peaking in spring.

Crabs and ghost shrimp make up the largest part of the mudsucker's diet; in turn, it is probably consumed by many shallow-water predators, including halibut, yellowfin croaker, spotted sandbass, barred sandbass, and striped bass. A commercial baitfishery exists for this species, but most taken for bait are used in fresh water.

The longjaw mudsucker's dorsal coloration is brownish to dark brown to bluish; back and sides are mottled (young often have eight vertical bars on their bodies and a dark blotch on the rear edge of their dorsal fin); below is yellowish. It lives to about two years and reaches a maximum length of 8¼ inches (21 centimeters).

AKA: Longjaw goby.

Blackeye Goby *(Coryphopterus nicholsi)*

Similar in configuration to the longjaw mudsucker (but with a shorter, rounder snout), the blackeye goby ranges from the Queen Charlotte Islands, British Columbia, to Punta

Rompiente, Baja California, but is most common from southern British Columbia southward. It is found on sand and mud bottoms near rocks, particularly around reefs, and usually near the rock-sand interface from the intertidal areas of quiet bays to deep water off the coast. Juveniles have been found near the surface far out to sea, and have turned up in the stomachs of albacore. Typically, though, the blackeye goby is a bottom-dweller, burrowing in rock crevices and ranging 3 to 5 feet (1 to 1.5 meters) onto the sand or into the water column to chase food (small crustaceans and mollusks) and ward off intruders. A diurnal fish, the blackeye retreats to its shelter at night.

Spawning takes place in nests beneath rocks from February to October, probably peaking in late spring and early summer. Blackeyes mature in about two years at a length of 1½ to 2 inches (4 to 5 centimeters). They live to about five years, with a maximum length of 6 inches (15 centimeters).

Elongate and nearly round in cross-section, the blackeye goby is tan (some specimens are nearly white) to olive above, usually with brown mottling. Its first dorsal fin is edged black, and there is an iridescent blue spot beneath its large black eye.

AKA: Blackspot goby, bluespot goby, onespot goby.

Killifishes (Family Cyprinodontidae)

These small schooling fishes inhabit quiet bays and estuaries, tidal creeks, marshes, and lagoons of tropical and warm-temperate waters. They are never found very far from shore. Killifishes can be distinguished from other small forage fishes by having only one short dorsal fin located far back on the body (closer to the tail than to the head). Also, the ventral fins are located on the abdomen, and the tail is rounded; the caudal peduncle is very thick. Most species are under 4 inches (10 centimeters) in length, but a few reach 6 inches (15 centimeters). Food consists of a variety of organisms and vegetable matter, depending on the species. The mouth of the killifishes is at the tip of the snout, adapted for surface feeding, and they can often be observed along grassy shorelines, dimpling the surface with their rises. Most are somber in color (except some breeding males), and many have dark vertical bars along the side. Killifishes are commonly used as bait, often for freshwater fishes. Killifishes are forage for many predacious species, including striped bass, bluefish, sea-run trout, snook, tarpon, and ladyfish.

Plate 3

Mummichog *(Fundulus heteroclitus)*

The mummichog inhabits marshy areas, brackish-water ponds, tidal creeks, river mouths, and estuaries, as well as sheltered and harbor shores from the Gulf of St. Lawrence to the Gulf of Mexico as far as Texas. It prefers shallow areas of submergent or emergent vegetation. Tolerant of a wide range of salinities, it sometimes ascends into fresh water. Whatever its habitat, the mummichog is usually found near the surface. During high tides, it can often be found in abundance among the grasses in only a few inches of water.

Spawning takes place in shallow water from April to August (with regional variation: earlier in the south, later in the north), depending on water temperature, and is reportedly associated with high tides of the new full moon. The mummichog's eggs are deposited on aquatic plants or, in the southern part of its range, in mussel shells. At one year, the mummichog is 1½ to 2 inches (4 to 5 centimeters) long; at age four, it is about 3½ inches (9 centimeters). Maximum length is about 5 inches (13 centimeters).

An omnivorous feeder, the mummichog consumes a variety of small crustaceans, fish eggs, small fishes, insects, and insect larvae (particularly mosquito larvae), as well as vegetable matter. The presence of mummichogs in the stomach contents of various fishes (such as bluefish and sea-run brook trout), as well as its use as bait, dispels the notion that it is toxic to other fishes.

The mummichog's body is stout, broad anteriorly and compressed posteriorly. Its head is broad, flat on top, with the snout bluntly rounded. The caudal peduncle is deep. Males are dark in color, dull green on the back and sides. The sides have numerous poorly defined silvery vertical bars and randomly distributed yellow and white spots. The belly is orange-yellow to greenish yellow, and the front edge of the pelvic and anal fins is yellow. At spawning time, the male's pigmentation becomes intensified. The body darkens, becoming nearly black on top in some cases, and takes on steel-blue reflections; the yellow becomes more brilliant.

Female mummichogs are plain olive green to green above and on the sides, lighter below. Some females are patterned with about fifteen indistinct vertical bars along the sides. These bars are a deeper tone of the same color as the body.

Mummichogs have the ability to change their color to more closely match their surroundings.

AKA: Barbel, choquemort (French), common killifish, common mummichog, chub, mummy, saltwater minnow. Mummichogs have been sold as bait under the erroneous label *tommy cod* in the northeast.

Gulf Killifish *(Fundulus grandis)*

Nearly identical in appearance to the mummichog, the Gulf killifish is found in the same habitat as is the mummichog in East Texas and Louisiana, ranging southward to Mexico and Cuba. *F. grandis* is sold as bait under a variety of names, including *chubs* and *minnows*, and it has also been incorrectly sold as *finger mullet*.

Striped Killifish *(Fundulus majalis)*   Plate 3

The striped killifish resembles the mummichog in general form, but is more slender, its body more fusiform, and its snout more pointed. *F. majalis* is found in estuaries, bays, and saltwater marshes as well as along open beaches (more likely in waters of higher salinity than is the mummichog) from New Hampshire to northeast Florida and in the northern part of the Gulf of Mexico.

A paler fish than the mummichog, the male striped killifish is dark olive green above; its sides are silvery, with fifteen to twenty black vertical bars; its belly is greenish yellow. There is a black spot on the rear part of the dorsal fin. Its pectoral fins and tail are a pale yellow. At breeding time—very early spring to early fall, with regional variation—the male turns more brilliant, its back becoming almost black, the lower sides and belly turning orange or golden, and the fins becoming bright yellow. The female is olive green above and white below. Atlantic Coast females have several dark vertical bars (virtually absent from some specimens) and two or three black lateral stripes; Gulf Coast females lack stripes, sporting several dark vertical bars only.

Food consists of small animals, including mollusks, crustaceans, small fishes, insects, and insect larvae. Maximum length for the species is 7 inches (18 centimeters), but is more commonly 6 inches (15 centimeters).

California Killifish *(Fundulus parvipinnis)*

Ranging from Morro Bay to northern Baja California, *F. parvipinnis* is common near shore in bays and marshes. Color is olive green above and yellowish brown below, usually with short dark vertical bars along the side. Breeding males are dark brown to blackish. Maximum length is 4½ inches (11 centimeters).

This is the only species of killifish native to the western United States. The rainwater killifish (*Lucania parva*), which lives primarily in fresh water but sometimes enters large brackish-water bays, was introduced accidentally. *L. parva* is similar in appearance to *F. parvipinnis*, but is smaller. It grows to only about 1¾ inches (4.4 centimeters), is straw-colored, and lacks vertical bars.

Anchovies (Family Engraulidae)

This family of delicate fishes is abundant in the tropical and temperate coastal waters and estuaries around the world, where they can occur in enormous schools. Although some species inhabit the open ocean, most prefer shallow bays and sounds. Characterized by an elongate, often silvery body (there is usually some degree of lateral compression) and a silver midlateral stripe, anchovies superficially resemble silversides (family Atherinidae). Belonging to the order Clupeiformes, however, anchovies are actually closer in relation to the herrings. They are distinguished from silversides and other forage fishes most obviously by a blunt, bulbous snout that projects over a large mouth. Anchovies range in color above from blue-green to translucent gray. The eye is usually large and placed well forward on the head.

The staple of the anchovy's diet is zooplankton, on which it filter-feeds (though there is strong evidence that some species selectively capture food), but larger anchovies might eat small fishes as well. In turn, anchovies are fed upon by many species of predacious fish, and support a commercial industry. Anchovies are widely used as bait and chum, particularly on the West Coast (though the delicacy of some species makes them unsuitable as live bait).

Anchovy species are similar in appearance and many are difficult to distinguish. Despite their importance (both commercially and in the food web), little is known of most species. About ninety species (including subspecies) inhabit waters of the Americas.

AKA: Anchoa (Spanish), bahía (Spanish; might refer specifically to the bay anchovy or a similar species), boquerón (Spanish); young-of-the-year anchovies are sometimes known as *glass minnows*.

Plate 4

Bay Anchovy *(Anchoa mitchilli)*

The bay anchovy is abundant within its range: Massachusetts (rarely as far north as Nova Scotia) to Yucatán, Mexico, including the Gulf of Mexico; most commonly south of Cape Cod and exceedingly abundant south of New Jersey; considered the most abundant fish species in the Chesapeake Bay; rarely found in the Florida Keys. The bay

American Sand Lance *Ammodytes americanus*

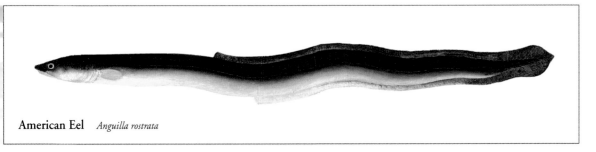

American Eel *Anguilla rostrata*

Atlantic Silverside *Menidia menidia*

Topsmelt *Atherinops affinis*

Alewife *Alosa pseudoharengus*

Plate 1

Atlantic Herring *Clupea harengus harengus*

Atlantic Menhaden *Brevoortia tyrannus*

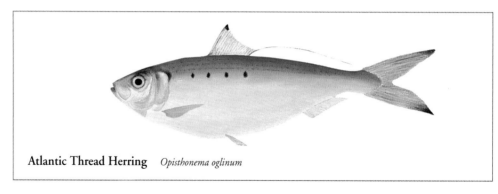

Atlantic Thread Herring *Opisthonema oglinum*

Scaled Sardine *Harengula jaguana*

Plate 2

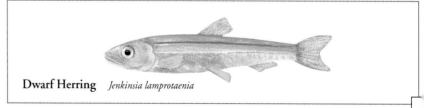

Dwarf Herring *Jenkinsia lamprotaenia*

Pacific Sardine   *Sardinops sagax*

Pacific Staghorn Sculpin   *Leptocottus armatus*

Code Goby   *Gobiosoma robustum*

Mummichog   *Fundulus heteroclitus*
(male, spawning colors)

Plate 3

Striped Killifish   *Fundulus majalis* (female)

Bay Anchovy *Anchoa mitchilli*

Northern Anchovy *Engraulis mordax*

Threespine Stickleback *Gasterosteus aculaetus*

Common Halfbeak *Hyporhamphus unifasciatus*

Plate 4

Balao *Hemiramphus balao*

Atlantic Needlefish   *Strongylura marina*

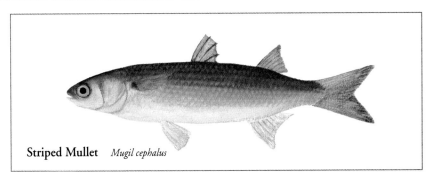

Striped Mullet   *Mugil cephalus*

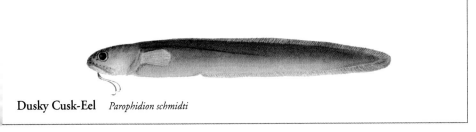

Dusky Cusk-Eel   *Parophidion schmidti*

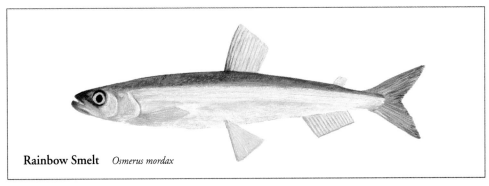

Rainbow Smelt   *Osmerus mordax*

Plate 5

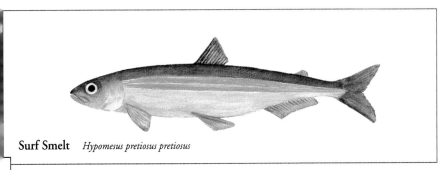

Surf Smelt   *Hypomesus pretiosus pretiosus*

Eulachon *Thaleichthys pacificus*

Atlantic Mackerel *Scomber scombrus*

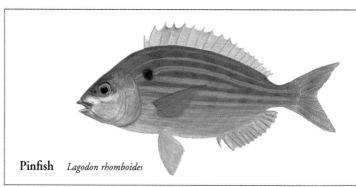

Pinfish *Lagodon rhomboides*

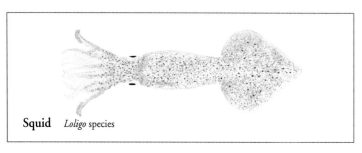

Squid *Loligo* species

Plate 6

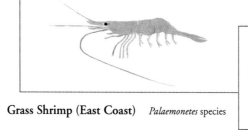

Grass Shrimp (East Coast) *Palaemonetes* species

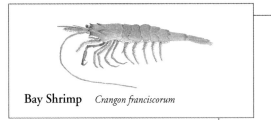

Bay Shrimp *Crangon franciscorum*

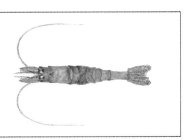

White Swimming Shrimp *Penaeus setiferus*

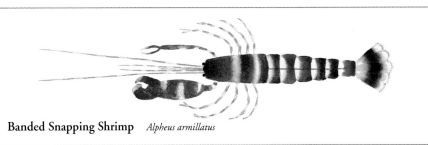

Banded Snapping Shrimp *Alpheus armillatus*

Blue Crab *Callinectes sapidus*

Green Crab *Carcinus maenas*

Plate 7

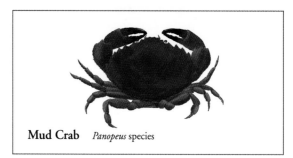

Mud Crab *Panopeus* species

Sand Fiddler *Uca pugilator* (male)

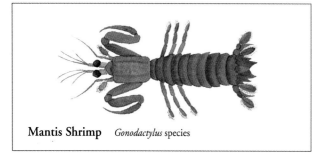

Sand Crab *Emerita analoga* (egg-bearing female)

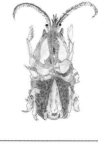

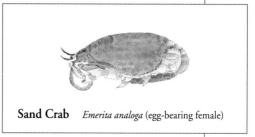

Mantis Shrimp *Gonodactylus* species

Plate 8

Green Clamworm *Nereis virens* (breeding colors)

anchovy occurs in schools over a variety of substrates and in a variety of habitats, primarily in shallow bays and estuaries, but also inshore along the open coast and sometimes a considerable distance offshore. It is common in brackish waters and often ascends into fresh water (juveniles have been taken nearly 40 miles [64 kilometers] above brackish water in Virginia rivers). Although its habitat is primarily estuarine, it also has been taken from hypersaline waters in Texas. As with salinity, temperature does not limit its distribution. There is no seasonal coastal migration for the species, and studies conducted in the warm-water discharge of a power plant found that bay anchovies were unaffected by water nearly 90 degrees F (32 degrees C).

The bay anchovy is a slender-bodied fish that is moderately compressed laterally. Dorsal coloration is reported in the scientific literature as greenish with bluish reflections. Carl Richards, however, who fishes Florida's Ten Thousand Islands area, reports the dorsal coloration of the bay anchovies there as golden gray. Similarly, Connecticut angler and author Ed Mitchell describes the dorsal coloration of the bay anchovies in his home waters as a faint yellowish brown or faint green. The bay anchovy has an indistinct silvery midlateral band (about the same width as the pupil of its eye, and often absent toward the front). Color below is pale and, like many species of silverside (family Atherinidae), its body is translucent. Distinguishing it from the silversides is its rounded snout, which protrudes over its large mouth. Abdominal walls are whitish silver, and the sides of the head and gill covers are silvery. Maximum size of the bay anchovy is reportedly 4 inches (10 centimeters), with an average of about 3 inches (7.5 centimeters); however, Carl Richards reports never having seen one in the Ten Thousand Islands area that exceeds 1 inch (2.5 centimeters), and Ed Mitchell reports the maximum size of the bay anchovies he has seen to be about 1¼ inches (3.1 centimeters).

Spawning takes place in estuaries throughout much of the year—most occurring from about late April to late September, but perhaps year-round in at least one Florida estuary (Indian River). Most spawning takes place in the evening or at night, probably at a depth of less than 60 feet (18 meters; 10 fathoms). The bay anchovy is a batch spawner, some females spawning in excess of fifty times per season.

Maturity comes quickly to the species. Those hatched early in the season can reach sexual maturity their first summer, reportedly at a length of 1⁷⁄₁₀ to 2⅓ inches (4.5 to 6 centimeters).

Mysids make up the principal food of the adult bay anchovy, which is presumed to be primarily a diurnal feeder. When the estuaries begin to warm, juvenile (and possibly some adult) bay anchovies move into fresh waters to feed. They return to more saline waters in early autumn, at which time they are found at the lower ends of estuaries schooling in tremendous numbers. (Ed Mitchell notes that schools of bay anchovies appear light yellowish brown, or sometimes reddish brown when seen from a distance.) By late November, all bay anchovies have returned to saline waters. Winters are spent in deeper estuarine and bay waters.

The bay anchovy is a primary forage of many gamefishes, including bluefish, striped bass (one of two dominant prey of the striped bass in the Chesapeake Bay in summer and fall, the other prey being the Atlantic menhaden), weakfish, spotted seatrout, white seatrout, snook, and tarpon.

AKA: Common anchovy, little anchovy, Mitchell's anchovy, whitebait.

Striped Anchovy *(Anchoa hepsetus)*

The striped anchovy is commonly found in shallow coastal waters, as well as waters extending out to the Continental Shelf, from Massachusetts (rarely as far north as Nova Scotia) southward. It is a common species along the entire west coast of Florida (particularly abundant in Florida Bay between October and May), throughout the Gulf of Mexico (rarely found in the Florida Keys), and throughout the Caribbean to Uruguay. While the striped anchovy is commonly taken in estuarine waters, it is more often associated with deeper bay waters and waters of higher salinity; it is usually found farther offshore than is the bay anchovy (*A. mitchilli*).

Elongate and moderately compressed, the striped anchovy is reportedly dusky green or greenish blue above, and whitish below with a silver midlateral band whose width is 75 percent the width of its large eye (the width of the eye is somewhat larger than the length of the snout). Above the midlateral band are yellow and green iridescent reflections. The head (whose snout is somewhat longer than that of the bay anchovy) has a noniridescent yellowish tinge to it, and there is yellow around the midlateral band as well. Carl Richards describes the striped anchovies he has seen in Florida's Ten Thousand Islands area as having a translucent yellow-tan body and a silver midlateral band that turns black when light strikes it at a certain angle.

The striped anchovy spawns in the early spring, and while some spawning takes place in the estuaries, most occurs farther offshore. The fish matures sexually at about one year at a length of 3 inches (7.5 centimeters). Maximum length is about 6 inches (15 centimeters).

AKA: Piquitinga (French).

Silver Anchovy *(Engraulis eurystole)*

Similar to the flat anchovy (*Anchoviella perfasciata*), the silver anchovy is usually found from Woods Hole, Massachusetts, to Beaufort, North Carolina (tentatively from Florida to the Gulf of Mexico), and is most common offshore and in deeper inshore waters. It probably enters shallows mainly at night. *E. eurystole*'s stripe is broad and black-bordered on top, as on the Atlantic silverside (*Menidia menidia*). It reaches a length of 6 inches (15 centimeters).

AKA: Anchois argenté (French).

Bigeye Anchovy *(Anchoa lamprotaenia)*

Occurring in southeastern Florida to Panama, including the Bahamas and the West Indies, *A. lamprotaenia* is entirely marine and is not found in estuaries. Its color above is gray (the top of its head is iridescent), and its silver stripe is broad. As indicated by its name, its eye is large (the diameter of the eye is much greater than the length of the snout). *A. lamprotaenia* reaches a length of 3½ inches (9 centimeters).

AKA: Longnose anchovy.

Dusky Anchovy *(Anchoa lyolepis)*

The dusky anchovy is found in bays and cuts (but apparently only in waters of full salinity) in southeastern Florida and the northern part of the Gulf of Mexico to Venezuela. Its body is elongate and dusky and somewhat iridescent above. The silvery midlateral stripe widens toward the tail and is bordered above by a narrow dark stripe. There is an iridescent golden spot on the top of its head. Its snout is long. The dusky anchovy reaches a length of 3½ inches (9 centimeters).

Cuban Anchovy *(Anchoa cubana)*

Similar to the bay anchovy (*A. mitchilli*), the Cuban anchovy is found along both coasts of Florida and the northern Gulf Coast southward to the Caribbean and Guatemala, mostly in shallow water (except along the Gulf Coast). *A. cubana* grows to 3 inches (7.5 centimeters).

Flat Anchovy *(Anchoviella perfasciata)*

As implied by its name, the flat anchovy is elongate and strongly compressed. The broad midlateral band (nearly as wide as the eye) is widest above the anal fin and ends in a dark crescent. The top part of the eye is orangish, and the top of the head has green and gold reflections with a pair of blue spots on top of the head behind the eyes. *A. perfasciata* ranges from North Carolina (but possibly as far north as New York) to the northern Gulf Coast and southward to the West Indies. The flat anchovy inhabits bays and coastal waters, but is not known to enter brackish water. Maximum length is 4 inches (10 centimeters).

Slough Anchovy *(Anchoa delicatissima)*

The overall range of the slough anchovy is from Long Beach Harbor, California, to southern Baja California. Although it is abundant in many southern California estuaries, it is of no commercial value, though it is used occasionally as bait. All life stages occur primarily in estuaries, bays, bay backwaters, and lagoons, although juveniles and adults are sometimes found along the outer coast. All life stages are pelagic and are found over various substrates. *A. delicatissima* usually forms small schools.

During the spring and early summer, adults move into spawning areas: the lower reaches of bays and estuaries. Spawning takes place at night from May to September, most probably occurring in July. Adults show post-spawning movements to other bay areas.

Juveniles range in length from 1 to 2 inches (2.5 to 5 centimeters). The species matures in one year, at which time it is at least 2 inches (5 centimeters) long.

The body of the slough anchovy is compressed, greenish above and white below with a silver midlateral band. It lives to about three years and attains a maximum length of about 3½ inches (9 centimeters). It is probably preyed upon by many species of fish.

AKA: Southern anchovy.

Deepbody Anchovy *(Anchoa compressa)*

Like the slough anchovy, the deepbody anchovy is of little commercial value, though it is used occasionally as bait. It is abundant in many bays and estuaries from Morro Bay, California, to Bahía de Todos Santos, California, but is most common south of Alamitos Bay. All life stages are primarily estuarial, but schools of juveniles and adults are found occasionally along coastal shores. Like the slough anchovy, *A. compressa* is found over a variety of substrates.

Spawning occurs from March to August, when adults move into the upper reaches of bays and estuaries (unlike *A. delicatissima*, which utilizes the lower reaches). Most spawning activity takes place at night from April to June. One-year-olds range in length from 2¾ to 3½ inches (7 to 9 centimeters). Adults reach 6½ inches (16 centimeters). The species can live to six years, but most die before age five.

The deepbody anchovy feeds primarily on small crustaceans, utilizing the entire water column for its search.

As its name implies, the species has a deeper profile than do most other anchovies, more herring-like in shape. Color above is brownish to green, silvery below with a broad silver midlateral band.

The deepbody anchovy is probably forage for many backwater fish species.

AKA: Anchovy, California deepbody anchovy, deep-bodied anchovy, sardinus, sprat.

Northern Anchovy *(Engraulis mordax)*

Plate 4

One of the most abundant fishes in the California Current, the northern anchovy inhabits coastal waters from northern British Columbia, Canada, to Cabo San Lucas, Baja California (most commonly from San Francisco southward), and has recently extended its range into the Gulf of California, Mexico. It is fished commercially from British Columbia to northern Baja California. *E. mordax* is a primary forage for many species of predacious fish, and is perhaps the most important baitfish for marine recreational fisheries off southern California. It is also used as bait for sturgeon, salmons, and other fishes in the Pacific Northwest.

Adults occur offshore (the bulk of the population occurs within about 25 miles [40 kilometers] of shore), from the surface to about 985 feet (300 meters; 164 fathoms), but they can also be abundant in shallow inshore areas and estuaries (though in the outer, higher salinity areas). Studies supervised by NOAA indicate the greatest estuarial abundance to be from Tomales to San Pedros bays, California; all estuaries within this range support abundant to highly abundant year-round populations of adults and juveniles.

All life stages are found over various substrates. There exist three genetically distinct populations.

The northern anchovy does not show predictable migrations, but studies show fairly extensive inshore-offshore movements (it has been found hundreds of miles at sea), as well as movements up and down the coast. In the Pacific Northwest, juveniles and adults move into estuaries during spring and summer, and then move out again in the fall. In southern California, yearling and young-of-the-year anchovies utilize shallow inshore areas. In summer, both adults and juveniles stay, to some extent, at depths below 330 feet (100 meters; 55 fathoms) during the day, though it is not unusual to see them at the surface. At night they come to the surface, dispersing into a thin layer. The northern anchovy forms dense schools when attacked.

Spawning has been reported from Barkley Sound and the Strait of Georgia, British Columbia, to south of Magdalena Bay, Baja California, and in the Gulf of California. Depending on the region (that is, subpopulation), spawning can take place throughout the year. In British Columbia, spawning occurs July through August; in Oregon, June to August; in central California, December to June; in San Francisco, May to September; and in southern California, January to May.

Most California spawning takes place in depths of less than 33 feet (10 meters; 5 fathoms), but spawning has been recorded several hundred miles offshore. The spawning of the northern subpopulation appears to be associated with the Columbia River Plume. The northern anchovy is a batch spawner and can spawn as many as twenty times per season.

Fish can mature in less than one year, at which time they are between 2¾ and 4 inches

(7 and 10 centimeters), but some can take up to four years, depending on location and population size. Maximum age is seven years, though specimens rarely live longer than four.

The northern anchovy is primarily a diurnal feeder, consuming phytoplankton and planktonic crustaceans as well as fish larvae. Juvenile and adult anchovies are consumed, in turn, by many species of predacious fish, including dolphin, halibut, kelp bass, chinook and silver (coho) salmon, white seabass, striped bass, rockfishes, yellowtail, barracuda, tunas, and sharks.

E. mordax is not as strongly compressed as are other anchovy species. Its color above is a metallic blue or metallic green (the green variation is preferred by bait fishermen, probably because it tends to be more lively), and silver below. Adults have a faint silver midlateral band. Maximum length is 9 inches (23 centimeters), but the species rarely exceeds 7 inches (18 centimeters).

AKA: Anchoa, anchovy, anchoveta, bay anchovy, California anchovy, North American anchovy, pinhead, plain anchovy.

Sticklebacks *(Family Gasterosteidae)*

This small family is distributed throughout the cooler waters of the Northern Hemisphere, from the East Coast of North America to Europe and from the West Coast to northern and central Asia. Tolerating a wide range of salinity, sticklebacks are found in marine, brackish, and fresh waters. They have been the subject of many important physiological and behavioral studies.

Threespine Stickleback *(Gasterosteus aculaetus)* Plate 4

The most common of the four stickleback species found in North American oceans (and the only species found in salt water on the West Coast), the threespine stickleback inhabits marine, brackish, and fresh waters. The vast majority of sea-dwelling populations are found in estuaries, usually in the shallow-water areas along shore (but sometimes offshore, at which times they are usually found among floating grasses), and usually at or near the surface. When not breeding, sticklebacks form fairly loose schools, which become more compact (that is, they ball up) when threatened.

The East Coast range of *G. aculaetus* is from Baffin Island to New York, and possibly as far south as Cape Hatteras, North Carolina. On the West Coast, it is found from the Bering Sea to northern Baja California, though in salt water only as far south as Monterey Bay, California. Studies supervised by NOAA showed common to highly abundant populations of all life stages in all West Coast estuaries from Puget Sound to Southern San Francisco Bay (both Elkhorn Slough and Morro Bay, California, showed common abundance of adults and juveniles only).

There has been much written about the unique body structure and unusual mating habits (and colors) of the sticklebacks (for a comprehensive history of the family, refer to Wootton's *The Biology of the Sticklebacks*); but for our limited purposes, we will regard only several points as being of interest.

The sticklebacks are small fishes (*G. aculaetus* grows to a maximum length of 4 inches

[10 centimeters]). For purposes of defense, they are armed with a number of dorsal spines (hence the common name). These spines can be locked in the erect position so securely that they cannot be depressed by the jaws of a predator even after death, making sticklebacks much more difficult for predators to handle than other forage fishes. Evidence (both observance of natural populations and evidence gained in the laboratory) demonstrates the importance of these spines as a deterrent to predation. Given mixed groups of minnows, ninespine sticklebacks (*Pungitius pungitius*, whose spines are more numerous but very short—much shorter and not nearly as threatening as those of *G. aculaetus*), and threespine sticklebacks, perch always opted to take minnows first, avoiding the threespine sticklebacks until nearly all other prey had been devoured. Even when prey were given one at a time, the perch still tended to avoid the threespines. Results of this experiment using pike as a predator were similar, though it is interesting to note that if the threespine sticklebacks had their spines removed, they were consumed with about the same frequency as the other food forms—that is, the pike were able to detect the presence or absence of spines.

Spines, however, provide only a deterrent to predation and are not an absolute defense, for the threespine stickleback is devoured by many shallow-water fishes, including striped bass. Although it is probably not a primary prey of any marine fish, it is doubtless taken readily if abundant.

The second point of interest to the angler is the breeding colors of the stickleback. During the breeding season, the coloration of male sticklebacks turns from silvery below to brilliant red (the red coloration often extends up the sides of the fish). This coloration seems to have two functions: to attract females and to intimidate rival males (during breeding, males become extremely territorial and aggressive). But such conspicuous coloration is conspicuous to predators as well. It has been observed in some freshwater populations of sticklebacks that heavy pressures from predation have caused a shift in the gene pool such that a large percentage of the males have lost their red breeding coloration altogether (evolution in action). While males that still display their red breeding colors are more likely to attract females, they are also more likely to be preyed upon by other fishes. Such tradeoffs exist everywhere in nature.

In the spring, marine populations of threespine sticklebacks move into brackish or fresh water to spawn.[1] At this time the belly and flanks of the male turn a brilliant red, its eyes become bright blue, and the dorsal coloration becomes very pale. The females turn color also, but the change is much more subtle, their throat and belly assuming a pinkish cast.

In North American waters, spawning takes place primarily in June and July in shallow water, usually on bottoms of sand or soft mud near vegetation. It is on such bottoms that the male, using various materials (twigs, sand, algae) glued together by a kidney excretion, constructs a small tubular nest. The male then entices the female into the nest by a series of nipping and zigzagging actions. The female deposits the eggs (as many as six hundred have been counted in a single nest), and is followed by the male, who fertilizes them. The male, seemingly having lost all fleeing instincts, guards the nest from predators (including other sticklebacks) that might devour the eggs, continuing to watch over the hatchling fish until they are able to fend for themselves.

Growth is fastest in the first year of life. Threespine sticklebacks reach between ½ inch to just over 1 inch (1.5 to 3.3 centimeters) their first year (at which time the fish are sexually

1. Several studies have shown the existence of populations of threespine sticklebacks that spawn in full marine waters (such as Vancouver Island, British Columbia, and Isles of Shoals, New Hampshire).

mature). Life span is from three to three and one-half years (about two and one-half years in Alaska). Maximum size is 4 inches (10 centimeters), but few specimens exceed 3 inches (7.6 centimeters). The threespine stickleback is a voracious predator. Food items consist primarily of small invertebrates (copepods and isopods, for instance), but also include small fishes, fish eggs, and aquatic insects.

In the fall, the sticklebacks move out toward deeper marine waters where they spend the winter.

The body of the threespine stickleback is elongate, tapering to a slender caudal peduncle (which in marine forms is usually keeled). The head is pointed and the mouth is small, the lower jaw projecting. The jaws are lined with sharp slender teeth. The eye is large. The dorsal fin of the stickleback is composed of three (rarely four) spines, behind which is a dorsal ray. The threespine stickleback has no true scales; rather, there are a number (up to thirty) of oblong bony plates along the sides of the fish (scientists speculate that these plates also play a role in deterring predators).

Colors of threespine stickleback are highly variable. Dorsal coloration can be silvery green, greenish brown, gray, olive, or sometimes blue; the effect is often mottled. Sides are paler with silvery reflections, and the belly is silvery. (Breeding coloration of the threespine stickleback is detailed above.) Very young sticklebacks are silvery.

AKA: Banstickle, common stickleback, eastern stickleback, épinoche à trois épines (French), European stickleback, needle stickleback, New York stickleback, pinfish, saw-finned stickleback, thornback, thornfish, three-spined stickleback, tiddler, twospine stickleback.

Halfbeaks and Needlefishes
(Order Atheriniformes)

These families are ordered with the flying fishes (family Exocoetidae) and share several characterisics: elongate bodies whose pectoral fins are placed high on the sides; the abdominal pelvic fins and dorsal and anal fins are located posteriorly.

Halfbeaks (Family Hemiramphidae)

Characterized by a body that is usually cylindrical (but sometimes compressed) and an elongated lower jaw that resembles a flattened blade, halfbeaks inhabit tropical and temperate waters worldwide. Halfbeaks are schooling fishes found in coastal and bay waters (some enter estuaries) as well as the open sea. Most species are surface dwellers capable of swift movement, and they can be seen skipping along the top of the water when chased. Omnivorous, halfbeaks eat both small surface-dwelling fishes and crustaceans as well as floating seagrasses. They are usually blue to green above, silvery white below. Most are under 12 inches (30 centimeters) in length. Halfbeaks are preyed upon by a variety of gamefishes, including yellowtail, dolphin, kingfish, king mackerel, barracuda, tunas, and billfishes. They are a popular trolled bait. Life histories of these families are poorly known, probably due to their lack of commercial importance.

Plate 4

Common Halfbeak *(Hyporhamphus unifasciatus)*

The common halfbeak is found from Maine to the northern Gulf of Mexico and throughout the Caribbean to Argentina, but it is only a stray in its northernmost range and is most abundant south of Chesapeake Bay. It also inhabits the Pacific from San Diego southward (though rare in U.S. waters), where it is known as the *silverstripe halfbeak*. It is usually found on the surface, out to sea as well as near shore, often entering bays and estuaries.

The common halfbeak is elongate and slightly compressed. Its body is much less deep in profile and more rounded than is either the balao's or the ballyhoo's (*H. balao* and *H. brasiliensis*, respectively). Color above is greenish with three dark lines running along the middle of the back. Below is silvery, with a darker silver midlateral band. Both the tip of its lower jaw and the upper lobe of its tail are a yellowish red. The eye is large. *H. unifasciatus* grows to 11 inches (27 centimeters).

The common halfbeak can be seen leaping across the water to flee predators. It is a favorite prey of the larger predators, including sailfish and tunas.

Researchers note that *H. unifasciatus* might actually consist of several species.

AKA: Balourou (French), skipjack.

Plate 4

Balao *(Hemiramphus balao)*

The balao is found from New York (rare north of Florida) to southeastern Brazil, including the Gulf of Mexico and the Caribbean. Its body is deeper and more fusiform than is that of the common halfbeak (*H. unifasciatus*). Dorsal coloration is dark bluish, silvery on the sides and below. The upper lobe of the tail is bluish violet with a red tip. The tip of the lower jaw is red. The balao grows to a maximum length of 16 inches (40 centimeters).

Ballyhoo *(Hemiramphus brasiliensis)*

Adult ballyhoo are abundant in bays and shore waters (young are pelagic; in the southeast United States, adults are also abundant near reefs) from Massachusetts to Brazil, including the Gulf of Mexico and the Caribbean. *H. brasiliensis* is a more abundant species than is *H. balao*. The ballyhoo is similar in shape and coloration to the balao. Dorsal coloration is dark greenish or bluish, white on the sides and below (overall appearance is silvery). The tip of the ballyhoo's lower jaw and its entire upper caudal-fin lobe are orange-red. The ballyhoo grows to 16 inches (40 centimeters). A favorite of Atlantic sailfish, most halfbeaks used for bait are of this species.

AKA: Ballyhoo halfbeak, Brazilian halfbeak, démi-bec brésilien (French).

Flying Halfbeak *(Euleptorhamphus velox)*

The body of the flying halfbeak is elongate and compressed to the extent that it is ribbonlike. Like the flying fishes (with which halfbeaks are ordered), its pectoral fins are large, and it uses them to glide across the water's surface when being pursued.

The northern range of *E. velox* is Rhode Island, but it is rare north of the Gulf of Mexico.

It ranges southward to Bermuda and Hispaniola. The flying halfbeak is oceanic, seldom entering coastal waters. Maximum length is 20 inches (50 centimeters).

Hardhead Halfbeak *(Chriodorus atherinoides)*

The only North American halfbeak species without an elongated lower jaw, the hardhead halfbeak inhabits bays and waterways—especially around seagrass beds—from southeast Florida to Yucatán, Mexico, including the Gulf of Mexico, Cuba, and the Caribbean. Color above is translucent tan or olive with a series of dots on the scales suggesting dark horizontal streaks. Below is pale with a narrow silver midlateral band that is widest below the dorsal fin. In this way it superficially resembles the silversides (family Atherinidae), with which it is ordered, but it can be distinguished from them in having only a single dorsal fin (silversides have two).

The hardhead halfbeak grows to 10 inches (25 centimeters).

California Halfbeak *(Hyporhamphus rosae)*

The California halfbeak is similar in color and configuration to the common halfbeak (*H. unifasciatus*), except that its lower jaw is longer. It is found near shore (frequently in bays), at or near the surface, and often in small schools from Santa Ana, California, to Costa Rica. Dorsal coloration is greenish with a silver midlateral stripe. Its lower jaw is tipped red. The California halfbeak reaches 6 inches (15 centimeters) in length.

Ribbon Halfbeak *(Euleptorhamphus longirostris)*

The ribbon halfbeak is found throughout the tropical Pacific and Indian oceans, and from southern California to the Galapagos Islands. A surface dweller, it is usually oceanic, but sometimes enters large open bays. Color above is greenish, silvery below. Pectoral fins are large. It grows to 18 inches (46 centimeters).

Longfin Halfbeak *(Hemiramphus saltator)*

The longfin halfbeak is similar to the California halfbeak (*H. rosae*), differing primarily in size and in color. Color above is brownish, below is silvery. The longfin halfbeak occurs from southern California (rare north of Baja California) to Ecuador, including the Galapagos Islands. An oceanic surface dweller, it grows to 18¾ inches (47.6 centimeters). It is a choice prey of billfishes and is a popular trolled bait.

Needlefishes *(Family Belonidae)*

Quite elongate and cylindrical (though sometimes compressed), needlefishes are a family of usually small, swift-swimming, predacious fishes whose species inhabit the surface of warm and temperate seas. Needlefishes are abundant in bays and harbors (usually in schools), but a few species prefer the open oceans. Some travel through brackish water to enter fresh water.

In all marine species, both jaws are long and beaklike, filled with sharp teeth that they use to capture and kill small fishes. In coastal waters, dorsal coloration is greenish; in oceanic waters, it is bluish. All species are white or silvery on the sides and below.

Needlefishes are easily startled and can be seen skipping along the surface when pursued. They are disoriented and startled by artificial light, and sometimes leap from the water when it is shone on them at night. Larger species such as the houndfish (*Tylosurus crocodilus*) are dangerous in this regard. Fatalities have occurred when leaping houndfish have impaled fishermen.

There are eight species of needlefish in North America. They are eaten by such predators as striped bass, bluefish, barracuda, tarpon, and Atlantic sailfish.

AKA: Aiguille (Cajun).

Plate 5

Atlantic Needlefish *(Strongylura marina)*

The Atlantic needlefish ranges from Maine southward into the northern Gulf of Mexico (being quite common to the latter in the spring and summer) and thence to Brazil, including Cuba and Jamaica. It inhabits coastal waters and is known to enter freshwater coastal streams. The body of the Atlantic needlefish is elongate and cylindrical, thicker than it is deep. Color is greenish to bluish green above, silvery on the sides, and white below. There is a bluish silvery stripe along its side, widening and becoming less distinct toward the tail. The lower half of the head below the middle of the eye is pale; the snout is darker to match the dorsal coloration. There is a blackish blotch on the upper part of the cheek. The tail is bluish at the base.

S. marina often occurs in small schools and is most active at night. Its diet consists mainly of small fishes. Spawning habits are little known, but it is thought to take place in both fresh and salt water. The Atlantic needlefish grows to a length of 25 inches (64 centimeters). I have seen many of these fish (always in small schools, and all of which were half their maximum size or less) in brackish Massachusetts rivers, particularly in August. Despite repeated efforts, however, I have yet to make one strike a small fly.

AKA: Needlegar, saltwater gar, sea pike, silver gar.

Flat Needlefish *(Ablennes hians)*

The flat needlefish is usually oceanic, but is also found in clean coastal waters from Chesapeake Bay (perhaps as far north as Massachusetts) southward, throughout the Gulf of Mexico and ranging as far south as Bermuda, the Caribbean, and Brazil. The body of the flat needlefish is strongly compressed laterally, less than half as thick as it is deep. Its color is greenish to bluish above. Its lower sides and abdomen are bright silvery. Some specimens have fifteen to twenty dark to sooty vertical bars along their sides (other specimens show blotches rather than bars); these bars are most obvious in young specimens. The species reaches 43 inches (110 centimeters).

AKA: Garfish.

Keeltail Needlefish *(Platybelone argalus)*

The only western Atlantic needlefish with a broad lateral keel on each side of its caudal peduncle, *P. argalus* ranges from North Carolina throughout the Caribbean, including the Gulf of

Mexico. It is an oceanic species, however, and is seldom found in shallow water (except in very clear waters around islands and reefs). Color is greenish above and silvery below, with a lateral streak margining the edge of the dorsal coloration.

The beak of *P. argalus* is long and slender, the lower jaw longer than the upper. It grows to 15 inches (38 centimeters).

Timucu *(Strongylura timucu)*

This species is so closely related to the Atlantic needlefish (*S. marina*) and is so similar in appearance that it has been listed under that common name. It is found inshore from southeastern Florida to Brazil, including the Gulf of Mexico, and grows to 24 inches (61 centimeters).

Redfin Needlefish *(Strongylura notata)*

The redfin needlefish inhabits bays, inlets, and tidal creeks (it is known to enter fresh water) from Florida southward throughout the West Indies. It is the most common needlefish within its range. As its name implies, its dorsal, caudal, and anal fins are tipped reddish or orangish, sometimes a pale shade. Another distinguishing feature is a black vertical bar along the front edge of its gill cover. Dorsal coloration is pale greenish and reflects silvery. There is a greenish streak from the base of the pectoral fin to the tail. The iris is silver. The redfin needlefish grows to 24 inches (61 centimeters), but is usually less than 15 inches (38 centimeters).

Agujon *(Tylosurus acus)*

The agujon is found primarily offshore (but it does enter shallow bays) from Massachusetts to the Caribbean, including the Gulf of Mexico. Its beak is relatively short, the upper jaw shorter than the lower. Young of the species pass through a "halfbeak" stage, the lower jaw being disproportionately longer; the discrepancy lessens with age. Color above is blue, sides are silver, and the belly white. The agujon can exceed 36 inches (90 centimeters).

Houndfish *(Tylosurus crocodilus)*

This largest species of needlefish ranges from New Jersey to Brazil, including the Gulf of Mexico and the Caribbean, preferring shallow waters over flats (around islands it prefers the seaward side). Dorsal coloration is greenish. Young specimens display a black lobe on the dorsal fin and dark vertical bars along the side, especially posteriorly. The beak is short. The houndfish grows to 60 inches (150 centimeters). Its size and nervous habits make it a dangerous fish for persons in boats using lights at night.

California Needlefish *(Strongylura exilis)*

The only needlefish in the California area, *S. exilis* is found in bays and harbors (at or near the surface and usually in small schools) from San Francisco (rare north of the Mexican border) to Peru, including the Galapagos Islands. It is greenish blue above and silvery below. The California needlefish grows to 36 inches (91 centimeters).

Mullets *(Family Mugilidae)*

These elongate, thick-bodied fishes inhabit warm and temperate coastal marine and brackish waters worldwide. Some inhabit fresh water, though as far as anyone knows, all mullets return to the sea to breed. Typically, mullets have a broad head, either cylindrical or flattened, with a blunt snout and a small, wide mouth. The eye is moderately sized. Mullets are round in cross-section in front, slightly compressed to the rear. Most are blue, green, or olive above and silvery below. Most school or form small groups. Mullets feed on microorganisms, algae, and detritus, which they take in mouthfuls from the bottom. They are taken commercially for food and are widely used as bait, particularly as trolled bait for larger gamefishes.

The six species of mullet in North America are sometimes difficult to identify.

AKA: Mulle (Cajun).

Plate 5

Striped Mullet *(Mugil cephalus)*

In the Atlantic, the striped mullet ranges from Maine (straying as far north as Nova Scotia) to Florida, including the Gulf of Mexico, and southward to Bermuda and Brazil. In the Pacific, it is found from San Francisco Bay southward, but is rare north of southern California (fairly common in San Diego and Newport bays). Occurring in large schools and frequently near the surface, *M. cephalus* is a common inshore and estuarine species in the mid-Atlantic and Chesapeake regions, especially in the smaller sizes, and is common to highly abundant in the southern United States and the Gulf of Mexico. Along Florida's Gulf Coast, the striped mullet supports a commercial fishery.

Striped mullet spawn at three-plus years of age. Most spawn offshore in the late fall and winter (though many southeast estuaries support common to highly abundant adult populations year-round). Usually this begins in October, peaks in November through December, and ends in February. There are, however, some local variations. On Florida's west coast, for example, striped mullet at Cedar Key spawn from October through May, and at Bayport from December to July.

Schools en route to spawning grounds are enormous, and predation on the migrating schools is heavy, particularly by tarpon and large snook.

Larval mullet come to inshore waters and estuaries at about ½ to ¾ inch (1.6 to 2 centimeters) in length, at which time they are a shiny silver and look so different from adults that they were once regarded as a separate species. Juveniles of 1½ to nearly 3 inches (4 to 7 centimeters) spend the rest of their first year in estuaries, salt marshes, and coastal waters. Some move to deeper water in the fall during the adults' spawning migration, but large numbers overwinter in the estuaries. After their first year of life, the mullet continue to inhabit the same areas they did as young juveniles, but they also inhabit the open sea as well as move upstream into fresh water, sometimes hundreds of miles.

Some striped mullet mature by their second year of life, most by their third year, at a length somewhere between 8 and 12 inches (20 and 30 centimeters). The striped mullet can live four or more years (maximum age recorded is thirteen years). It can reach 30 inches (76 centimeters) in the southern part of its range, but it seldom exceeds 12 inches (30 centimeters), and is usually smaller than this in the north. Food consists primarily of algae, but plankton is also eaten.

Adults are elongate, cylindrical toward the front, and compressed toward the rear. Dorsal coloration is brown, olive, bluish green, or bluish gray; sides and abdomen are silvery. Some side scales have dark centers, appearing as six or seven horizontal stripes along the fish's side. (Fish under 6 inches [15 centimeters] lack the horizontal stripes.) There is a bluish spot at the base of the pectoral fin. The fish's iris is brownish.

Striped mullet are used as bait for a wide variety of fishes, particularly for billfish along Florida's Gulf Coast. Large mullet are preyed upon heavily by sharks in Florida, and mullet up to 13½ inches (35 centimeters) are eaten by spotted seatrout.

AKA: Black mullet, cobb (abbreviation of *corn cobb*, to denote large mullet), common mullet, finger mullet (small specimens), gray mullet, jumping mullet, muge cabot (French).

White Mullet *(Mugil curema)*

The range and habitat (as well as general habits) of the white mullet are similar to those of the striped mullet, but its northernmost range appears to be Cape Cod, Massachusetts (larvae and juveniles [to 6 inches; 15 centimeters] have strayed to Nova Scotia), and it is also found in the Bahamas. It is a spring spawner that tends to prefer waters of higher salinity than does the striped mullet. Color above is blue, olive, or dark green; its sides are silvery, and its belly is paler. There are no lateral stripes. Its iris is light brownish. It can grow to 24 inches (61 centimeters).

The white mullet is the most abundant mullet in tropical America. While both the white mullet and the striped mullet are found on both sides of Florida, Carl Richards observes that the white mullet is more abundant on the east coast, while the striped mullet is more abundant on the west.

The white mullet is often used as bait in the southern states, particularly for sailfish off southern Texas.

AKA: Muge curema (French).

Liza *(Mugil liza)*

M. liza is similar in appearance to the striped mullet, but with a smaller head that is wedge-shaped when viewed from the side. Dorsal coloration is dusky to bluish black, below is silvery. The liza ranges from Florida to Argentina, including Bermuda and the Bahamas. It grows to 24 inches (60 centimeters).

AKA: Lebrancho.

Fantail Mullet *(Mugil gyrans)*

Similar in appearance to the white mullet, the fantail mullet is found from Florida and the Gulf of Mexico to Brazil, including Bermuda and the Bahamas (the most common Bahamian mullet). It prefers clearer-water shallows than do other mullets. It grows to 18 inches (46 centimeters).

Redeye Mullet *(Mugil gaimardianus)*

The redeye mullet is found near mangroves in shallow coastal bays of eastern Florida. As its name implies, the iris of the redeye mullet is red-orange. It grows to a length of 27 inches (67 centimeters).

Mountain Mullet *(Agonostomus monticola)*

Adult forms of the mountain mullet inhabit freshwater streams of North Carolina, Florida, Louisiana, and Texas—young to 1½ inches (4 centimeters) are found in coastal and offshore waters. They are more commonly found south of this, however, in the bays and fresh waters of the West Indies and eastern Mexico. The species' range extends to Colombia, and it is also found in the tropical eastern Pacific. Dorsal coloration is brown. Young (and often adults) have a dusky stripe along the side. There is a bright red stripe along the side of the front half of the body. The tail is yellowish with a dusky spot at the base. Both the dorsal and anal fins are yellow at the base. The head of the mountain mullet is flattened. It reaches a maximum length of 12 inches (30 centimeters).

Cusk-Eels (Family Ophidiidae)

Members of this family are not true eels, but rather belong to the order Gadiformes, which includes the codfishes. They are included in this text because it was reported by A.J. McClane that in his examinations of the stomach contents of bonefish, cusk-eels and snake eels (see

Northern Mullets

Little has been documented scientifically concerning the occurrence of mullets in mid-Atlantic and northeast waters. Mullet aficionado Bob Popovics detailed for me the brief and mysterious seasonal appearance of mullets in his home waters around Seaside Park, New Jersey.

In late July or August, mullet of 3 to 4 inches (7.6 to 10 centimeters) suddenly appear in large numbers, densely schooled, in New Jersey's Barnegat Bay. Their residence is short-lived, however, for come the beginning of September they start their southward migration. At that time, mullet of about 6 inches (15 centimeters) appear in coastal waters. These are fast-swimming fish whose schools are generally less dense than those of the smaller mullet. As each week goes by, progressively smaller mullet appear in the surf until, by the end of September, mullet of 2 to 2¼ inches (5 to 5.7 centimeters) prevail. Smaller mullet, Bob observes, tend to travel much slower than do larger ones; also, they tend toward the bottom in small, densely packed schools.

Succeeding weeks bring larger mullet (though they look somewhat different from the previous mullet, and Bob speculates that more than one species might be involved). Sometime in October, large striped mullet or *cobbs* (sometimes as large as 5 or 6 pounds) make their appearance and generally signify the end of the mullet run (around the first or second week in November in New Jersey).

Mullet are also seasonally common for a brief period of time in the fall as far north as Rhode Island.

Order Anguilliformes) were more abundant than their density suggested they should be, indicating that bonefish might feed on them selectively.

Bottom dwellers, most cusk-eel species are dull tan to dark brown.

Dusky Cusk-Eel *(Parophidion schmidti)*

Plate 5

Usually pale brown, darker dorsally and lighter ventrally, the dusky cusk-eel inhabits the shallow coastal waters of Florida to the Central American coast, including Bermuda, the Bahamas (the most common Bahamian cusk-eel), the Virgin Islands, and Jamaica. It is usually found around beds of turtle grass over a sand bottom. It grows to about 4 inches (10 centimeters).

Smelts (Family Osmeridae)

These slender, silvery fishes are usually found in schools in shallow coastal and brackish waters. Most species are marine, but a few are anadromous, entering fresh water to spawn; two native North American species have landlocked populations. The ten or so species occurring in North America can be distinguished from similar species by the presence of the adipose fin common to trout and other members of the order Salmoniformes.

Capelin *(Mallotus villosus)*

The capelin is a marine species found in deep waters from the northern Atlantic to the Gulf of Maine (but seldomly that far south), and in the northern Pacific from Arctic Alaska to the Strait of Juan de Fuca. In the Atlantic, capelin are plentiful off the north shore of the Gulf of St. Lawrence, but are most abundant off the Newfoundland and Labrador coasts.

In the spring, Atlantic coastal populations of capelin migrate inshore in vast schools to spawn. Spawning begins around the first part of June and can continue through July, depending on tides, winds, and water temperature. Late spawning sometimes occurs, having been observed as late as the end of August. Spawning takes place on beaches of coarse sand or fine gravel. Wave action brings the fish up onto the beach, where the eggs are deposited and fertilized in the gravel, and where they remain during development. Beach spawning occurs at night or during times of heavy overcast; it is most intensive during the intermediate tide. Evidence suggests that females might be batch-spawners, spawning more than once during a season. Mass mortalities occur during beach spawning, yet those that survive spawn yearly.

Not all capelin spawn on beaches, however. Significant amounts of eggs have been found 6½ to 9 feet (2 to 3 meters; 1 to 1½ fathoms) deep at Bryant Cove, Newfoundland. Offshore spawning also occurs: Gravid females and ripe males have been found on various offshore banks at depths up to 260 feet (80 meters; 43 fathoms).

Spawning begins at age three, at which time the males average 6½ inches (17.4 centimeters); females of the same age average about 6 inches (15.8 centimeters). Capelin live to about five years and reach a maximum size of 8½ inches (22 centimeters), though few grow larger than 7½ inches (19 centimeters).

Spawning of West Coast populations of capelin occurs in September and October along shallow beaches at night. Like the East Coast populations, the capelin of the Pacific Northwest wriggle out of the water to spawn among the sand and pebbles, and are often gathered by beachgoers and fried whole.

The capelin feeds on planktonic organisms; feeding is most intense during the pre-spawning period and ceases during spawning. The capelin makes up a significant portion of the food of many predacious birds, mammals, and fishes. Chief pisciverous predators on the East Coast are the Atlantic salmon and Atlantic cod, though they are also likely eaten by a number of other fishes, such as sea-run trouts and chars. Cod are known to follow capelin inshore during their spawning migration, and have often been seen chasing them at the surface.

Slender, elongate, and laterally compressed, the capelin is olive green above and silvery below; the belly is white. There are usually black dots on the gill covers. Dorsal coloration darkens to nearly a bottle green at spawning time.

AKA: Angmagssat (Greenland), capelan (French), caplin (Newfoundland), lodde, Pacific capelin, whitefish (young fish, Newfoundland and Labrador).

Plate 5

Rainbow Smelt *(Osmerus mordax)*

The abundance and schooling behavior of the rainbow smelt make it an important forage for many large predacious fishes on both the East and West coasts of North America.

In the Atlantic, *O. mordax* is found from Labrador to Delaware Bay; in the Pacific, it occurs from Alaska to Vancouver, British Columbia, but is rare south of Alaska. Anadromous, it enters fresh water to spawn. (There are also landlocked freshwater populations in the rivers and lakes of the northeastern United States and southeastern Canada.)

The rainbow smelt moves into estuaries in fall and winter. In the Atlantic, spawning takes place in the spring in brooks and streams above (sometimes below) the head of the tide, and the smelt can often be seen in large schools in estuaries and rivers during a run. In the Miramichi River, New Brunswick—the area of the smelt's greatest abundance in the Atlantic—spawning has been reported from late April into June. Spawning begins progressively earlier toward the southern part of the fish's range. Depending on water temperatures, it can begin as early as February in the south. Spawning lasts for about two months overall. All spawning takes place at night.

Fry are carried downstream to brackish water, where they can be found in May. Early hatchers can reach a length of 2½ inches (6 centimeters) by November.

The rainbow smelt mature in two to three years at a length of 5 to 8 inches (13 to 20 centimeters). These fish make up the bulk of the commercial smelt catch, although 7- to 8-inch (18- to 20-centimeter) fish are also caught. Females grow faster, live longer, and reach greater size than do males. Maximum length of the rainbow smelt is about 13 inches (33 centimeters). West Coast specimens are usually less than 8 inches (20 centimeters).

The rainbow smelt is a voracious carnivore. Fry feed on mysids, shrimp, and marine worms, changing primarily to small fishes as they grow. Fall and winter fishing for rainbow smelt is popular on the East Coast. Smelt are taken on small baited hooks and have even been known to take a small artificial fly.

During the warmer East Coast months, the smelt move to cooler waters offshore, probably within 6 miles (9.6 kilometers) of the coast, and not more than 18 feet (5.5 meters; 3 fathoms) deep, but probably farther and deeper in the fish's southern range. Evidence suggests migrations at sea, but little is actually known of this period in its life.

The rainbow smelt is elongate and slender, moderately compressed. Its head is moderately long, its snout elongate and pointed; the lower jaw protrudes slightly. The eye is moderately large. The rainbow's color is olive to green above and silvery on its sides, which emanate iridescent reflections of pink, blue, and purple (from which it gets its common name).

AKA: American smelt, Atlantic smelt, éperlan arc-en-ciel (French), freshwater smelt, frostfish, icefish, jacksmelt (large specimens, though the largest rainbows are actually jills), leefish, smelt.

Surf Smelt *(Hypomesus pretiosus pretiosus)* Plate 5

Similar in appearance to the California grunion (*Leuresthes tenuis*), the surf smelt ranges from Prince William Sound, Alaska, to Long Beach, California, but is rare south of Tomales Bay, California. Considered an excellent foodfish, this schooling species is taken commercially in California and Washington. It is an important forage for many predacious fishes, including salmons and striped bass.

Found primarily near shore off sandy beaches, the surf smelt is only occasionally present in California estuaries, but it is common to highly abundant, seasonally, in estuaries in Oregon and Washington. It sometimes enters brackish water.

This species contains many local breeding groups (ten in Puget Sound alone; the Puget Sound population is genetically different from coastal populations). Spawning takes place year-round throughout its range, though at specific sites at specific times of the year.

Except for Puget Sound and adjacent areas (Hood Canal and Skagit Bay), spawning takes place on coastal beaches. Beaches used for spawning are composed of coarse sand and fine gravel, typically have some freshwater seepage, and are often shaded by trees or cliffs. At the start of the spawning run, schools are usually composed of individuals of the same sex. Female schools arrive at the spawning grounds before the males. Spawning takes place in the upper intertidal area, within about 3 feet (1 meter) of the beach, primarily during late-afternoon high tides, continuing through the ebb into evening. Females spawn in batches over several consecutive days, and might return to spawn later in the season as well. A spawning run lasts four to five months.

Spawning occurs annually after the smelt reaches maturity. For most, this is in their second year, but some reach it in their first. Females grow faster and live longer than do males. A male will not live past three years; the female can live to age five. Adults range in size from 3⅛ to 7 inches (8 to 18 centimeters). Maximum length is about 10 inches (25 centimeters).

The surf smelt feeds on a variety of small crustaceans and fish larvae.

The surf smelt is elongate and compressed, spindle-shaped. Males are dull olive green above; females are bright blue-green or metallic green. Below is silvery with a golden tinge (more so in males). All have a bright silver midlateral stripe.

AKA: Day smelt (so called for its diurnal spawning habits), Pacific surf smelt, silver smelt.

Whitebait Smelt *(Allosmerus elongatus)*

Found over soft bottoms from Vancouver Island, British Columbia, to San Francisco (possibly as far south as San Pedro), California, the whitebait smelt is an important prey for larger fishes. A coastal schooling species, entirely marine, it spawns on subtidal sandbanks and is often abundant in bays. Similar in configuration to the surf smelt, the whitebait smelt's color above is greenish gray, with a distinct silver midlateral band. Its eye is large. The whitebait smelt grows to a length of 7 inches (18 centimeters).

Longfin Smelt *(Spirinchus thaleichthys)*

The overall range of the longfin smelt is from Prince William Sound, Alaska, to Monterey Bay, California, though it is rare south of San Francisco Bay. Inhabiting deep waters inshore during the day, adult longfins move to the upper water column at night. They are strong swimmers and are found over a variety of substrates. Anadromous, the longfin enters fresh water to spawn (there are a few landlocked populations, such as those in Harrison Lake, British Columbia).

In the fall, juveniles and adults move from the lower to the upper estuarine areas. Spawning occurs in freshwater areas at night from October through March. Spawning is thought to take place over sandy-gravel areas or in such areas supporting aquatic plants. Nearly all adults die after spawning.

Juveniles range in length from about 7/8 to 3½ inches (2 to 9 centimeters). Spawning occurs at age two. Spawning adults range in length from 3½ to 6 inches (2 to 15 centimeters), the average being around 4 inches (about 10 centimeters). Larvae, juveniles, and adults are carnivorous planktivors, preying on a variety of crustaceans.

The longfin's color is greenish brown above, silvery below.

Studies supervised by NOAA indicate a somewhat patchy estuarial distribution. Central San Francisco and Suisun and San Pablo bays, California, all support year-round adult populations and are the sites of greatest abundance. Other estuaries supporting year-round adult populations include Skagit Bay, Gray's Harbor, and Willapa Bay, Washington; the Columbia River estuary, bordering Oregon; Yaquina and Coos bays, Oregon; and southern San Francisco Bay, California. Most estuaries with year-round presence of adults also support year-round populations of juveniles. Other estuaries supporting year-round juvenile populations are Puget Sound, Washington, and Humboldt Bay and the Eel River estuary, California.

The longfin is prey for many species of fish, birds, and mammals.

AKA: Long-finned smelt, Pacific smelt, Puget Sound smelt, Sacramento smelt.

Night Smelt *(Spirinchus starksi)*

Similar in appearance to the longfin smelt and occurring in similar habitat as the whitebait smelt, the night smelt ranges from Shelikof Bay, Alaska, to Point Arguello (central), California. Little is known of the night smelt's life history other than that it spawns in the surf at night (hence its name). Color above is brownish to greenish, shading to silvery below. It grows to 9 inches (23 centimeters).

Delta Smelt *(Hypomesus transpacificus)*

The delta smelt inhabits the fresh and brackish waters of the Sacramento–San Joaquin River system of central California. Mostly silvery, it has a faint speckled midlateral stripe. It grows to 4½ inches (11 centimeters).

Eulachon *(Thaleichthys pacificus)* Plate 6

Ranging from the Bristol Bay, Alaska, to Monterey, California, the eulachon smelt is most abundant from Oregon northward. In the United States, major spawning runs occur in the Klamath River, California, and the Columbia River, Washington/Oregon, with many other coastal streams supporting small runs.

At sea the eulachon forms dense schools. Adults are found from the intertidal zone (often in coastal inlets and rivers) to the edge of the continental shelf, but most frequently at depths greater than 150 feet (45 meters; 25 fathoms). Movements at sea are unknown.

The eulachon spawns in fresh water. Spawning migrations begin around December, with spawning taking place from January to April (March to May in British Columbia) and peaking in February and March. During its spawning migration, the eulachon is found near the bottom of estuarine and riverine channels. Spawning occurs at night, usually just a few miles above the estuaries, in waters of moderate velocities. Most eulachon die after spawning.

Planktivorous, the eulachon eats a variety of crustaceans, but does not usually feed during its spawning migration.

Adults range in size from 5½ to 10 inches (14 to 25 centimeters). The average length of spawning adults is just under 7 inches (17 centimeters). Spawning usually occurs at age three, but some specimens live to age five.

Color above is blue-brown with black speckling along its back and often on its tail. Dorsal coloration shades to bright silver below. During spawning, the eulachon's dorsal coloration turns gray-brown. It is the only smelt with striations on its gill cover.

The largest Pacific Coast smelt, the eulachon is prey for the many species of predacious fish, birds, and mammals that habitually follow its spawning migrations. At sea it is eaten by salmons and other fishes. The eulachon has traditionally been a major source of food for the native peoples of the Pacific Northwest, who capture them with nets during spawning runs. The eulachon is an oily fish, its oil particularly high in vitamin D. Dried, it can be inserted with a wick and used as a candle, from which it gets its common name of candlefish. Often the oil is rendered and used to cook and flavor foods.

AKA: Candlefish, chucka, Columbia River smelt, fathom fish, hooligan, little candlelight fish, oilfish; oolachan, oolachon, oolakan, etc.; salvation fish, small fish, swaive, yshuh.

Mackerels (Family Scombridae)

This family of fast-swimming torpedo-shaped fishes is found worldwide in tropical and temperate waters. It includes the bonitos, the wahoo, and the true tunas. Smaller species are often food for larger ones.

AKA: Maquereau (Cajun).

Atlantic Mackerel *(Scomber scombrus)* Plate 6

This inhabitant of temperate waters is one of the most active and migratory fishes in North America. Occurring in open seas from Newfoundland to Cape Hatteras, North Carolina, Atlantic mackerel spend their winter in moderately deep water—

230 to 650 feet (70 to 200 meters; 38 to 108 fathoms)—along the Continental Shelf from Sable Island Bank, Nova Scotia, to Chesapeake Bay. With the coming of spring, there is a general inshore and northeastward migration. The population splits, half moving toward United States coastal waters, the other half migrating northeast toward the Gulf of St. Lawrence.

The Atlantic mackerel utilizes two regions in the northwest Atlantic for spawning: the coastal waters between Cape Cod and Cape Hatteras, and the Gulf of St. Lawrence. Spawning takes place from mid-June to mid-July. Upon completion of spawning, adults move to various feeding areas.

Early growth of the mackerel is rapid. Approximately ⅛ inch (3 millimeters) long upon hatching, the fish reach 6¼ inches (16 centimeters) in ninety days, and 8 inches (20 centimeters) in another thirty. At one year, mackerel grow to about 10 inches (26 centimeters). Atlantic mackerel live at least fourteen years and attain a maximum length of about 22 inches (56 centimeters).

The Atlantic mackerel's food consists primarily of small fishes and squids, but it also eats planktonic organisms, which it obtains by filter-feeding. It is considered to feed the heaviest in the spring. A strong schooling species, mackerel schools usually consist of similarly sized fish.

The Atlantic mackerel's body is fusiform, streamlined, and slightly compressed. Its snout is pointed and its eye moderate. Color above is greenish, bluish, or greenish blue, with dark wavy vertical bars extending just below the lateral line. Sides and abdomen are silver-gray to silvery white, often with a pinkish iridescence.

Mackerel are eaten by many species of predacious fish, including swordfish, the tunas, and bluefish, which follow the mackerel northward during their spring migration. Mackerel is a popular chunk bait for striped bass and bluefish; small mackerel (tinkers) are a popular live bait for bonito and false albacore around the island of Martha's Vineyard.

AKA: Common mackerel, maquereau bleu (French), tinker (small or half-grown specimens).

Pacific Mackerel *(Scomber japonicus)*
(also listed in the genus *Pneumatophorus*)

Inhabiting all three coasts, *S. japonicus* occurs in the Atlantic from Cape Cod to southern Florida and throughout the entire Gulf of Mexico, but is rare north of Chesapeake Bay. In the Pacific, it ranges from Alaska to Mexico, but is most abundant between Point Conception, California, and southern Baja California; it is sometimes found in abundance as far north as Monterey, California. Overall abundance goes through boom and bust cycles.

A schooling fish—often found schooling with the Pacific sardine (*Sardinops sagax*)—the Pacific mackerel is usually found at or near the surface of open waters both offshore and nearshore. It is attracted to light, and is often found at night around lighted piers and oil platforms.

Pacific spawning can occur from January to October, but most occurs from April to August. Spawning takes place from Point Conception to the Gulf of California. A fast-growing species, *S. japonicus* reaches 12 inches (30.5 centimeters) in two years. Food consists of large zooplankton and small fishes and squids.

Similar in color pattern to the Atlantic mackerel, the Pacific mackerel is greenish to bluish above, shading to silvery below. Black wavy vertical bars span the head and back, breaking into a series of dusky spots along the lower side. There is a black spot inside the base of the pectoral fin. The Pacific mackerel has been aged to eleven-plus years. It reaches a maximum length of about 25 inches (64 centimeters), though it is usually no bigger than 18 inches (46 centimeters). It is a primary food of many West Coast predators, including billfishes, sharks, yellowtail, bonito, dolphin, and white seabass.

AKA: Blue mackerel, chub mackerel, striped mackerel.

Porgies (Family Sparidae)

Oblong, compressed fishes with large heads and steep profiles, porgies are found over a variety of substrates and in a wide range of salinity. Porgies are most common in bays, estuaries, and shallow coastal waters where the shellfish on which they feed are abundant. There are sixteen species in North America, only one of which occurs in the Pacific.

Scup *(Stenotomus chrysops)*

The overall range of the scup is from Nova Scotia to Florida, but it is rare north of the elbow of Cape Cod and south of North Carolina. Most northern populations are migratory, arriving in Rhode Island's Narragansett Bay and along southern Massachusetts in early May from wintering areas offshore of Virginia and North Carolina. They are present in Chesapeake Bay in April. From spring to fall, the scup is found in the high-salinity areas inshore (most within 5 or 6 miles [8 or 9.5 kilometers] of the coast), usually in schools of like-sized individuals. Scup four years old and older remain in nearshore areas and do not enter estuaries, while scup younger than four years move into estuaries in schools in early spring, the larger fish entering first.

Spawning takes place in inshore high-salinity waters (sandy and weed-covered bottoms are believed to be preferred) from May to August, peaking in June. Early growth is fairly rapid, for juveniles of 2 to 3 inches (5 to 8 centimeters) are common in September. Young fish are often found close to shore in only a few feet of water. At 1½ inches (4 centimeters), juveniles obtain the basic look of the adults. Most scup reach sexual maturity by the end of their second year at a length of just over 6 inches (16 centimeters). Scup can live to fifteen years.

Scup are opportunistic bottom feeders (primarily diurnal), eating crustaceans, annelid worms, sand dollars, young squid, and fish fry. Feeding ceases during spawning.

The scup is about half as deep as it is long (to the base of the tail). Its mouth is small, its eyes placed well up on the side of the head. One long dorsal fin begins just over the pectorals. In configuration, the scup superficially resembles freshwater bream or sunfishes: oval and compressed. Overall color is dull silvery (darker above) with twelve to fifteen indistinct horizontal stripes and pale blue flecks. The belly is white. There are five or six faint vertical bars along the body. The scup's head is silvery, marked with irregular or dusky blotches. Maximum length is 14½ inches (37 centimeters), but 12 inches (30.5 centimeters) is more common. Most larger scup are caught at depths between 90 and 120 feet (27 and 37 meters; 15 and 20 fathoms).

Scup are eaten by such predators as cod, bluefish, and weakfish. They are a popular live bait for striped bass.

AKA: Fairmaid, ironside, maiden, mishcup, porgee, porgy, scuppaug, spare doré (French).

Plate 6

Pinfish *(Lagodon rhomboides)*

Found along the coast and in estuaries, the pinfish ranges from Massachusetts (rare north of Maryland) southward throughout the Gulf of Mexico to Yucatán, Mexico, and also in Bermuda. The species' area of abundance is from the Virginia estuaries to the northern Gulf of Mexico (except the turbid brackish waters of western Louisiana). Adult pinfish—which can reach 15 inches (38 centimeters)—prefer waters of higher salinities and depths of 98 to 164 feet (30 to 50 meters; 16 to 27 fathoms). Juveniles of ½ to 4 inches (1.5 to 10 centimeters) can be found in abundance in shallow coastal and estuarine waters, primarily over grassy flats.

Spawning takes place in deeper waters in fall and winter, though some estuaries (New River and Cape Fear River, North Carolina; North and South Santee rivers, South Carolina; St. Johns and Indian rivers and Biscayne Bay, Florida) support common to highly abundant year-round populations of adults. Most estuaries within the area of abundance support common to highly abundant year-round populations of juveniles.

The pinfish is essentially non-schooling, though dense schools have been reported. Primarily a daytime feeder, the juvenile pinfish preys on shrimps, mysids, and amphipods, while adults eat a variety of items, including fish eggs, crabs, worms, and plant matter.

Of the same basic configuration as the scup—oval and compressed—the pinfish is olive, sporting numerous blue and yellow stripes and spots on its sides; overall appearance is silvery. Along its body are five or six faint dusky vertical bars. There is a dark shoulder spot just behind the gill cover.

Pinfish are a popular live bait for tarpon. They are also preyed upon by snook, redfish, and seatrout, among other fishes.

AKA: Bream, butterfish, chopa espina (Spanish), pin perch, poisson beurre (Cajun), sailor's choice, sand perch, sargo selema, sar selema (French).

SQUIDS (ORDER DECAPODA)

Classed with the octopus and other cephalopods, squids are found in every ocean, from dime-sized Lilliputian species to the 60-foot monsters of nautical lore. Among the seas' larger inhabitants, squids are exceeded in abundance only by the fishes.

Squids are invertebrates, and thus lack skeletons. In place of the backbone is a thin flexible internal shell called a *pen*. The surrounding body or *mantle* (attached to the pen along the interior dorsal surface) forms a more or less detached stocking over the squid's internal organs. The mantle is often long and tapered to a point at the rear, where there are a pair of fleshy lateral fins, also often tapering to a point. The rear end of such squids superficially resembles a broadhead arrow, thus giving the creature its British name of sea arrow. This hydrodynamic shape makes the squids among the swiftest swimmers in the sea. At the forward end of the mantle are the squid's head and ten arms or *tentacles*. Like the tentacles of an octopus, the squid's tentacles are lined with rows of suction cups, which are used for grasping prey. Centered at the base of the tentacles is a sharp, horny beak, much like a parrot's beak except with an underbite. These mandibles are used for killing and cutting up food (be careful when handling live squids—they can inflict a nasty bite). The squid's eyes are well developed and similar in structure to those of fish—amazing when you consider that the squid is actually more closely related to clams and oysters. Its keen eye, coupled with a well-developed brain and nervous system, rank the squid among the most highly evolved of invertebrates.

Squids swim in two ways: Leisurely forward movement is accomplished by a rippling motion of the lateral fins; rapid movement and quick thrusts (to capture prey or escape from predators) are executed by ejecting water through the *siphon*, a small nozzle protruding from beneath the mantle on the squid's underside. By changing the direction of the siphon, the squid can move in bursts either forward or backward (most movement, however, is backward). So strong are these jet-powered thrusts that some squids are able to jump clear of the water and, aided by their lateral fins, glide through the air for over 100 feet (30 meters).

Within the squid's skin are *chromatophores*—elastic sacs filled with various pigments—appearing as a multitude of dots covering the squid's body. Chromatophores can be brown, black, red, blue, yellow, or orange—but no more than three colors have been found on any squid. By expanding and contracting the sacs, the squid can alter its colors, and by regulating the display of various pigments it can create a variety of hues. Color change is virtually instantaneous and is most often done for camouflage, allowing the squid to blend with backgrounds of sky, sand, seagrass bed, or rock. Color changes have also been attributed to periods of excitement, particularly those associated with mating activities.

In addition to its chromatophore system, the squid also has a built-in ink jet for defense. This is usually likened to a smoke screen that blinds the predator to the escaping squid. However, research has shown that a threatened squid will shoot a stream of ink (known as sepia; ink ranges in color from light brown to black) that coagulates in the water to a cloud of approximately the same size and shape as the squid. The squid then turns transparent and darts off, leaving the predator to attack the inky decoy.

Squids are preyed upon by a variety of fishes and other marine creatures. Predacious carnivores themselves, squids eat fishes, crustaceans, worms, and mollusks (including other squids, sometimes even those of the same species). Schools of the South American Humbolt squid, which reaches 12 feet (3.6 meters) in length, have been known to strip 600-pound (272-kilogram) marlin to the bone. Some squids are attracted to lights at night and can be captured then with a long-handled dip net.

Family Loliginidae

This family of small schooling squids is found primarily in fairly shallow coastal waters within the Continental Shelves. While many species are commonly seen near the surface in shallow waters at night, trawl captures suggest that most species tend to stay toward the bottom during the day. The two species outlined here are abundant on the East and West coasts, respectively.

Common Squid *(Loligo pealei)*   Plate 6

 The common squid ranges from southern Labrador (in the summer; in the winter, the northernmost location is Georges Bank) to Florida (though rare south of South Carolina). In the spring and summer, it is found in shallow water near shore to a depth of 300 feet (91 meters; 50 fathoms). The general appearance of *L. pealei* is long and fusiform (the mantle swells slightly toward the middle). The fins, which are attached to the mantle toward the dorsal, are longer than they are broad, and are half the length of the mantle. They are triangular and slightly lobed in front. Eight of its arms are short (these are known as sessile arms), each with two rows of suction cups. The two longer (tentacular) arms are club-like near the end and are lined with four rows of suction cups. These tentacular arms are retractable and are used mostly for seizing prey, so they are seldom noticed by the observer. Chromatophores are reportedly yellow, blue-green, and reddish brown—more numerous dorsally than ventrally or along the sides. The squid's overall appearance, though, is usually a translucent pearl or pale gray ranging to amber or pale ginger. When excited or aroused (particularly during mating), the squid can be flushed with waves of purple.

Breeding takes place near shore from spring to early summer in schools from ten to one hundred individuals or more. The male, using its left tentacular arm, removes a packet of spermatophores from within its mantle and places it in the mantle of the female. After fertilization, the eggs are laid in clusters and attached to seaweed, rocks, shells, and other structures. The eggs hatch within a few weeks, and by fall the young squids are approximately 2 inches (5 centimeters) in length. The squids mature about one year after hatching. *L. pealei* can grow to 18 inches (45.7 centimeters), but maximum size rarely exceeds 12 inches (30.5 centimeters); males are slightly smaller and more slender than females. Life span is probably one to three years.

Common squid are forage for a number of East Coast gamefishes, particularly striped bass and bluefish, from which they will shoot clear of the water when attacked. They are taken commercially for both food and bait.

Market Squid *(Loligo opalescens)*

Closely related to *L. pealei*, the market squid is found in coastal waters from Alaska (though most commonly from Queen Charlotte Sound, British Columbia) to Baja California. Very similar in appearance to its East Coast counterpart, the body of *L. opalescens* is slender, elongated, fusiform, and pointed at the rear; the triangular fins are nearly half as long as the mantle and are slightly lobed in front. The arms are short. Both sexes of this species reach about 8 to 12 inches (20.3 to 30.5 centimeters), but the male's arms are longer than the female's. As indicated by its common name, opalescent squid, *L. opalescens* usually appears pale and iridescent. Excitement or arousal (particularly that associated with breeding activity), however, can bring about radical changes in color—often waves of purple, red, and maroon.

Breeding takes place year-round, with local variation, mostly in semi-protected bays and usually over a sand bottom with rocky outcroppings. Breeding has been recorded in March in the Strait of Georgia and the Queen Charlotte Strait, British Columbia; June through July around Victoria and West Vancouver Island, British Columbia; April through May and July through August in the San Juan Islands, Washington. Mass spawning in central California runs from about April to November; in southern California, mass spawning begins around October and lasts until April or May (some years, however, spawning can take place year-round). Breeding market squid form huge schools. Hatchling squid mature in about one year. Spawning takes place at one year to one and one-half years of age (occasionally a squid reaches two years of age), after which they die.

The market squid is prey for a variety of West Coast fishes, including striped bass, white seabass, dolphin, salmons, sharks, and tunas. There is a sport fishery for large kelp bass (4 to 5 pounds [1.8 to just over 2 kilograms]) off Catalina Island in the winter that is famous because the bass essentially strike only squid. Like the common squid, *L. opalescens* is fished commercially for food and bait.

AKA: Opalescent squid.

CRUSTACEANS
(CLASS CRUSTACEA)

Most gamefishes prey primarily on other fishes, consuming crustaceans only as opportunity allows. (For bonefish and permit, however, crustaceans are the staple of their diet; refer to Randall Kaufmann's *Bonefishing with a Fly* for scientific studies of the stomach contents of bonefish from Florida, the Bahamas, and Puerto Rico.) Regardless, the place of crustaceans in general angling should not be overlooked, for even striped bass will forgo all other offerings to feed selectively on shrimp and crabs if their abundance is sufficient to warrant it.

As with annelid worms, the number of crustacean species (some 26,000 worldwide, including freshwater forms)—forever being shuffled about their convoluted taxonomical hierarchy of subclasses, superorders, orders, infraorders, series, and divisions—is truly mind-boggling. This text can offer only a slice of that complex world, but it is a slice, I believe, that can be useful.

The North American angler need be concerned with only two orders of crustaceans: Decapoda (most shrimps and crabs) and Stomatopoda (mantis shrimps).

Order Decapoda

The order Decapoda comprises all ten-legged shrimps, crabs, and lobsters.

The decapod body is divided into two major sections: a head-thorax section (called the cephalothorax, which includes the eyes, antennae, and mouth parts) and an abdomen consisting of six movable segments (*somites*) and a tailpiece (*telson*). Most crabs have evolved such that their abdomens are fixed beneath their cephalothorax and between their walking legs. The crab's abdomen is obvious only when the crab is turned on its back, or when it unfolds for mating.

The crustacean's body is enclosed by an exoskeleton or shell (called the *carapace* where it covers the cephalothorax), which is intermittently molted and replaced with a larger shell to accommodate a growing body.

Originating beneath the cephalothorax are a pair of claws (*chela*) and four pairs of walking legs (*periopods*). (In some species, the claws are on the second pair of walking legs rather than on the first. Also, in some species, more than one pair of walking legs is clawed.) Beneath the abdomen on shrimps and lobsters are three or more pairs of appendages called *pleopods* or *swimmerets*. These fan water for steady forward movement, and also bear the eggs on females. On both sides of the telson are two flaps called uropods, which along with the telson form the tail fan.

Coloration among Crustacea is highly variable, both from species to species and often within the same species. Most color patterns conceal the crustacean from predators by allowing it to successfully merge with a particular environment. Many crustaceans are able to adjust their color pattern to some degree by regulating the display of their various pigments.

Decapod Shrimps

Grass Shrimps (Families Palaemonidae and Hippolytidae)

These small shrimps are abundant in estuarine and marine waters on all three coasts, and are forage for a variety of gamefishes.

Plate 6

Grass Shrimp (East Coast; *Palaemonetes pugio* and *Palaemonetes vulgaris*)

Five species of palaemonid shrimp inhabit the Atlantic and Gulf coasts—all similar in appearance and habits—two of whose life histories are well documented. They are common prey for many gamefishes, including striped bass, white perch, speckled trout, spotted seatrout, redfish, and juvenile tarpon, as well as a number of forage fishes (such as large killifish). There is a limited bait fishery for grass shrimps within their range, which extends from the Gulf of St. Lawrence to Corpus Christi, Texas; *P. vulgaris* has also been recorded at Rio Champoton and near Progresso, Yucatán, Mexico.

Grass shrimps inhabit estuarine and marine waters from the water's edge rarely to a depth of 49 feet (15 meters; 8 fathoms), particularly in areas of emergent and submerged vegetation. (Vegetation type is unimportant; in shallow water, grass shrimp are found over a variety of substrates, but in deeper water, bottoms littered with oyster shell are preferred.) Patches of vegetation are home to many of the small animals on which the shrimps feed, and are used as nursery areas by breeding shrimps as well. Vegetation also provides the shrimps with refuge from predators.

P. vulgaris is associated with larger rivers whose salinity levels range between 15 and 35 percent (waters of very low salinity can be fatal; *P. vulgaris* can tolerate waters exceeding 40 percent salinity). *P. pugio* is found in waters of lower salinities, most abundantly in the 10- to 20-percent range.

Adult grass shrimps are free-swimming, moving most often in a forward direction, propelled steadily by their swimmerets, but they are capable of rapid bursts of more than 5 inches in either direction (I have seen them leap clear of the water when being chased by small searobins). Although grass shrimps are active during the day, they might be more active at night, at which time they are more likely to be found feeding throughout the water column. (Their diet consists of zooplankton, meiofauna, algae, and detritus.) Populations of grass shrimps vary between twenty and three hundred individuals per square meter. Even at their lower densities, grass shrimps are a readily available forage. At night, look for shrimp by shining a small flashlight along the water's edge (especially along a sandy river shore). Sometimes they traverse the shoreline en masse, convoy-style (particularly in June in the Northeast).

Spawning seasons and habits of the two species are similar. In general, spawning takes place in shallow waters from early spring (February in southern waters, around May in Rhode Island, and perhaps as late as July in northern extremes) to October (ending earlier in northern waters), and is continuous within the season. Female *P. pugio* migrate toward waters of higher salinity to release their newly hatched larvae.

Maturation of the hatchling shrimp is rapid. Those hatched in spring can spawn later that summer at a length from 1/10 to 7/10 inch (5 millimeters to 18 millimeters). Growth is most rapid from late summer to fall. Winters are spent offshore or in deep holes within the estuaries, and growth ceases during this time. With the coming of spring, the grass shrimp again appear in the shallows and growth is resumed. Male *P. vulgaris* can attain a length of just over 1 inch (3 centimeters); females, just over 1½ inches (4.2 centimeters). Male *P. pugio* can attain a length of 1 3/10 inches (3.3 centimeters), while females can grow to nearly 2 inches (5 centimeters)—but the averages are usually much less: just under 1 inch (2.35 centimeters) for males and just over 1 inch (3 centimeters) for egg-bearing (ovigerous) females. Life span of grass shrimps is about one year, but a few see their second winter.

The two species of *Palaemonetes* outlined here are nearly identical in appearance, but can be differentiated by the color of their eyestalks: red brown for *P. vulgaris* and yellowish for *P. pugio*. Body color is more or less transparent, but the shrimps can vary the display of four pigments (red, yellow, white, and blue) under hormonal control. Pigment regulation allows grass shrimps to more effectively match their surroundings. Depending on their environment (and perhaps to some extent, what they have been eating), grass shrimps can be tinted light to deep tan or green. Often there are a few brown spots on the carapace and abdomen. Egg-bearing females cast a fairly good shadow against the sand when a flashlight is shone on them at night, so in deeper water they doubtless present an obvious silhouette to any fish lurking below.

When fishing for striped bass in estuaries at night, take note of any rises that don't quite break the surface (similar to the bulging rise of a nymphing trout). If the rises are numerous, it's a good bet the bass are taking shrimp. During such times a shrimp fly fished with a floating line and worked in very short strips can be deadly. Even if you see no rises, but shrimp are numerous in the area and nothing else seems to be working, try a shrimp fly. This has saved the night for me more than once.

AKA: Glass prawns, glass shrimp, hardbacks, jumpers, popcorn shrimp, seed shrimp.

Arrow Shrimp *(Tozeuma carolinensis)*

The arrow shrimp is found in marine waters from Vineyard Sound, Massachusetts, through the Gulf of Mexico to Yucatán, Mexico, southward to Panama, throughout the West Indies to Curaçao, and from Pernambuco to Bahía, Brazil. It is common in shallow water—the intertidal to 246 feet (75 meters; 41 fathoms)—and is often found in beds of vegetation.

Color of the arrow shrimp is dependent on habitat and diet. Colors range from light yellowish green to deep green, depending on habitat; it can also be brownish red or even purple when found around alcyonarian corals.

The arrow shrimp grows to a length of 2 inches (5.4 centimeters).
AKA: Grass shrimp.

Grass Shrimp (West Coast; *Hippolyte clarki*)

The West Coast grass shrimp ranges from Sheep Bay, Alaska, to Santa Catalina Island, California, where it is found from the intertidal area to a depth of 100 feet (30.5 meters; 16½ fathoms). It is found among eelgrass, clinging lengthwise to the blade, and between the fronds of kelp. The body of *H. clarki* is slender and moderately compressed, and generally resembles the palaemonid grass shrimps. *H. clarki* reaches a maximum length of just over 1 inch (3 centimeters). Color is mostly green, often with brown mottlings along the carapace. The cornea of its eye is pinkish. Spawning occurs from May to October, though the specifics are poorly known.

Caridean Shrimps (Family Crangonidae)

Caridean shrimps are found on both the East and West coasts, and are easily distinguished from the grass shrimps by their larger size, distinctive shape, and prominent coloration.

Sand Shrimp *(Crangon septemspinosa)*

Found from the Gulf of St. Lawrence to eastern Florida (also in Alaska from Eschholtz Bay to the Shumagin Islands), *C. septemspinosa* commonly occurs along bay shores and sea inlets. It has been reported 25 miles (40 kilometers) upstream from the mouth of the Potomac River. It is found from the intertidal area to a depth of 115 feet (35 meters; 19 fathoms), but it can exceed depths of 908 feet (277 meters). The sand shrimp is so named because it is usually found over a sand bottom (the densest populations are found in areas of silty mud flats and sandy mud around eelgrass). It has also been found in a variety of habitats, including areas of boulders, stones, and gravel. An abundant East Coast shrimp species, *C. septemspinosa* is an important prey for many fishes, and has been found in the stomach contents of striped bass, white perch, croakers, haddock, hickory shad, bonito, bluefish, jack crevalle, and weakfish.

In such northern areas as the Penobscot River estuary in Maine, large numbers of adult sand shrimp are present in the shore zone from April to November. In more southern areas, such as Delaware Bay, they are present in the shore zone all year.

Spawning takes place year-round, but is seasonal according to region. In the Penobscot estuary, egg-bearing (ovigerous) shrimp of 1½ to over 2½ inches (3.8 to 6.8 centimeters) are found in the shore zone from about May to October. In Delaware Bay, large egg-bearing shrimp of 1³⁄₁₀ to 2¾ inches (3.4 to 7 centimeters) appear in March through May, and are replaced by smaller egg-bearing shrimp of slightly less than 1 to 1⁸⁄₁₀ inches (2.2 to 4.6 centimeters) in July and August; from then until the termination of spawning in fall, the smaller egg-bearing shrimp are replaced by larger ones. Spawning in Chesapeake Bay occurs in the channel and intratidal areas, probably from October through July. Sand shrimp can live two and one-half years.

As its name implies, the sand shrimp is sand colored: tan to ash to sandy gray (occasionally darker and sometimes brown), irregularly speckled with blackish brown spots (though depending on the environment, the spots are not always present). Color is regulated by five pigments within the chromatophore system, and varies according to background. (For a structural description, refer to the related bay shrimp [*C. franciscorum*]).

The sand shrimp is primarily nocturnal, most often remaining buried in the sand during the day and ascending into the water column at night to feed on various creatures (such as brine shrimp). I have seen them active during the day several times, however, most recently on the mudflats at the entrance to Massachusetts' Duxbury Bay. I suspect the striped bass cruising the shallow flats were feeding on sand shrimp, for I rousted a patch of them. When disturbed, the shrimp makes several short, rapid darts backward, coming to rest on the sand bottom and working its legs to burrow straight down into it.

Male sand shrimp reach a maximum length of almost 2 inches (4.7 centimeters), while females can grow to 2¾ inches (7 centimeters).

AKA: Salt-and-pepper shrimp.

Bay Shrimp *(Crangon franciscorum)* Plate 7

With an overall range from San Diego, California, to Alaska (but not normally found in estuaries south of San Francisco Bay), *C. franciscorum* (along with one of two subspecies, *C. franciscorum franciscorum*) is the dominant decapod shrimp in most Pacific Coast estuaries. Studies supervised by NOAA showed common to abundant year-round populations of juveniles and adults in most estuaries between Puget Sound and southern San Francisco Bay. All life stages of the bay shrimp seemed absent from Oregon's Rogue River estuary and California's Klamath River estuary; Humboldt Bay, California, supported a common to abundant year-round population of juveniles only. Estuaries outwardly adjacent to Rogue River and Humboldt Bay, however, each supported abundant year-round populations of both juveniles and adults. (As this species shows large annual fluctuations in abundance, and might be highly sensitive to the effects of short-term estuarine pollution, such findings are inconclusive.) An important prey for many West Coast predators—including green sturgeon, white sturgeon, and striped bass—the bay shrimp is fished commercially (primarily with trawls) in San Francisco Bay. While some are used for human consumption, most taken are used as bait for the aforementioned fishes.

Juvenile and adult bay shrimp are primarily bottom dwellers found over sand or mud. Adults are found in estuaries as well as offshore, from the intertidal areas down to 600 feet (183 meters; 100 fathoms). Juveniles primarily inhabit channels and flats in the upper reaches (that is, the low-salinity areas) of estuaries, especially in the summer months. Some adults are present in the upper reaches of estuaries, but they are less common there than are juveniles.

As they mature, bay shrimp move to the lower reaches of estuaries. In fall and winter, a spawning migration of sorts occurs, with reproductively active females and males moving to deeper, higher-salinity areas—often the nearshore areas just outside the estuaries. Usually there are two spawning periods, but sometimes only one, depending on the estuary. In Yaquina Bay, Oregon, spawning occurs from December to March, and then again from April to August. The first spawning period is composed primarily of males and older females, the second mixed with both first-time and repeat-spawning females. (Males are believed to spawn only once in their lives, while females can spawn twice.) The second spawning is usually larger than the first—that is, there are more spawners present for a longer period.

C. franciscorum is a fast-growing but short-lived species. Studies conducted in Yaquina

Bay show different growth rates for the two groups of hatchling shrimps. Larvae from the first spawning hatch in the early spring, become juveniles between May and July, and reach maturity in December. Larvae from the second spawning hatch in late summer, are juveniles by December, and reach maturity the following summer. Juveniles range in size from about ²⁄₁₀ inch to nearly 2 inches (6 millimeters to 4.8 centimeters; 1³⁄₁₀ inches [3.4 centimeters] for males). Both sexes mature at one to one and one-half years. Maximum size in San Francisco Bay is about 2 to 2½ inches (5.5 to 6 centimeters), though specimens larger than this are common off the Columbia River. Female bay shrimp can live to two and one-half years, males to one and one-half years. *C. franciscorum* is primarily carnivorous during all life stages. Food items include mysids, amphipods, copepods, and bivalves (occasionally detritus and plant material). At night, juveniles and adults move toward the surface to feed.

The bay shrimp's body is moderately stout and compressed ventrally, widest where the cephalothorax meets the abdomen and tapering toward the tail. Color is light to dark yellowish gray, mottled; eyes are moderately large, the cornea reportedly salmon colored in live specimens, though West Coast angler Hal Janssen (whose sense of color I trust) says the eye is pearl with a rust-colored cornea.

AKA: Bay crangon, California shrimp, Franciscan Bay shrimp, grass shrimp.

Swimming Shrimps *(Family Penaeidae)*

The largest decapod shrimps on the East Coast, swimming shrimps range from the United States (most commonly from the Carolinas southward) to Brazil, though they are uncommon in highly saline waters, such as those surrounding the Bahamas. Of great economic importance, they are fished commercially throughout most of their range, primarily for human consumption but also as bait for various fishes. There are three species of penaeid shrimp common to U.S. waters.

Colors detailed below are for adults. Juveniles to nearly 2 inches (4.7 centimeters) are similar in appearance to each other: in general, nearly transparent with a grayish cast, mottled with very small brown and slate-blue dots (chromatophores). Specifically, *P. setiferus* can have a greenish cast when found around beds of vegetation, and the dots on *P. aztecus* are brown and olive green. Each of the aforementioned species has brown to reddish-brown areas toward the end of the tail fan.

Juveniles larger than the aforementioned size take on adult colors progressively as they grow.

AKA: Commercial shrimps, white shrimps.

Plate 7   **White Swimming Shrimp** *(Penaeus setiferus)*

The white swimming shrimp is fished commercially throughout most of its range, adults being marketed for food while juveniles are sold as bait. They inhabit estuaries and the inner oceanic littoral zone (predominantly on mud bottoms, into which they burrow, though they do not burrow as extensively as do other species of swimming shrimps) from water's edge to a depth of 98 feet (30 meters; 16 fathoms), rarely deeper. *P. setiferus* ranges from Fire Island, New York, to Saint Lucie Inlet, Florida (rarely as far out to sea as the Dry Tortugas, Florida); in the Gulf of Mexico, it can be found from the Ochlocknee River, Florida, to Campeche, Mexico. *P. setiferus* is most abundant in areas featuring extensive inland brackish marshes that are connected by passes to offshore shallows of relatively high salinity. By far the greatest concentration of *P. setiferus* is found in and around Louisiana's Mississippi River Delta. However, distribution is not uniform and might be the result of a variety of factors, chief among them salinity. Studies show that the abundance of *P. setiferus* in a given area is linked to the total rainfall for the current year and the preceding two years: high rainfall is followed by good catches.

Spawning of the white swimming shrimp varies with location (that is, population). In the Carolina region, spawning begins around May and extends into September. In the Gulf of Mexico, the season runs from March perhaps into October. (It has been suggested that there are two spawning seasons in Texas waters.) Spawning occurs offshore, probably in depths between 29 and 102 feet (9 and 31 meters; 5 and 17 fathoms). The precise location of the spawning grounds off the Carolinas is not known, though NOAA studies indicate that at least some spawning might be taking place in Charleston Harbor. In Texas, spawning has been recorded 6 or more miles (9.7 kilometers) offshore in waters between 26 and 89 feet (8 and 27 meters; 4 and 15 fathoms).

Hatchling *P. setiferus* begin entering the sounds around June, making their way up into the estuaries. This "recruitment" period can last through September (longer in the Gulf of Mexico), but most probably occurs from June to July. Once in the estuaries, the young shrimp begin to grow rapidly, increasing their length by nearly 1½ inches (3.6 centimeters) each month on average. Young shrimp can be found at all depths during the day, but they tend toward the surface at night. During their early lives, they prefer the shallower, lower-salinity portions of the estuaries (hatchlings can utilize waters of somewhat lower salinity than those utilized by the young of other local penaeids). As they grow, they gradually move to deeper, more saline waters. Upon reaching sexual maturity, they finally return to sea.

White swimming shrimp north of South Carolina move southward in fall and winter, returning in the spring. Studies supervised by NOAA showed common to highly abundant year-round populations of adults in Winyah Bay and Charleston Harbor, South Carolina, and in the Savannah River, Ossabaw Sound, St. Catherine/Sapelo Sound, and St. Andrew/St. Simon Sound, Georgia. In the NOAA studies, adults were completely absent from the St. Johns River, Florida, and rare in Indian River and Biscayne Bay, Florida. Common to highly abundant year-round populations of juveniles were found in every estuary between Winyah Bay, South Carolina, and the St. Johns River, Florida. (Given the fluctuations of abundance of *P. setiferus*, the NOAA findings should be regarded as inconclusive.)

The white swimming shrimp is a translucent bluish white, with dusky bands and patches of scattered black specks. Its rostrum and sides are tinged pink. The blades of its pleopods are marked with dark red. Its antennae are dark brown and are twice the length of its body. The blades of its uropods are tipped with dark brownish purple, with a narrow stripe of yellowish green along the margin. Females grow to nearly 8 inches (20 centimeters); males reach a maximum length of about 7 inches (18.2 centimeters).

AKA: White shrimp (common names often exchanged with common names of *P. duorarum*).

Pink Swimming Shrimp *(Penaeus duorarum)*

Like the white swimming shrimp, *P. duorarum* is found in estuaries and the inner oceanic littoral zone from water's edge to a depth of about 115 feet (35 meters; 19 fathoms), but perhaps exceeding 1,180 feet (360 meters; 197 fathoms). It is fished commercially (primarily in its centers of concentration) for both food and bait. The species ranges from the lower Chesapeake Bay through the Florida Straits to the Dry Tortugas, the west coast of Florida, and around the Gulf of Mexico to the Isla Mujeres at the tip of the Yucatán Peninsula, Mexico. Areas of abundance are the entire west coast of Florida and in the Bay of Campeche, Mexico (there is a minor center of abundance around Beaufort, North Carolina). The pink swimming shrimp prefers a bottom of shell-sand, but it is also found on sand, mud-sand, and coral-mud bottom. It is usually burrowed during the day, and is active throughout the water column at night (at which time it can be attracted with a light and captured with a dip net).

As with *P. setiferus*, spawning season depends on population. A single spawning season is indicated for the northernmost population (Chesapeake Bay through North Carolina): May into July, at least some of which takes place off the Beaufort Inlet. Florida spawning extends from April to July, and year-round spawning occurs on the Tortugas Shelf.

Postlarval shrimp begin moving into the estuaries in June and continue to November (most recruitment occurring from July to September). During this time they occupy the shallower, somewhat less saline waters for their early lives (in Florida and Texas, young *P. duorarum* are particularly abundant in the grassy areas of estuaries in waters of at least 20-percent salinity). Once in the estuaries, growth of the omnivorous *P. duorarum* is rapid. Shrimp hatched in late March or April can reach 2½ inches (6.5 centimeters) in length by July (those hatched in May can be nearly 1½ inches [3.5 centimeters] by July). Many juveniles overwinter in estuaries. Among the East Coast estuaries supporting year-round populations of juveniles are Pamlico and Bogue sounds and New River, North Carolina; St. Johns and Indian rivers and Biscayne Bay, Florida (the latter being the highest year-round concentration of juvenile *P. duorarum* on the coast, according to NOAA studies). Harsh winters, however, can result in mass mortalities. Warming spring weather induces increased feeding, and the adult shrimp migrate to sea to spawn. It has been estimated that at one year, *P. duorarum* is about 5½ inches (14 centimeters).

Color of *P. duorarum* is variable. Juveniles and young adults are often light brown or reddish brown, but can also be various shades of gray, ranging to bluish gray. There is a distinctly darker spot at the juncture of the third and fourth abdominal segments; this spot and other bandings can be gray, blue-gray, blue, or purplish. The tail fan is nearly transparent and edged with blue. Older specimens (especially those from deeper waters) tend to be red, pinkish, blue-gray, or nearly white, the abdominal spots either being absent entirely, or being reddish or purplish brown. Other recorded variations of body color are lemon yellow or (in the area of the Dry Tortugas) a rosy tone with reddish-brown markings. Some specimens of *P. duorarum* live for more than two years. Males achieve a maximum length of 6½ inches (16.9 centimeters), while females can grow to 11 inches (28 centimeters).

Pink swimming shrimp are eaten by many species of predacious fish, including spotted seatrout, snook, mangrove snapper, red grouper, black grouper, and king mackerel.

AKA: Pink shrimp, pink night shrimp, pink spotted shrimp, spotted shrimp.

Brown Swimming Shrimp *(Penaeus aztecus)*

The brown swimming shrimp is found in the estuaries and oceanic littoral zone from Martha's Vineyard, Massachusetts, around peninsular Florida and the Gulf of Mexico to northwestern

Yucatán, Mexico. It occurs from water's edge to a depth of 360 feet (110 meters; 60 fathoms). Fished commercially throughout much of its range, *P. aztecus* is taken most abundantly along the coast of Texas and in the southwestern Bay of Campeche. Its overall harvest exceeds that of the other two penaeid species outlined here.

Like the pink swimming shrimp, the brown swimming shrimp is a burrower, but it prefers a bottom similar to that preferred by *P. setiferus:* mud, muddy sand, sandy mud, or loose peat. Like *P. duorarum*, *P. aztecus* is most active in the water column at night.

Research done on *P. aztecus* indicates an extended spawning period that probably varies with location (spawning grounds are probably farther offshore and in deeper waters than are those of *P. setiferus* and *P. duorarum*). Postlarval *P. aztecus* enter sounds from October to May (peak recruitment is from late March to early April). Once in the estuaries, young shrimp move to the low-salinity shallows (most abundant in waters of between 10- and 20-percent salinity). These are virtually the same nursery grounds occupied by young *P. duorarum*, but as recruitment times of the two species do not coincide, they do not occupy common territory simultaneously.

Young *P. aztecus* grow rapidly as the weather warms. It has been estimated that juveniles can increase their length by nearly 2 inches (5 centimeters) per month (in Louisiana; somewhat less, on average, to the north). Growth has been linked to temperature: warm years make for good catches. As with the other penaeids listed here, *P. aztecus* moves to deeper, more saline waters as it grows, eventually returning to sea.

The shell of *P. aztecus* is thin, smooth, and translucent. Juveniles and young adults from estuaries or nearshore oceanic waters are usually brown, grayish brown, or reddish brown (red and green specimens also occur), occasionally with darker spots or faint concentrations of chromatophores at the joints of the abdominal segments. Color is darker on the legs and tail fan; the tail fan is often darkly edged with blue, purple, or reddish purple. Large specimens found offshore are often orange or lemon yellow (deeper on the legs and tail fan).

Male forms of *P. aztecus* grow to a maximum length of 7½ inches (19.5 centimeters); females exceed 9 inches (23.6 centimeters). Some spawning individuals found off Texas were as small as 5½ inches (14 centimeters).

AKA: Brown shrimp.

Snapping Shrimps (Family Alpheidae)

These tropical crustaceans live along the shore regions within rock crevices and coral heads, in the passages of sponges, among oyster shells, or in burrows (often in pairs) they dig in the sand. Snapping shrimps look like a crayfish or tiny lobster, with one pincer inordinately large. Species of the genera *Alpheus* and *Synalpheus* are able to shoot a sharp stream of water with this large claw (known as the *snapping pincer*), the shock effect from which is used both in prey capture and as a defense mechanism. When this stream is fired, the shrimp's wrist joint produces a click, not loud but clearly audible above water. It was described by A.J. McClane as being "like one of those 'crickets' that kids used to take to school." This click is also used as a warning to trespassers (usually other snapping shrimps), and is most often heard by the angler when wading the flats.

Like crayfishes, snapping shrimps are able to dart backward in short but rapid bursts. McClane speculated "that when bonefish tail in quick starts and stops—this is what they are feeding on." In McClane's examinations of the stomach contents of bonefish, most alpheid specimens were about 2 inches (5 centimeters) in length.

Color of snapping shrimps is highly variable, both among the species in general and within some particular species.

AKA: Pistol crabs, pistol shrimps.

Plate 7

Banded Snapping Shrimp *(Alpheus armillatus)*

Reported by A.J. McClane to be the "dominant forage by frequency... among Florida and Bahamian bonefish," the banded snapping shrimp is abundant under rocks and shells (including those found among turtle grass), on reefs, in the passages of sponges, and in holes in rocks from the water's edge to a depth of 46 feet (14 meters; 8 fathoms). The range of *A. armillatus* extends from North Carolina to São Paulo, Brazil, including the Gulf of Mexico, the Caribbean, and Bermuda.

Body color of *A. armillatus* can be a base of light brown or orange-brown, banded with black. Base color can also be dark gray, greenish brown, greenish tan, or brown, banded with translucent white. (Basic color varies to some degree according to the background and light conditions.) In any case, bands total nine—three on the carapace and six on the abdomen. Width of the bands is equal to or slightly less than those of the alternating color. The tail fan usually sports a broad crossband near the edge and is sometimes tipped with orange. Claws sport whitish bands above, are thickly speckled with dark gray, and are tipped with white or pale pink. Antennae and walking legs are orange-yellow banded with white. The banded snapping shrimp grows to a maximum length of 1⁷⁄₁₀ inches (4.5 centimeters).

Brown Snapping Shrimp *(Alpheus armatus)*

Similar in appearance to *A. armillatus* (except that its brown or reddish-brown color is solid; also, antennae are red, banded with white), the brown snapping shrimp grows to 2 inches (5 centimeters) in length.

AKA: Red snapping shrimp.

Big-Clawed Snapping Shrimp *(Alpheus heterochaelis)*

Similar in appearance to the banded snapping shrimp, though not as abundant, the big-clawed snapping shrimp is found among stones and shells or in burrows in the mud (often among shells), from the shoreline to a depth of 98 feet (30 meters; 16 fathoms). It ranges from the lower Chesapeake Bay to Brazil, including the Gulf of Mexico, Bermuda, Curaçao, and Cuba. It is a common species throughout Everglades National Park, Florida, and is particularly abundant in the Florida mangrove *Juncus* system, in salinities ranging between 1 and 27.5 percent.

Color is dark translucent green, fused slightly with purple along the sides of the carapace. The claws are marked with white, and the walking legs are pale red. Tips of the tail fan are blue, bordered with orange along the outer edge. The outer blades of the tail fan sport a patch of red just above the blue, with a narrow white border. The big-clawed snapping shrimp grows to just over 2 inches (5.4 centimeters).

AKA: Common snapping shrimp.

Green Snapping Shrimp *(Alpheus normanni)*

The green snapping shrimp is found in shallow water on shelly or rocky bottoms, in sand burrows, or on pilings from Cape Charles, Virginia, and the lower Chesapeake Bay to São Paulo, Brazil, including the Gulf of Mexico, the West Indies, and Bermuda (also from the Gulf of California to Panama).

Color is gray or dull green. Sometimes there is a whitish median and lateral stripe, which is often mottled with dark green or brown. There is a pale spot behind each eye. The snapping pincer is dark green, its inner surface usually banded with two stripes of yellow or yellowish brown. The fixed finger of the snapping pincer is blackish, and the moving finger is reddish. The small pincer and walking legs are a paler green than that of the snapping pincer, and often sport dull gray or reddish bandings. The body is sometimes banded with red and pale yellow. Maximum length is just over 1 inch (3 centimeters).

Yellow Snapping Shrimp *(Synalpheus brevicarpus)*

This common snapping shrimp is found in dead corals and throughout sponge passages. Body color is yellow (a green-bodied variation is common), the snapping pincer is reddish (the red claw more closely matches the body color in younger specimens).

Crabs

Swimming Crabs *(Family Portunidae)*

Composed of several subfamilies, each containing a number of genera, the family Portunidae comprises the entire family of swimming crabs. While crabs are usually thought of as bottom dwellers, swimming crabs are indeed strong swimmers, their rearmost pair of walking legs having evolved into paddles that allow them to move throughout the entire water column.

Swimming crabs are found in both estuarine and marine waters over a variety of bottoms from the water's edge to great depths. The carapaces of some species are roughly elliptical, being about one-quarter wider than they are long; others, such as that of the blue crab (*Callinectes sapidus*), can be as many as two and one-half times wider than they are long, and superficially resemble the blade of a medieval axe in outline. Coloration varies widely from species to species, within species, and from juvenile to adult forms. In general, various shades of olive, green, gray, tan, and brown predominate, both in solids and in mixtures and mottlings (for comprehensive color descriptions of specific species, refer to Williams' *Shrimps, Lobsters, and Crabs of the Atlantic Coast of the Eastern United States, Maine to Florida*).

Blue Crab *(Callinectes sapidus)*

Plate 7

 The blue crab is one of the most important crab species, both economically and environmentally (it is harvested throughout its range and is significant in the diets of many fishes). The blue crab is found from Massachusetts (most commonly from the south side of Cape Cod; rarely as far north as Nova Scotia) to northern Argentina, including Bermuda, the West Indies, and the Antilles. It occurs in a variety of coastal and estuarine habitats from the water's edge to depths of about 295 feet (90 meters; 49 fathoms), but primarily inhabits the shallows to depths up to 114 feet (35 meters; 19 fathoms). Tolerant of extremes in salinity, *C. sapidus* has been found in hypersaline waters as well as in fresh water (recorded over 180 miles [290 kilometers] above the ocean in the St. Johns River, Florida).

Although the blue crab can be found in virtually any habitat within its range, studies have shown vegetated areas and seagrass beds to be important areas for juveniles and adults. These areas not only contain the crab's forage (plant matter, fishes, bivalves [especially oysters], and crustaceans, including other crabs and even members of its own species), they also provide it with refuge from predators (particularly during moltings). Several estuaries within the Gulf of Mexico that are devoid of bottom vegetation (such as Mississippi Sound and Mobile Bay, Alabama) also support large populations; in these areas, blue crabs are associated with soft mud bottoms.

Like other members of the family Portunidae, the blue crab is a swimming crab and is quite mobile within the water column. While we normally associate crabs with sideward movement, Carl Richards observes that the blue crab can swim in any direction and will often swim backward when frightened. Swimming crabs in general, Richards further notes, descend from the water's surface at approximately a 45-degree angle.

Mating occurs during the summer, and from late summer to fall the impregnated females migrate to more saline waters at the lower reaches of the bays and estuaries. Sperm is stored over the winter by the females, and the eggs are fertilized the following spring (a single crab can carry up to 8 million eggs). Hatching occurs from June to September. The crab larva (known as a *zoea*) swims to the surface and is swept by tidal currents to offshore waters, where it completes development and returns to the bays and estuaries as a post-larva (*megalops*) or young juvenile (of about 2.5 millimeters in width) during late summer and fall. Adults spend winter months in deeper waters; small crabs burrow beneath shallow vegetation in shallow muddy bottoms, or in the bottoms of deeper waters. Growth ceases during the winter months. As the water warms in the spring, the small crabs emerge and begin feeding, and both adults and juveniles move into shallower bay and estuarine waters.

Color of the blue crab, as well as other morphological features, is highly variable—much of which is the result of genetic variation. The carapace is two and one-sixth to two and one-half times as wide as it is long. In general, coloration of the carapace and dorsal surface of the claws is mottled with varying shades of grayish, bluish, blue-gray, or brownish green. Carl Richards also reports blue crabs of sand color, grayish green, bluish green, and brown. Not always are the crabs mottled, he notes, but are sometimes solid in color. The claws of some specimens are shaded bright blue on the dorsal surface and sometimes on the inside surface. Ventral surface of the claws is white, and the fingers of the claws are sometimes tipped with red. The spines along the front of the carapace can also be red (the younger the crab, the fainter the red). Legs vary blue and white, with traces of red or brownish green; leg joints are orange. Ventral surface (abdomen and sternal area) is off-white with tints of yellow and pink. Full and partial albinos—albinos of any species are rare in nature because of their conspicuousness to predators—have also been recorded.

Juvenile blue crabs are eaten by many fishes, including striped bass (one study found as many as twenty-five small blue crabs in the stomachs of striped bass), bluefish, permit, crevalle jack, redfish, tarpon, bonefish, spotted seatrout, weakfish, red drum, black drum, Atlantic croaker, largemouth bass, cobia, and also bull, sandbar, and bonnethead sharks.

Green Crab *(Carcinus maenas)*

Plate 7

Although a member of the family of swimming crabs, the green crab lacks the overt swimming paddles that characterize the family and is more or less restricted to bottom dwelling. It occurs over a variety of shallow bottoms, both in marine and estuarine environments, from Nova Scotia to Virginia. It is a common prey and popular bait for tautog and striped bass.

The carapace of the green crab is about 25 percent wider than it is long, and is usually multicolored: grayish green, dark green, bluish green, reddish, or occasionally light blue (juveniles are often mottled with white). Legs vary from olive to yellowish white to violet. Ventral coloration (abdomen and sternal area) is yellowish white. As with the blue crab (*Callinectes sapidus*), some albino specimens have been recorded.

AKA: Shore crab.

Mud, Stone, Rock, Coral, and Reef Crabs
(Family Xanthidae)

Plate 8

A large, complex group, the family Xanthidae comprises many species on all three coasts, occurring in a variety of habitats and salinities. It is found from northern waters and ranging throughout South America, including many island habitats in between. Species identification is difficult. In general, xanthid crabs are either transversely oval (mud, stone, and coral crabs) or transversely hexagonal (reef crabs). Color varies widely depending on species and habitat (drab mottled olives in a mud environment to rich reds, oranges, blues, and purples around stones or corals; some species are nearly colorless). Fingers of the claws are often dark—usually black, red, or purple—and the carapace and claws are often spotted or bear numerous dark spines to that effect.

Xanthid crabs are eaten by a variety of gamefishes, including bonefish and permit.

Fiddler Crabs (Family Ocypodidae)

Fiddler crabs live straddled between land and water, occupying burrows in the mud or sand within the intertidal areas of estuaries. They emerge during low tides (especially at night) to feed on algae, bacteria, and detritus. Estuarine areas housing fiddler crabs are easily recognized: numerous dime- to quarter-sized holes in the sand or mud, outside of which are piled the little balls of sand or mud cleared from the burrows. In all species, one of the male's claws is inordinately large with long, thin fingers. This large claw is used to signal females during the breeding season, and also to fight off rival males. Both claws of all females are small and of equal size.

During breeding, the carapace of the male fiddler lightens, and in some species there is a patch of color at the cardiac region (middle of the crab's underside), which helps signal females.

I've seen fiddler crabs in such numbers along the south side of Cape Cod that in the moonlight it appeared the beach was moving. Despite this, I'm not convinced they are significant in the diet of any gamefish, given their burrowing habits and low-tide emergence (and thus will treat them briefly). However, fiddlers work as bait, and fiddler patterns catch fish as well—though perhaps less because they look like fiddlers than they do crabs in general. Carl Richards has taken snook, redfish, and even tarpon on his fiddler patterns; Bill Catherwood (originator of the Giant Killer series of flies) has been tying a fiddler-crab imitation for over twenty years to catch tautog, but I believe his impetus for doing so was the fiddler's use as bait. As tautog are primarily marine, entering estuaries only on occasion, it is doubtful they have much opportunity to encounter fiddler crabs under natural conditions.

The three species of fiddler crabs found along the East Coast—red-jointed fiddler, sand fiddler, and mud fiddler—are similar in appearance and life history. These three species are summarized below.

Red-Jointed Fiddler *(Uca minax)*

Range: Cape Cod, Massachusetts, to Matagorda Bay, Texas.
Carapace: Only slightly (about one and three-tenths times) wider than long and rounded at each end, an H-shaped depression near the center. Maximum size of male carapace about 1 inch (2.5 centimeters) in length, and about 1½ inches (3.8 centimeters) in width; female to a length of just under 1 inch (2.2 centimeters), and a width of just over 1 inch (3 centimeters).
Color: Carapace is chestnut brown, lightening to gray in front; legs are olive or grayish brown. The large claw has red spots at the joints; hands are ivory white.
Breeding Color: Carapace grayish white or dull yellowish white, dull orange at the front. Cardiac region displays a red spot. Large claw is grayish orange to yellowish orange, joints are edged with red.
Breeding Season: July to the beginning of September.
AKA: Brackish-water fiddler.

Plate 8

Sand Fiddler *(Uca pugilator)*

Range: Cape Cod, Massachusetts, to about Pensacola, Florida.
Carapace: As much as one and one-half times wide as long. Male to about ⁷⁄₁₀ inch (1.7 centimeters) in length, and just over 1 inch (2.6 centimeters) in width; females to just over ½ inch (1.4 centimeters) in length, and just over ⁷⁄₁₀ inch (1.9 centimeters) in width.
Color: Carapace is brown with small gold or light-brown spots; walking legs are olive to white. Large claw is buff white to yellowish white; the base of the claws is often pale orange. Eyestalks are grayish white.
Breeding Color: Carapace is whitish (usually yellowish white). Purplish violet patch on cardiac region.
Breeding Season: July to mid-August in the species' northern range, and April to October in the south.

Mud Fiddler *(Uca pugnax)*

Range: Provincetown, Massachusetts, to Daytona Beach, Florida.
Carapace: Male to ½ inch (1.5 centimeters) in length, and nearly 1 inch (2.3 centime-

ters) in width; females to nearly the same length (1.3 centimeters), but only to about ⅗₀ inch (1.8 centimeters) in width. There is an H-shaped depression near the center.

Color: Usually brown; eyestalks and the rearward part of the carapace are often blue or turquoise (often faintly in the southernmost range). Walking legs are dark and banded. Large claw of male is usually yellowish white to yellowish orange, but sometimes light brown or simply yellowish. Fingers of large claw are white, as is entire small claw.

Breeding Color: Often fails to lighten. When it does, color is pale gray.

Breeding Season: Observed in Massachusetts from early to mid-July, early July to mid-August in New Jersey, and as early as April in Florida.

Mole Crabs *(Family Hippidae)*

These burrowing crabs inhabit the surf zones along sandy beaches of all three coasts. They less resemble crabs than they do some aquatic scarab. Their carapaces are olive-shaped, quite convex dorsally, and marked with a series of transverse ripples. Legs are short (first pair of legs with poorly developed pincers; fifth pair of legs are threadlike and generally hidden) and adapted for swimming and burrowing rather than for walking. All movement—swimming, burrowing, crawling—is backward. When burrowed, mole crabs allow their long hairy antennae (which are normally coiled beneath the mouth parts) to extend out of the sand, collecting the plankton and particulate matter on which they feed. (The filaments of the antennae can also intermesh to form a sort of breathing tube to draw water into the gill chambers.)

Mole crabs are used as bait both live and dead, and are preyed upon by various shallow-water fishes.

AKA: Sand bugs, sand crabs, sand fleas.

Mole Crab *(Emerita talpoida)*

This crab is found in aggregations along sandy beaches in and below the surf line (to 11½ feet [3.5 meters; 2 fathoms] in winter) from Harwich (Cape Cod), Massachusetts, to Yucatán, Mexico. Color is a uniform pale yellowish brown, or whitish tinged faintly with purple on the carapace. Length of the male carapace can reach nearly ⅘₀ inch (2 centimeters); egg-bearing females can reach almost 1½ inches (3.6 centimeters). The antennae are nearly twice the length of the carapace. Spawning occurs from winter to autumn. The eggs, which are cradled between the ventral part of the thorax and the abdomen, are bright orange when first laid, their color fading to translucent gray just prior to hatching. (For an imitation, see Tom Lentz's Sand Flea.)

Sand Crab *(Emerita analoga)*   Plate 8

This close relative of *E. talpoida* is found abundantly in its same environment from Oregon to the South American coast. Length of the female carapace can reach just over 1 inch (2.9 centimeters), while males only grow to a length of just under ½ inch (1.2 centimeters). Color of the adult carapace is steel gray flecked transversely with a lighter shade (to better blend with the wave-washed sand). Legs and ventral surface are white with a pinkish tinge. As with its East Coast counterpart, the breeding season of *E. analoga* takes place from winter to autumn. Bright coral in color when first laid, eggs fade to dull grayish brown just before hatching.

Sand crabs are a principal food of such gamefishes as barred surfperch and corbina. Marine biologists speculate that sand crabs might compose as much as 90 percent of these fishes' diets.

Mantis Shrimps *(Order Stomatopoda)*

The order Stomatopoda might exceed 365 species worldwide (over 60 of which inhabit the Florida-Caribbean region), and although mantis shrimps are doubtless eaten by a number of piscine predators, they are of main interest to the bonefisherman.

Mantis shrimps are coastal bottom-dwellers (a few have been found as deep as 4,265 feet [1,300 meters; 711 fathoms] and several species might enter brackish water). In appearance, mantis shrimps less resemble what we normally think of as shrimps than they do some sort of aquatic insect. Superficially they resemble the freshwater hellgrammite (the larval stage of the dobson fly) with a large flattened abdomen and a fan-shaped tail. Unlike other crustaceans, the head of the mantis shrimp is jointed, the foremost part capable of independent movement. But perhaps the most characteristic feature of the mantis shrimp is its pair of large "jackknife" claws, so similar to those of the praying mantis that they are the source of the order's common name. Like the claws of the praying mantis, the raptorial claws of the mantis shrimps are used for catching food (the claw's inner edge is serrated on some species, smooth on others; some claws are more clublike than scythelike). These strong appendages, however, might also be used for defense. Anyone handling live specimens should be cautioned, for mantis shrimps are able to slice into human flesh as well, hence the local names *thumbbuster, thumbcracker,* and *split thumb.*

Mantis shrimps live in burrows (either those they excavate themselves or ones they usurp from other creatures) in sand or mud bottoms, or in crevices in coral reefs. Most species are predominantly nocturnal predators and are largely inactive during the day. Some species lie in wait near their burrow entrances for prey to happen by; others are stalkers, creeping up on prey and cutting it down with lightning speed. The claws of mantis shrimps are strong enough and sharp enough to sever many prey in half with a single swipe. Prey include fish, crabs and shrimps (particularly in the molting stage and sometimes including members of their own species), worms, and sea anemones. For anyone interested in collecting specimens, mantis shrimps can be lured from their burrows by using the viscera of sea cucumbers.

As they are largely nocturnal, most mantis shrimps consumed by daytime-feeding bonefish are probably flushed from their burrows by the bonefish's rooting or are happened upon by chance. Mantis shrimps are excellent swimmers, using their swimmerets to move rapidly in any direction. By bending and stretching their bodies, they can also jerk either backward or forward. Some species can reach 12 inches (30 centimeters) or more in length. Although they are eaten by humans, they are solitary in their habits and so in most areas cannot be collected in sufficient quantities to support a commercial industry (though there is something of a commercial fishery for them in Japan).

As colors vary widely both from species to species and within species, color descriptions are only of cursory use. Mantis shrimps can range from cream to black and all colors in between, often in a variety of barrings, mottlings, or other patternings. Differences in coloration within species can be the result of genetics, habitat, or to some extent even light levels or temperature.

A.J. McClane noted that in his examinations of the stomach contents of bonefish, most stomatopod specimens were only 2 to 3 inches (5 to 7.6 centimeters) long.

Golden or False Mantis *(Pseudosquilla ciliata)*

In the Atlantic, *P. ciliata* occurs in all tropical areas from Florida to Brazil. In Florida, at least, it is most commonly found on grass banks in shallow water, often swimming freely rather than burrowed. *P. ciliata* is also found on reefs, though less frequently.

Color has been reported as yellow-brown, dark green, pea green, bright green, or nearly white, with the appendages and thoracic segments edged in bright yellow and the dactylus of the raptorial claw pink. Color has also been reported as a mottled dark green and brown with the appendages edged in bright red. Color is sometimes bluish green.

Males can reach a length of 3 inches (8 centimeters), while females can grow to 3½ inches (8.9 centimeters). In addition to having been found among the stomach contents of bonefish, *P. ciliata* has also been found in the stomachs of mutton snapper, Nassau grouper, and bonnethead shark.

WORMS (PHYLUM ANNELIDA)

The number of worm species inhabiting our oceans is overwhelming, and no work such as this could even hope to put a respectable dent in the subject as a whole. However, considering the place of marine worms in the diets of many gamefishes—mostly during their spawning periods, but also as opportunity allows—it is a subject that deserves our attention. Various worms are popular bait for many fish species throughout the season, and the spin-fishing community is only just realizing the effectiveness of plastic worms and their progeny—longtime standards for freshwater bass—on striped bass and other saltwater fishes. Given the proper circumstances, some of our baitfish imitations are as likely taken for worms as they are for fish.

For the fly-rodder, a knowledge of marine worms is most valuable during their spawning periods, when certain gamefishes might feed on them quite selectively. This I learned the hard way one night in a bay on the south side of Cape Cod, when rising bass ignored everything I threw at them. It never occurred to me that those 2-inch worms squirming around the lighted dock were what the bass were feeding on; it never occurred to me the bass would ignore baitfish for a smaller offering.

The phylum Annelida comprises the three main classes of segmented worms, but for our purposes I have decided to concentrate on those two families within the class Polychaeta that have caught the attention of our most knowledgeable saltwater fly-rodders.

In brief, polychaete worms are characterized by distinct segmentation and *parapodia*—feetlike appendages along the sides of the body. Most polychaetes have a pair of these appendages on nearly every body segment. A definite head, usually having eyes, is also present. Polychaetes are often highly colored, many being tinted red, yellow, blue, and green. They can be found in nearly every type of marine habitat, from the intertidal zone down to great depths, from rocky shores to sandy beaches to mud flats to ocean bottom. Many live in self-built tubes of calcium carbonate or other materials, while others burrow in the sand or mud or in rock crevices. Still others are free-living (but these species confine most of their activities to the undersides of rocks, among seaweed, or in other places where they are sheltered from predators). A few species are even found swimming freely in the water, but these are usually transparent. Some polychaetes feed on plankton, detritus, or other kinds of organic substances, while the remainder are predacious, eating other worms, small crustaceans, and the larvae of various marine animals. Some species are omnivorous. Despite their own desirability as forage, polychaetes are a highly successful and abundant class of marine animals.

All polychaetes reproduce by means of sperms and eggs—a few species can also reproduce by means of *budding*, or breaking in two—the sexes being separate in most species and each releasing sperms or eggs into the water, where they unite randomly. Of most interest to the angler is the phenomenon of *swarming*—mass spawning at the water's surface. During such episodes, the males usually appear first at the surface and are soon joined by the females. Both sexes then swim excitedly about the water, the males somewhat more quickly than the females, in a manner not unlike skywriting airplanes, each leaving its trail of eggs or sperms. Spawning times differ for each species. In some, spawning can take place several nights in succession, or it might be stretched out over several months, recurring only during particular phases of the moon. Other influential factors can include time of day, tide, light conditions, temperature, or water calmness. Most swarming species die after they are spawned out, while a few live to spawn repeatedly. As we can imagine, it is during their swarming phase that such worms are most vulnerable to predation by fishes.

Clamworms *(Family Nereidae)*

Nereids are slender worms, elongate and flattened, with numerous parapodia at each side and along the entire length of the body. For the most part, they are burrowers and bottom dwellers, living in crevices, under rocks, and in holes they excavate in the sand and mud. Most are predacious, armed with a pair of strongly developed hooklike jaws (usually darkly colored) that open and close on prey, drawing it toward the elongated mouth (*proboscis*) and engulfed whole. Any angler who has handled these worms, which are widely sold as bait, has likely been bitten.

The nereids of most interest to the fly-rodder are those that swarm at the surface when spawning; in North America, these include various species of the genera *Nereis* (sometimes listed as *Neanthes*) and *Platynereis*. Precise identification of swarming worms is difficult because of the metamorphosis they undergo prior to spawning. This phenomenon is called *epitoky*. As the sex organs of the worms mature, the rearward parapodia become elongated and transformed (only slightly in some species, significantly in others) into scooplike oars, allowing the animal to swim to the surface. Also, the segmentation becomes compressed, making the spawning worm significantly stouter than its mature nonspawning form. Unlike their burrowing and bottom-dwelling counterparts, these reproductive forms are positively phototropic, being attracted to light (both natural and artificial) at the surface. So different in structure and behavior are these sexually active forms from the nonsexual ones that they were once placed in a separate genus,

Heteronereis, and even today the sexually active worm is referred to as a *heteronereid* or *epitoke*.

AKA: Cinderworms, mussel worms, pileworms, ragworms (Britain), rockworms, sandworms, seaworms.

Green Clamworm *(Nereis virens)*   Plate 8
(also listed as *Neanthes virens*)

The green clamworm inhabits both coasts from Newfoundland to Virginia on the East Coast (most commonly from Labrador to Long Island Sound, Long Island being perhaps the species' greatest area of concentration) and along the entire West Coast. *N. virens* is also one of the largest and most common of the North American nereids, some specimens growing to 18 inches (45.7 centimeters) in length and nearly ½ inch (1.25 centimeters) in width. Tolerant of a wide range of salinity, it is found in the sheltered areas of both estuaries and sounds—particularly common in the flats outside river mouths. It is found burrowed in mucus-lined tubes from about the low-water mark to almost the high-water mark, and in the ocean proper to a depth exceeding 500 feet (153 meters; 84 fathoms). *N. virens* occurs in a variety of soils: firm mud fixed with sand; muddy, coarse, or gravelly sand; clay; peat; and among the roots of decaying marshgrass and eelgrass. On rocky shores, it is found under rocks and stones. It is also found burrowed in the sand among mussel beds. Burrows range from 2½ to 18 inches (about 7 to 45 centimeters) deep, the largest specimens usually burrowing the deepest.

N. virens often feeds by protruding its fore end out of its burrow to seize food and pulling it down into the burrow to be devoured. Unlike most other worms, however, it sometimes emerges from its burrow (especially at night) to swim about the surface to feed. (Burrows are only semipermanent; after exiting the burrow, the worm might tunnel anew.) *N. virens* is a swift and voracious predator, eating worms and other types of marine animals, but it also consumes the alga commonly known as *sea lettuce* (*Ulva*).

N. virens is peach colored, with a sheen ranging from iridescent green to steel blue, sometimes tinged with orange or red, particularly on the parapodia (though the orange or red tinge is most common to breeding females).

Heteronereids of *N. virens* are only somewhat modified, their parapodia enlarged only slightly into diamond-shaped paddles. They are reportedly somewhat shorter and thicker, proportionally, than their mature nonspawning length because of compression of the body segments. However, on the *N. virens* heteronereids I've examined (collected along Massachusetts' South Shore in March), this compression was virtually unnoticeable. With the exception of their color—which was iridescent steel blue with crimson legs—and their slightly elongated and slightly broadened legs, they looked very much like those you would find at a bait shop.

A heteronereid of about 10½ inches (27 centimeters) in length is reportedly just under 1 inch (2.5 centimeters) in width. A 6-inch (16-centimeter) heteronereid is about ½ inch (1.3 centimeters) in width. When spawning, the worms emerge from their burrows with the rising of the tide and swarm about at the surface, sometimes in immense numbers (though the heteronereids I've collected in March were swimming leisurely beneath the surface and reminded me of Chinese dragon kites). During these times they have been observed in shallow waters along shores and in tide pools. Swarming can take place either during the day or at night.

Spawning can take place from very early spring to August.

Swarming has been recorded in Maine from the middle of March to late June, sometimes extending into August. At the mouth of the Oyster River in New Hampshire, swarming has been observed in April. In Massachusetts, swarming has been recorded as early as the end of February (in Barnstable), though the bulk of the breeding in Massachusetts appears to occur in March. Spawning has also been recorded in the evenings along the Cape Cod Canal in May, shortly before or just after the turning of the tide during the new moon and full moon.

After spawning, virtually all the spent heteronereids die.

N. virens is an important forage for many fishes, some of which (such as tautog) dig them out of their burrows. Clamworms are commonly dug and sold as bait.

AKA: King ragworm (Britain).

Platynereis dumerilii (might be synonymous with *Platynereis megalops*)

Inhabiting shallow waters from southern Newfoundland to Florida and the Gulf of Mexico, *P. dumerillii* is found on shelly bottoms, in rock crevices, in pilings and wharfs, in sponges, and particularly among algal masses (*Fucus*) and floating seaweed (*Sargassum*). When inhabiting algae, it constructs transparent, parchment-like tubes into which it might incorporate foreign matter such as sand.

P. dumerilii is a small worm, reaching a maximum length of about 3 inches (7.5 centimeters) and a width of about ⁹⁄₁₀ inch (6 millimeters). Heteronereids are highly modified. Because of the greater compression of the body segments, the male heteronereids are smaller than the females. Male heteronereids achieve a maximum length of just under 1 inch (2.4 centimeters). They are greenish anteriorly, and pinkish to reddish posteriorly (the impression you get from observing the male is of a red worm with a white head). Female heteronereids grow to a maximum length of almost 2 inches (4.7 centimeters), and are pale green or yellowish, often nearly white. (As spawning takes place exclusively at night, colors of heteronereids are only of passing interest.)

In the Woods Hole region, swarming takes place at the surface for about two hours every night during the dark of the moon (I've seen them just before the full moon on Massachusetts' South Shore) from June into September, though most probably occurs in July and August. In Beaufort, North Carolina, swarming occurs in June and July. The spawning season is greatly extended in Naples, Florida, where swarming heteronereids can be found from October to May, tending to coincide with the first and third quarters of the moon.

Swarming occurs generally at the surface, the male heteronereids swimming rapidly with jerky movements and rotating in spirals. The females swim rather slowly, usually at a greater depth than the males. When swarming, these worms can be attracted by artificial lights at the surface. All heteronereids die after spawning.

Nereis succinea (also listed as *Neanthes succinea* and *Nereis limbata*)

N. succinea is found from the Gulf of St. Lawrence to Florida and in the Gulf of Mexico, occupying U-shaped burrows from the high intertidal area and into the ocean down to about 150 feet (46 meters; 25 fathoms). Tolerant of a wide range of salinity, it is found both in marine and brackish-water environments, but prefers protected areas—coves and harbors, bays and sounds, estuaries and marsh ditches—to open shoreline. It burrows among oyster shells, barnacles, or in a variety of soil types, such as peat, the mulch of brackish-water areas, soft or firm mud (especially mud mixed with shells, sand, or gravel), or coarse sand. Areas of particular abundance include Great Bay, New Hampshire, and its associated rivers; it is common throughout the harbor in New Jersey (except in pure sand) and in Delaware Bay (particularly in the mid-bay region). *N. succinea* is the most common annelid in Chesapeake Bay and the most common nereid around Beaufort, North Carolina. It can be found in abundance in many intertidal areas along the Gulf Coast.

Nonspawning adults of *N. succinea* are brownish anteriorly and greenish, greenish yellow, or pale red posteriorly (jaws are light amber). They can attain a length of 7½ inches (19 centimeters). Heteronereids are vastly different from the nonspawning form. Both males and females are considerably shorter because of compression of body segments, and both forms have enlarged, photopositive eyes. Male heteronereids are 2 inches (5.5 centimeters) long at most, and ³⁄₁₀ inch (5 millimeters) wide. Males are bright red with a white posterior end. Female heteronereids can be 3 inches (7.5 centimeters) long and nearly ³⁄₁₀ inch (7 millimeters) wide. Females are pale yellow-green and often nearly white. Male heteronereids swim in either a swift gyrating motion or in wide circles. Females swim more slowly.

N. succinea has been observed swarming in immense numbers, both in the daytime and at night. Swarming has been recorded in June in Miramachi Bay, New Brunswick. In the Woods Hole region and in Vineyard Sound, they have been observed swarming in March and in every month from May through October first, generally during the dark of the moon. Rhode Island reportedly has large numbers in May. They have been observed in immense numbers in Long Island Sound in August, where they touched off a feeding frenzy among bluefish. In the Cooper River, South Carolina, they have been observed swarming in April. Heteronereids die after spawning.

Nereis pelagica

This species is found on both coasts—on the East Coast from Hudson Bay to Key Largo, Florida, and on the West Coast from southeastern Alaska to San Pedro, California (though most commonly from Puget Sound southward). *N. pelagica* is rarely found in mud, preferring bottoms of sand, gravel, shells, stones, and rocks (under which, or in whose crevices, it can hide). It can be found among mussels and sponges, on pilings, or on algae or floating kelp (upon which it builds membranous tubes). It is associated with clean, circulating water from the low rocky intertidal areas to depths of perhaps 3,600 feet (1,097 meters; 600 fathoms).

N. pelagica is a slender worm, reaching a length of nearly 8 inches (20 centimeters) and a width of perhaps ½ inch (1.4 centimeters). Color varies greatly from light to reddish to golden brown or iridescent greenish brown to olive green, yellowish, or violet.

Swarming is sporadic and does not always take place at the surface. Spawning has been recorded in August in Labrador, but at a depth of 360 feet (110 meters; 60 fathoms). Heteronereids have been recorded at depths from 1 to 30 feet (to 9 meters; 5 fathoms) around the Eastport/Penobscot/Mount Desert region of Maine in October. Surface spawning has been observed in Woods Hole in March and in the Cape Cod Canal in May. On the West Coast, heteronereids have been observed at night in the lights of Friday Harbor, Washington, during the summer months.

Nereis brandti (also listed as *Neanthes brandti*)

This West Coast nereid is perhaps the largest polychaete in North America, growing to about 1 yard (1 meter) in length. Very similar to the green clamworm (*N. virens*) in appearance *N.*

brandti is found in bays and harbors, burrowed in the soft mud near algal mats. Heteronereids from 12 to 23½ inches (30 to 60 centimeters) in length have been reported swarming at night—mid-June through August—in the Friday Harbor, Washington, area (presumably attracted to the lights), most abundantly on nights immediately preceding the highest low (neap) tides.

Large Mussel Worm *(Nereis vexillosa)*

This worm is common in nearly all types of environments, from surf-pounded shores to the shores of protected bays, among both rocky shores and gravel beaches (including muddy gravel), in mussel beds, and among wharf pilings. It is found from Alaska to San Diego, and is abundant throughout its range. *N. vexillosa* is dark brown, blue-green, or green-brown (often iridescent; green-brown appears to be the most common color). Adults range in size from about 2 to 12 inches (5 to 30 centimeters); the largest specimens are found burrowed in the mussel beds of the open coast.

During spawning, the posterior segments swell with either eggs or sperm and show through the worm's body. The posterior of the female is red, while that of the male is white (the male worms tend to be smaller than the females). Swarming takes place at night, usually beginning one or two hours before midnight, during the dark of the moon from March to August.

AKA: Clamworm, pileworm.

Small Mussel Worm *(Nereis grubei)*
(formerly *Nereis mediator*)

Similar in appearance to *N. vexillosa* (but considerably smaller), *N. grubei* is common among seaweed fronds and holdfasts (where it inhabits mucus tubes), and also on pilings and in mussel beds, from British Columbia to Mexico. *N. grubei* is usually green, though females containing developing eggs are turquoise. Adults rarely reach 4 inches (10 centimeters) in length.

Spawning season depends on population. One population studied in central California (Pescadero Point, San Mateo County) showed large heteronereids swarming nearly every month between mid-February and mid-June, while a study done in southern California (Point Fermin, Los Angeles County) found considerably smaller heteronereids present all months of the year.

Palolo Worms (Family Eunicidae)

Found in all marine environments—but particularly in tropical shallows, coral reef rubble, and mangrove swamps—most eunicid species spend their lives burrowed in cracks and crevices in rubble, rock, and sand. Like the nereids, they are of most interest to the angler during their brief lunar-governed spawning periods, when they may occur in such abundance as to create a surface layer several yards thick.

Atlantic Palolo Worm *(Eunice fucata)*
(also identified as *Eunice schemacephala, Mayeria gregaricus,* and *Staurocephalus gregaricus*)

Common to the Florida Keys, the Atlantic palolo worm lives burrowed inside coral rock in shallow water, emerging to feed only under cover of darkness or dim light. At sexual maturity, the worm's posterior undergoes a metamorphosis similar to that undergone by nereid worms, except that during the palolo's spawning this modified section, or *epitoke*, separates completely from the anterior, or *atoke*, and swims toward the surface, where the sperms or eggs are released. The atoke remains burrowed within the coral and regenerates a new epitoke that will spawn the following season.

The small body of literature regarding the Atlantic palolo worm is plagued with inconsistencies and is of little use to the angler; hence, I asked Tom Kokenge, a professional guide (one of Steve Abel's favorites) in Big Pine Key, Florida, to share with us his years of experience fishing the palolo swarmings:

Swarmings of the Atlantic palolo worm cannot be predicted with any great accuracy, but they occur most consistently in the Florida Keys at the end of May and the beginning of June[2] and are associated with the extreme low tides brought about by the full moon.[3] Several factors lead Tom to speculate that high water temperatures are critical to triggering the swarmings. First, extreme low tides allow the water to warm to its maximum. Also, swarming seems always to take place in the afternoon (he's never seen a morning swarming), when the sun is at its peak and its warming effect greatest. These swarmings sometimes last into the evening. Finally, palolo swarmings may be thwarted by inclement weather. During periods of overcast skies or rough seas—which prevent the water from reaching peak temperatures—swarmings are, in Tom's experience, nonexistent.

Locating palolo swarmings is touch-and-go at best. That one area produces a good swarming one afternoon is no guarantee it will produce anything the next. Likewise, a spot that is dead one day may be hot the following day. Some years, Tom notes, it is as if the swarmings don't take place at all—or in any case, no one can locate them. Steve Abel fished the Keys for several years in a row, at the appropriate times, before getting into his first swarming. At their most productive, the palolo swarmings of the Florida Keys can in no way be likened to the great insect hatches we have on some of our trout rivers, and the most any Keys angler can hope to encounter in a single season is three successive days of swarmings.

Palolo swarmings orginate only from coral ("live rock") bottom—home to the natural. Tom has witnessed swarmings in 2 to 20 feet of water (0.6 to 6 meters), though in the Dry Tortugas swarmings have been reported in water as deep as 30 feet (9 meters; 5 fathoms). Tarpon are the gamefish most commonly associated with the palolo worms, though the swarmings attract a variety of other fishes, including bonefish, permit, jacks, grunts, and snappers. Tom has often seen schools of tarpon loitering around coral just prior to a swarming, pre-

---

2. Kokenge notes swarmings sometimes take place later in June and have been reported by some Keys guides to have taken place at the beginning of July. Various writers have reported swarmings as occurring within three days of the full of the July moon (no mention of location); during the three days prior to the third moon quarter between June 29 and July 28 (no mention of location); A.J. McClane reported swarming at the end of May and the beginning of June within three days of the full or new moon tide (presumably in the Florida Keys), or as early as April and into July at other locations within the species' Western Atlantic range.
3. Although extreme low tides are brought on by the new moon as well as the full, Kokenge has never witnessed swarmings then.

sumably in anticipation. Although all swarmings originate from coral, the effect of tide may cause the actual feeding to take place some distance away.

The palolo epitoke has been described in the scientific literature as ranging from 2 to 4 inches (5 to 10 centimeters) in length, although Tom relates that, in his experience, most epitokes are from ¾ to 1½ inches (1.9 to 3.8 centimeters) in length and from about ⅟₁₆ to ⅛ of an inch (1.6 to 3 millimeters) in diameter. The body of the epitoke is reddish (Steve Abel describes it as a "burnt cherry red") or reddish orange, tapering gradually to a point at the tail. The head is small, grayish white, and slightly larger in diameter than the body. The palolo epitoke swims quickly and erratically, its movements not unlike those of swarming heteronereids ("skywriting"). It may actually leave a wake as it swims.

Much has been written about the abundance of palolo worms during their swarmings, some writers having described the epitokes as creating a surface layer several meters thick and resembling vermicelli soup. Such abundance may occur in some instances, but Tom has never witnessed this, reporting the numbers of worms seen during the most productive swarmings to be much more conservative. He recalls having jumped as many as thirty tarpon during a swarming while actually seeing only about ten worms throughout (though he concedes that during a swarming he is much too busy to be counting worms).

The tarpon's rise to the palolo epitoke is deliberate, and it sips the worm off the surface with an audible slurp (slurping tarpon are a telltale sign of a palolo swarming, though worms are also taken subsurface). Tarpon may become quite selective when feeding on palolo worms, especially as regards length and shape (though Tom also feels that flies in the red/orange spectrum produce better than colors outside this range). Steve Abel recalls fishing a swarming with Kokenge when, having sacrificed all of their (Fitz Coker) Palolo flies to the fish, they were forced to trim orange Stu Apte Tarpon Flies to more closely match the epitokes.

Some anglers believe palolo worms might have a narcotic effect on fish, as the fish seem to act "stoned"—or in any case, reckless and less boat-shy—during the swarmings. One Keys guide is said to have crushed a palolo epitoke in his fingers, after which his fingers went numb.

PART III

DIRECTORY OF
FLY PATTERNS

Fly Patterns are listed alphabetically by common family name.
All flies in photographs are dressed by their originators
unless otherwise noted.

All flies catch fish. However, no fly is, as Bob Stearns so aptly puts it, a silver bullet. That is to say, no fly works for every fish in every situation—which is a bit of luck for those of us who write books about them.

The following flies represent a wide variety of tying styles, from conventional bucktail streamers to recent innovations in synthetics. Traditionalists might regard some of these patterns as less fly-dressing than model-building, but in a scientific sense, that's exactly what we're doing when we tie a fly: We are constructing a model of a prey configuration to elicit predatory behavior from a gamefish.

In compiling this directory, I met with a decided undercurrent of disdain for specific imitation. By the reaction I got from some anglers, one would think a fish had never been caught on a specific imitation.

To choose a fly based on the size of the fish's desired prey is a giant step toward specific imitation; to choose also by the prey's color, another step—no matter which school of imitative theory you prefer. Some tyers have been criticized as exact-imitation fanatics. Nothing could be further from the truth, and the notion of "exact imitation" is itself an oxymoron and should be dropped from our vocabulary. Dan Blanton considers his Sar-Mul-Mac series mere impressions of forage fishes—a step away from a feathered hook and toward the baitfish—whereas no better example of flagrant Expressionism is to be found than in some of Bill Catherwood's Giant Killers. Hal Janssen's Striper Fly, a simple pattern by any standards, uses bucktail flared around a tinsel body to effect a grunion's bulk and translucence—a better attempt at Realism I cannot conceive. And despite its name, Steve Abel's Anchovy is more of an attractor pattern than many of the flies that are lumped into that category.

Fly-fishing is an intensely personal game. You must fashion your game to suit *you*, using flies you have confidence in and that reflect *your* beliefs. Our fly is our dream, wrote Lee Wulff rightly; but it is also our red rag to the bull—a tool we use to push the fish's predatory buttons. How we push these buttons—attractor pattern, suggestive pattern, or meticulous imitation; Impressionism, Expressionism, or Realism; natural or synthetic materials—is irrelevant. Aesthetic arguments and debates among the various schools of imitative theory are ultimately decided by the fish.

The anglers whose work appears in this book are no different from anglers anywhere: No two agree on everything, and a few, I'm sure, agree on nothing save their passion for the sport. Their differences of opinion, expressed in their work, are their contributions to the game. Each has something to teach us.

FISHES
Anchovies

Despite the number of anchovy species and their importance as forage, established imitations are relatively few. As is implied by the similarity between anchovies and silversides, silverside patterns should suggest some anchovy species fairly well, and vice versa.

Abel's Anchovy

Plate 9

Hook:	Mustad 7692 (Abel's preferred hook for tarpon) or equivalent; 1/0 to 5/0.
Thread:	Black or chartreuse; size A.
Body:	Silver or pearl Diamond Braid or Mylar tubing wound around the hook shank. Stop one-third the length of the shank back from the eye of the hook.
Underwing:	White bucktail, FisHair, or Polar Hair, the same length as the wing, secured to the underside of the shank where the body stops.
Wing:	Bucktail, Polar Hair, or FisHair—blue over green over white. Both the wing and underwing should be 3 to 5 inches long,[1] and each section of the wing and collar should compose 25 percent of the entire wing in thickness.
Topping:	Ten to fifteen strands of peacock herl or black Krystal Flash, over fifteen to twenty strands of pearl Flashabou, over the same amount of silver Flashabou—all the same length as the wing.
Throat:	Red Flashabou, Crystal Hair, or Krystal Flash, ½ to ¾ inch long.
Head and Eyes:	While rotating the fly, apply a coating of clear hot-melt glue to the head (it helps to use a vise with a rotating head). Attach a 5- or 6-millimeter plastic doll's eye (white with a black pupil) to each side of the head before the glue sets completely. Shape the head with wet fingers. After the glue sets completely, coat the head with Jolly Glaze (available in hobby shops), or brush it with clear nail polish to help secure the eyes.

Steve Abel began designing his Anchovy in the mid-1980s for shark fishing. His technique was to chum blue and mako sharks to the boat with ground mackerel or bonito, and then toss frozen anchovies to the circling sharks. When the sharks began to feed, he would cast.

When standard saltwater patterns went largely ignored, Steve tried to more closely match the frozen anchovies. Early prototypes fared a little better than had the standard patterns, but were still far from effective.

Over the years, Steve noticed that sharks and barracuda attacking a balled-up school of

---

1. To convert dimensions, use the following: 1 inch = 25.4 millimeters or 2.54 centimeters; 1 millimeter = 0.03937 inch; 1 centimeter = 0.3937 inch.

anchovies first slash through the bait, and then make a return pass to snatch up the cripples. The injured anchovies, he observed, were surrounded by a halo of scales—a phenomenon he terms *scale fall*. This halo of scales, Steve eventually concluded, is one of the indicators sharks and barracuda use to distinguish injured from uninjured prey. When Steve noticed that scale fall surrounds frozen anchovies as well, he added silver and pearl Flashabou to his flies in hopes of suggesting it.

The Flashabou increased the pattern's effectiveness dramatically. At this writing, Steve has set world records for blue and mako sharks and for wahoo. (He was once briefly connected to a cartwheeling mako in the 250-pound range.) The Abel Anchovy has also taken Pacific bonito, skipjack, and most other species of tuna, yellowtail, dolphin, barracuda, all species of jacks, sandbass, striped bass, bluefish, African pompano, king salmon from Alaska, a world-record peacock bass from Venezuela, and most recently tarpon from Florida.

When chumming from a boat, Steve uses an Anchovy that matches the size of the whole frozen baits tossed overboard. Technique varies between dead-drifting the fly and a full retrieve. Wahoo in a chum line want a fly sitting, he notes, whereas sharks usually prefer some movement—erratic twitches to full strips.

Steve dresses his Anchovy in several variations. His Wahoo version uses strictly Krystal Flash in the appropriate colors for all wing, underwing, and throat materials. Another variation is topped with two peacock swords, á la the Streaker Streamer (refer to Joseph D. Bates, *Streamers and Bucktails*), to enhance the profile. Despite its name, the Abel Anchovy is intended to imitate two important West Coast forage species other than the northern anchovy: the Pacific sardine and the Pacific herring. Abel Automatics, Inc. (165 Aviador Street, Camarillo, California 93010, Tel. 805-484-8789) produces these flies commercially.

Bay Anchovy (Carl Richards)

Plate 9

Hook:	Mustad 3406B Accu-Point; 4 to 6.
Thread:	Coats & Clark transparent thread (available at fabric stores).
Belly or Underwing:	Mixture of half raw silk and half white lamb's wool.
Wing:	Polar bear Fish Fuzz. The entire fly should be ¾ inch long.
Topping:	A very few fibers of gold Fish Fuzz.
Midlateral Band:	One strand of pearlescent or silver Flashabou or Krystal Flash tied at each side of the shank.
Eyes:	Witchcraft eyes (Witchcraft Tape Products, Coloma, Michigan) secured with 5-minute epoxy.

Cal's Glass Anchovy (C.P. Calhoun)

Plate 9

Hook:	Long-shanked; 2/0 to 6/0.
Body:	3M glue-backed lead tape folded over the shank and cut to suggest the ventral curve of a fish. Over this, slip a length of Mylar tubing and secure at each end with thread. Then coat the body with 5-minute epoxy. After the epoxy sets, use permanent marking pens to tint the body to your liking.
Tail:	A few strands of pearl Krystal Flash over sparse white bucktail or calf tail.

Wing:	Green bucktail topped with peacock herl, over a few strands of pearl Krystal Flash, over sparse white bucktail.
Head:	Large yellow eye and black pupil, painted on.

(Dressed by Bill Peabody.)

Green-and-White Glass Minnow

Plate 9

Hook:	Mustad 34007; to 1/0.
Body:	Silver Mylar overwrapped with clear 12- to 20-pound monofilament.
Wing:	Bucktail—green over white—extending no more than one shank length past the bend. The wing is flanked by a ⅛-inch-wide strip of silver Mylar the length of the wing.
Head:	Painted green, and then painted with an eye (white with a black pupil).

(Dressed by Bill Peabody.)

Developed by Carl Hansen, Glass Minnows presumably represent young-of-the-year anchovies and herrings (most likely, the *Jenkinsia* species). They have been particularly popular along Florida's Atlantic Coast for snook, redfish, and seatrout.

Striped Anchovy (Carl Richards)

This fly is tied in the same way as is the Bay Anchovy, and uses most of the same materials. Substitute brushed-out yellow-tan egg yarn for the polar bear Fish Fuzz wing, and disregard the topping. The length of the fly should be from ¾ to 3 inches.

Along with his Sardine patterns (see "Herrings"), Carl uses his Bay and Striped Anchovy patterns for snook, baby tarpon, ladyfish, redfish, and jack crevalle in Florida's Ten Thousand Islands area. He concentrates his efforts around lights at night, where anchovies congregate in immense swarms and tarpon and snook can become ultraselective. Use a floating line and retrieve these flies in short, quick strips. During the day, Carl prefers the Striped Anchovy in the larger sizes, casting it around mangrove roots and retrieving it with quick, medium-length strips. For tarpon lying a bit deeper (8 to 10 feet of water), he uses an intermediate line.

Cusk-Eels

Cusk-Eel (A.J. McClane)

Hook:	Size 4 keel.
Thread:	Brown.
Body:	Beige chenille.
Wing:	Bucktail or equivalent, brown over yellow, 3½ inches long.

This was A.J. McClane's imitation of the dusky cusk-eel (*Parophidion schmidti*), which he used for bonefish. See "What the Bonefish Eats" in *The Compleat McClane*.

Plate 10

Cusk-Eel

Hook:	Mustad 34007 or equivalent; to size 1.
Thread:	Brown monocord.
Tail:	Six slim brown saddle hackles fastened concave sides together on top of the shank at the bend.
Head:	Fasten brown lamb's wool to flare around the shank, and trim it to shape. Leave some longer wool at the rear of the head to veil the tail and give a smooth flow to the fly's silhouette.
Eyes:	Small to medium bead-chain fastened to the shank in figure-eight wraps, painted white with a black pupil, and then coated with epoxy or Hard As Nails before the actual tying begins.

Puff

Hook:	Regular shank.
Tail:	Eight cree feathers tied splayed. These are flanked by badger or opossum fur not quite as long as the feathers.
Collar:	Several turns of soft black hackle immediately in front of the tail.
Eyes:	Glass eyes or painted lead eyes attached just behind the midpoint of the shank.
Body:	Light tan chenille tied in at the collar and wrapped to create a body that tapers to the front.

This letter from Lee Wulff to J. Edson Leonard, reprinted from Mr. Leonard's book *Flies*, might also be of interest:

Sushan, New York, March 2, 1949

The best fly I know for bonefish is the Rhode Shrimp fly which is made of three hackles wound around the shank of a No. 1/0 hook with three hackles going out on each side of the shank pointing backward from the bend, a sort of forked tail. This fly has a lot of action in the water and I like it best in natural (or dyed tan) plymouth rock hackles. Homer Rhode, Miami Beach Rod and Reel Club, Hibiscus Island, Miami Beach, Florida designed the fly.

It seems likely that Homer Rhode's Shrimp Fly—a precursor of the Sea Ducer series (refer to Kreh's *Salt Water Fly Patterns*), which is effective for a number of gamefishes—could have been taken by the bonefish as a cusk-eel, as the fly fits the natural's general description. Having read nothing of the pattern in recent years, however, I presume it has lost favor.

Eels

Because of the eel's general resemblance to the sand lance (family Ammodytidae), the patterns for each are often interchangeable, especially at night.

Bay-Delta Eelet

Plate 10

Hook: Mustad 34007 or equivalent; 2/0 to 4/0.
Thread: Black; size A Nymo.
Eyes: ⅛-inch silver bead-chain, tied in first slightly back from the eye of the hook, and then wrapped at last with medium black chenille.
Body: Medium black chenille, secured after the undertail and horse mane are fastened, and wrapped progressively during construction.
Undertail: Six black saddle hackles, 4 to 5 inches long, secured toward the underside of the hook near the bend. On top of this, secure an equal length of black horse mane or synthetic hair (optional). Wrap the chenille halfway toward the bead-chain and secure it in place with hackle pliers or a material clip (but *do not* cut it).
Wing: Fasten six black saddle hackles—three to a side, concave sides together—on top of the shank where the chenille stops. Then flank the wing with a generous amount of black Krystal Flash. Also, add one long grizzly saddle to each side of the wing. Total number of feathers in the undertail and wing is fourteen. Wrap the chenille forward, figure-eight style, over the bead-chain and tie it off close to the eye of the hook. Form a neat head and whip finish.

This pattern was developed in 1972 by Dan Blanton for West Coast striped bass during their spring spawning runs up the Sacramento and San Joaquin rivers. It is suggestive of a number of eel species on all coasts, as well as juvenile forms of the Pacific lamprey, which occupy the same rivers as Pacific stripers and often fall victim to them.

Bullet-Head Eel

Hook: Mustad 34007 or equivalent; 1/0 to 3/0.
Thread: Black monocord.
Tail: Four black saddle hackles tied concave sides together at the bend.
Head: Black bucktail tied Thunder Creek style, extending half a shank length beyond the hook bend. In front of this, secure bead-chain eyes. A coat of epoxy over the head and wrappings is optional.

A simple yet effective fly for night-fishing.

Catherwood's Eel

Plate 10

Hook: Mustad 94151; to 7/0.
Thread: Heavy black cotton-wrapped polyester.
Marabou: One or two khaki feathers (depending on the fullness of the feathers or the desired fullness of the fly), tied concave side up on top of the shank near the bend of the hook to form the belly.

Wing:	The wing numbers either eight or ten feathers total. Either two or four black saddle hackles (depending on the desired fullness), flanked by one blue-dyed grizzly hackle. Another black hackle covers each grizzly hackle. The wing is flanked along the bottom with one khaki saddle.
Head:	Several clumps of deer body hair flared around the shank and clipped to shape (refer to Catherwood's Herring for construction technique).
Eyes:	Glass—¼-inch diameter for the largest flies—secured to the shank with figure-eight wraps.

Whitlock's Eelworm Streamer

Hook:	Noncorrosive, regular or long-shanked; to 3/0.
Thread:	Danville's single-strand unwaxed floss.
Head:	Bead-chain or lead dumbbells.
Tail:	Four narrow black saddle hackles, outside of which are two more black saddle hackles half the length of the rest.
Rib:	One or two soft black saddle hackles wound forward and tied off just behind the bead-chain.
Body:	Dubbing of 50-percent Orlon and 50-percent natural fur (such as rabbit), all dyed black. Wind this the length of the shank around the bead-chain in figure-eights to form the head, and tie off at the hook eye.

This pattern was developed by Dave Whitlock. It is usually tied with grizzly hackles in a variety of colors for largemouth bass. It can also be tied with a monofilament weedguard.

Halfbeaks and Needlefishes

Although naturals of both families are found along the Northeast coast, imitations have not gained wide favor there; however, needlefish casting plugs are commonly used for striped bass and bluefish. Most flies and many lures used for barracuda are needlefish imitations. Most tarpon flies, even those that are clearly attractor patterns, are also suggestive of needlefish.

Ballyhoo (Lefty Kreh)

Hook:	2XL to 3XL; 1/0 to 3/0.
Thread:	White.
Wing:	Ten to twelve white saddle hackles, 3½ to 5 inches long, fastened at the bend. These are flanked by six strands of pearl Flashabou the same length as the wing. (One grizzly saddle on each side and twelve strands of peacock herl on top are optional.)

Head: Thread tapered along the hook shank to form the head and beak. Coat the wrappings with clear head cement and paint medium green along the top. Encircle the last ¼ inch of shank behind the hook eye with bright red paint.

Janssen's Halfbeak

Plate 11

Hook: Long-shanked. Wright & McGill 66 SS or Mustad 79574ST; 1/0 to 4/0.

Thread: Heavy white.

Wing: Medium chenille, white or yellow, secured just above the barb of the hook and wrapped around the shank to build up a ball. Just in front of this, tie a medium amount of crinkly white bucktail to flare around the ball to all sides evenly, forming a veil. Cut the butts off at an angle rather than straight, and then lacquer and wrap them with thread. Directly in front of the ball and on top of the hook, secure four black saddle hackles, two on each side (concave sides facing in), and lacquer the butts. Over these, tie six white saddle hackles, three to each side, splayed; then lacquer the butts. All hackles in the pattern should be 3 to 4 inches long. Over these, tie two grizzly saddle hackles—concave sides facing in, one hackle to each side (preferably long and thin with very dark, close barring). Again, lacquer the butts. Next, secure eight olive-brown saddle hackles over the top of the deer hair on the top side of the hook—four to each side—with the concave sides facing in and positioned tent-style to imitate the baitfish's back.

First Collar: Olive-brown marabou feather tied in at the tip (and just in front of the wing) and wound like a hackle, and then pulled back and secured as a wet-fly hackle would be.

Cheeks: Golden-olive marabou tied on the down side. This suggests the long golden-yellow fins of the natural.

Second Collar: Two more olive-brown marabou feathers tied in at the tips, wound as hackles would be, and secured as on the first collar.

Eyes and Beak: Two small glass eyes secured just in front of the collar at each side of the shank, the stems of the wire secured approximately ⅜ inch toward the eye of the hook. After securing the eyes, wind the thread to just in front of the ends of the wires and tie off. Then wind white Danville nylon floss over the wires and between the eyes figure-eight style to reinforce them. After reinforcing the eyes, wind the floss as thinly as possible to the eye of the hook and whip finish.

Paint: Lacquer the floss with several coats of clear Pactra Aerogloss enamel. To paint the beak, mix small amounts of yellow and green Aerogloss enamel with a lesser amount of orange to match the olive brown of the saddle hackles and collar. Apply this to the top of the head, between the eyes, to the butt ends of the marabou collar, and along the top of the beak to the eye of the hook. When this has dried, mix a bit of orange with a bit of yellow Aerogloss enamel to get a pale golden olive. Use this to paint a thin line at the edge of the olive, from just behind the eye down the length of the beak to the eye of the hook. The underside of the beak should be left white. Allow this to dry, and then coat the head and beak with Hi-Build Hi-Gloss Epoxy (manufactured by Epoxy Coatings of Hayward, California).

Hal Janssen invented the Halfbeak on his first trip to Mexico. He dressed the prototypes in the bar of the Oasis Restaurant in Loreto to resemble a small baitfish he had foul-hooked the first day of his stay (given the dressing, probably a longfin halfbeak [*Hemiramphus saltator*]). These flies proved deadly on surface-feeding yellowtail, and have subsequently caught many gamefishes, including dolphin, Sierra mackerel, and barracuda. The bucktail flared over the ball of chenille reduces fouling and prevents the saddle hackles from being drawn tightly together, creating an illusion of bulk while keeping the fly castable. The long-shanked hook not only represents the fish's beak, but in many cases eliminates the need for a shock tippet for toothy predators. This might also be aided by the rearward position of the glass eyes, which Hal feels directs the gamefish's bite farther back on the shank.

Plate 11

Janssen's Ballyhoo

The construction of Hal Janssen's Ballyhoo is the same as for his Halfbeak, with some minor substitutions in the dressing. Dress the Ballyhoo in the same way as the Halfbeak, substituting pale-blue grizzly hackle for the natural grizzly, and eight royal-blue hackles for the olive-brown saddles. These grizzly hackles should go under, not over, the blue saddles. The saddles are flanked by a bit of pearl or silver Krystal Flash or Flashabou. Use blue-gray marabou for both collars, and pale-blue marabou for the cheeks. The glass eyes are painted orange on the back. Paint the top of the beak with corsair-blue Pactra Aerogloss enamel. Then mix some corsair-blue enamel with a little white enamel and paint a thin line at the edge of the corsair blue (as on the Halfbeak). The underside of the beak should be left white. Wrap a bit of orange-red floss at the tip of the beak, and then finish with Hi-Build Hi-Gloss Epoxy (as on the Halfbeak).

Needlefish imitations abound in a variety of tying styles and materials. Those listed below are representative of various styles.

Plate 11

Catherwood's Needlefish

Hook:	Mustad 34011; to 4/0.
Thread:	Heavy green cotton-wrapped polyester.
Marabou:	One feather for each color (maybe two for white, depending on the fullness of the feather): green over pink (both tied concave side down) over blue dun over white (both tied concave side up, as on Catherwood's Herring). The marabou feathers are tied on top of the shank near the hook bend, their stems laid between the glass eyes.
Wing:	Six hackles, two of each color: silvery blue dun outside blue outside green.

| Eyes: | Glass—¼-inch diameter for the largest flies—secured to the hook with figure-eight wraps. |
| Beak: | Tying thread wrapped the length of the hook shank and heavily lacquered with aircraft nitrate cellulose tautening dope. |

Lentz's Needlefish

Plate 11

Hook:	Mustad 34007 or equivalent; 1 to 3/0.
Thread:	Chartreuse 6/0, pre-waxed.
Tail:	White bucktail fastened at the bend of the hook, on top of which are tied two medium-blue saddle hackles (concave sides together), the same length as the bucktail. The tail is flanked with five or six strands of gold Flashabou.
Collar:	Green marabou tied in at the base of the tail.
Eyes:	Large bead-chain painted yellow, fastened ⅛ inch forward of the collar just above the point of the hook.
Body:	Formed with tying thread, wrapped heaviest toward the rear, tapering toward the front. Chartreuse floss wrapped for ⅛ inch just behind the eye of the hook.

(Dressed by Bill Peabody.)

Page's Bonito Needlefish

Plate 11

Hook:	Long-shanked, straight eye, noncorrosive.
Thread:	Danville's flat waxed nylon, white.
Tail:	Bucktail tied sparse: olive over light green over fluorescent yellow over white. A few strands of lime-green Superpearlescent Fly Flash on each side.
Head:	Built prominently with tying thread and whip finished at the hook eye. Apply a good coating of head cement, and then paint or use a marking pen to color the top of the head olive. Paint a black eye and coat the entire head with cement or epoxy.

Page Rogers reports that this easy-to-tie fly (impressionistic of needlefishes, sand eels, and silversides) is very effective on bonito and false albacore, as well as on striped bass.

FisHair Needlefish Fly

Hook:	Regular shank, noncorrosive; 1 to 3/0.
Thread:	Red, or to match dorsal color.
Wing:	FisHair, 8 to 10 inches long, secured at the bend or secured at the hook eye and wrapped back to the bend. The end of the tail is whip finished or glued with Pliobond or Flexament to keep it from blossoming on the retrieve.

This pattern is tied in a number of colors: all orange, orange over white, pale blue over pale green over white. Plastic doll's eyes are sometimes glued to the sides.

Braided FisHair Needlefish Fly

This pattern is tied in essentially the same way as is the FisHair Needlefish Fly, but with a braided wing. It is often tied in color combinations such as dark green over pale green over white. After braiding, the wing is whip finished or glued at the tail. Doll's eyes are optional.

Plate 11

Steve Bailey's Cuda Fly

Hook:	Regular shank; 2 to 2/0.
Thread:	Flat waxed nylon, color to match dorsal coloring.
Wing:	FisHair, 6 to 8 inches long, secured at the bend or at the hook eye and wrapped back. The wing is then whip finished 1 inch from the end. The tail is given two coats of Flexament and trimmed to shape.
Body:	Built up with nylon tying thread. Red is used to suggest gills. Painted eye is yellow with a black pupil. The whole pattern is given a final coating of epoxy.

(Dressed by Bill Peabody.)

This pattern is tied in various color combinations, such as blue over white, or dark green over chartreuse over white.

When used for barracuda, needlefish imitations are best retrieved quickly.

Herrings

Plate 12

Alewife (Dave Whitlock's Match-the-Minnow Series)

Hook:	Noncorrosive, long-shanked.
Thread:	Danville's white single-strand unwaxed floss.
Body:	Pre-cut body form of aluminum, lead tape, or plastic. Attach the body to the hook shank with Zap-A-Gap cyanoacrylate glue so that the underbody faces away from the point (that is, the hook will ride point up on the finished fly). Over this, slip a length of flattened Mylar tubing secured at both ends with thread.
Wing:	Two to four olive saddle hackles tied in at the head and glued along the top of the body with a cyanoacrylate glue.
Cheeks:	Barred teal.
Eyes:	Wapsi solid-plastic doll's eyes glued to the cheeks with Goop.

This construction technique can be used to suggest a host of forage fishes in both fresh and salt water, and is particularly good for simulating any deep-bodied baitfish.

Catherwood's Herring

Plate 12

Hook:	Mustad 94151; to 7/0.
Thread:	Heavy blue cotton-wrapped polyester.
Marabou:	One fluffy white marabou feather tied on top of the shank near the bend of the hook and over the barb, with the concave side facing up (to form the belly). Over this, tie a silvery blue dun marabou feather, also with the concave side facing up. Over the dun, fasten a pink marabou feather—with the end section cut out to form a V—concave side down (the pink feather should be a bit shorter than the others). Next, tie in a blue marabou feather the same length as the white, concave side down.
Wing:	Four to eight long saddle hackles (depending on the fullness desired)—equal numbers of blue and silvery blue dun. Blue dun should be fastened outside the blue. The original pattern calls for one light-colored emu or rhea feather tied in along the sides. However, since legal sources of these feathers are few, commercial Herrings produced by Umpqua are flanked with flash material.
Head:	White deer body hair. The first bunch of hair should be exceptionally long, and the fine ends should flow back over the wing. Each clump is given three wraps of thread and forced—not spun—around the shank to flare. After the third bunch of hair is fastened, tie in the eyes figure-eight style. Tie in one or two more bunches of hair and tie off, and then trim the head to a bullet shape.
Eyes:	Glass, ¼-inch diameter for the largest flies.

Unlike most tyers, Bill Catherwood trims from back to front, holding the scissors against one glass eye and the eye of the hook as a guide to form the bullet-shaped head. He feels it is of the utmost importance to trim away any hair extending over the top of the wing so that the flow of water over the saddle hackles is not impeded. This, he believes, ensures optimal action.

The hair head doesn't simply float the fly—Catherwood's hair-head patterns are also fished subsurface with sinking or sink-tip lines—it pushes water, thereby alerting predators. When fishing around dense schools of forage, you will often foul-hook baitfish during the retrieve. Bill notes that with a hair-head pattern, snags are virtually nonexistent, and the hair head telegraphs the baitfish as well.

Catherwood's Herring can also be tied without a hair head. To do this, fasten the eyes figure-eight style before you begin to tie the pattern, and secure the marabou farther forward on the shank, laying the stems between the eyes.

Whether tying a hair head or not, Bill uses aircraft nitrate cellulose tautening dope (used to repair aircraft-control surfaces; available from hobby shops or aircraft repair facilities) as the cement. He lays it over the thread-wrapped shank before fastening any materials, and also uses it as a final head cement.

With one exception (Catherwood's Capelin—a silverside imitation), Bill never uses flash material and wings his flies with natural materials only, layering various colors of marabou feathers and saddle hackles. In the water, these materials pulsate and intermingle to effect the iridescent reflections of various baitfishes.

Catherwood's Herring is not a specific imitation as such, but rather is a composite of several similar herring species. Nevertheless, it has taken fish all over the world, including Atlantic salmon in Norway and all species of Pacific salmon. One of Bill's customers used it to win a salmon tournament in Oregon while all of the competition used natural herring as bait. Reduced, the pattern is also effective on sea-run trout and sea-run white perch.

Bill was one of the first fly-dressers concerned with imitating specific saltwater forage, developing a number of his Giant Killers years before the tackle that could cast such large flies had even been invented. Bill's vision and innovation have exerted a tremendous influence over saltwater fly patterns, most obviously in the work of such tyers as Dan Blanton, and he has been described by noted California angler Hal Janssen as a genius. Surprisingly, many saltwater fly-fishers have yet to hear of him. Make no mistake: Bill Catherwood was doing thirty years ago what many of us discovered only last week.

Catherwood's Giant Killer series numbers nearly forty patterns, most of which were developed for salt water. Not only are these flies great works of art, but they have been fished the world over and have accounted for no fewer than half a dozen world records.

Tom McNally, who named Catherwood's revolutionary oversized imitative streamers "Giant Killers," wrote in the February 1968 issue of *Outdoor Life*: "After years of fishing them for all kinds of fish under varying conditions, I'm convinced they are the best big-fish streamers ever developed. . . . In designing his flies, Bill has strived to duplicate real marine life as closely as possible."

Plate 12

Page's Menemsha Minnow
(Atlantic Herring and Baby Bunker Versions)

Hook:	Extra-long shank, straight eye, noncorrosive.
Thread:	Danville's flat waxed nylon.
Tail:	Clump of calf tail or marabou tied in at the bend (either white or to match dorsal coloration), and topped with metallic Flashabou (to match dorsal coloration). The tail is then whip finished and cemented.
Lower Body:	Witchcraft prismatic tape, cut and folded so that it snugs up against the tail and drops down ¼ to ½ inch at the hook eye. Leave two sides of the tape open at the hook eye. Trim the leftover tape flat along the length of the hook shank.
Upper Body:	Witchcraft prismatic tape in a color to match the dorsal coloration of the baitfish species. Cut a thin strip and fold it over the top part of the lower body tape and hook shank, snugging it tight to the tail and angling it slightly up from the hook eye. Cut a notch down toward the hook eye in the upper body, and a swag in the belly of the lower body up toward the hook eye.
Lateral Line: **and Gill Plate**	Use a black Sharpie pen; or, gill may be painted on with a red Testors paint marker.
Eye:	Witchcraft press-on eyes.
Epoxy:	Devcon 5-Minute Epoxy. Fill the fly well with epoxy and smooth the outside with a thin coat over the tape body. Rotate the fly as the epoxy cures and keep pushing the epoxy inside the fly.

Page Rogers considers her Menemsha Minnows the fly-rodder's answer to the KastMaster. Extraordinarily durable, an early version of the Minnow took seventy bluefish before it was finally retired. Because they sink readily, these are good flies in rolling surf and in rips. Larger sizes work well for bass and blues, while smaller sizes are effective for bonito and false albacore; very small sizes are good on largemouth and smallmouth bass, trout, and landlocked salmon.

Janssen's Sardine

Plate 12

Hook:	Mustad 79574ST or equivalent; 1/0 to 4/0.
Thread:	Heavy white.
Wing:	Medium chenille, white or yellow, secured just above the barb of the hook and wrapped around the shank to build up a ball. Just in front of this, tie a medium amount of crinkly white bucktail to flare evenly around the ball to all sides, forming a veil. Cut the butts off at an angle rather than straight, and then lacquer and wrap them with thread. Directly in front of the ball and on top of the hook, secure the following tent-style in this order: two natural grizzly saddles, two bright-blue grizzly saddles, two fluorescent-green saddles, and two olive grizzly saddles.
Collar:	Two olive saddle hackles wound, pulled back, and tied off as a wet-fly hackle would be.
Topping:	Twenty strands of peacock herl.
Cheeks:	Olive-brown marabou to suggest fins.
Eyes:	Secure two small glass eyes (painted yellow on the back) just in front of the collar on each side of the shank. Secure the stems of the wire approximately ⅜ inch toward the eye of the hook. After securing the eyes, wind the thread to just in front of the ends of the wires and tie off. Then wind white floss over the wires and between the eyes figure-eight style to reinforce them. Wind the floss as thinly as possible to the eye of the hook and whip finish.
Paint:	Lacquer the floss with several coats of clear Pactra Aerogloss enamel, and then paint with colored enamel: pale olive on bottom, bright green along the sides, and to match the peacock herl on top. Paint several black dots along each side over the bright green. Allow the enamel to dry, and then epoxy all wrappings with Hi-Build Hi-Gloss Epoxy.

Hal Janssen's Sardine, which is a variation of his Halfbeak, is effective on most Pacific Coast gamefishes, including yellowtail, dolphin, tunas, wahoo, and amberjack.

Bunker (Bill Peabody)

Plate 13

Hook:	Mustad 34007; 4/0 to 7/0.
Thread:	White; 6/0.
Tail:	Start with a generous amount of white bucktail fastened at the bend

of the hook to encircle the shank. On top of this, fasten a sparse amount of white FisHair (70 denier) 4 inches long, and then two or three strands each of blue and pearl Flashabou to extend ¼ inch past the FisHair. Next, tie four neck hackles—three white and one light yellow (the yellow on the inside)—to each side of the shank, splayed.

Body: Fasten Pearl Bodi-Braid or braided Mylar where the hackles are tied in. Wrap two turns over the butts of the materials, then tie in the first section of wing—both top and bottom—then take two more wraps with Bodi-Braid. Repeat the process until you get to the dark-gray top wing. Each top wing section (up to, but excluding the dark gray) is flanked with two strands each of blue and pearl Flashabou.

Wing/Throat: Tie the following along the top and bottom of the hook shank, Hi-Tie style, from the rear forward, reading top/bottom: white/white, light gray/white, light gray/white, light olive/white, dark olive/white, dark olive/yellow under red (for the final, forwardmost throat). Finish the wing with dark gray bucktail on top.

Topping: Eight to twelve strands of peacock herl, as long as the dark gray bucktail. Form a head with the thread and tie off.

Eyes: 10-millimeter plastic eyes, yellow with a black pupil, glued to the sides of the head with Goop. Then coat the entire head area with Devcon 5-Minute Epoxy, making sure the eyes are seated in the epoxy as well.

Bill likes to substitute bright gold Flashabou for the blue in at least one wing section, and he also likes to add three or four strands of blue, red, and yellow FisHair to the white FisHair in the tail; though sparse, this gives a rainbow of color to the rear of the fly. Wing/throat sections may be added or deleted as necessary for larger or smaller flies.

A custom fly-dresser, Bill markets Bodi-Braid and a number of other products through his Narragansett Bay Flies, 87 Lisa Terrace, Portsmouth, Rhode Island 02871, Tel. 401-683-2510.

Plate 13

Catherwood's Pogy

Hook: Mustad 94151; to 7/0.

Thread: Heavy blue cotton-wrapped polyester.

Wing: Scottish blackface (sheep) hair. Each bunch should be about ¼ inch in diameter when loose. The first bunch should be white and about 3 inches long. The next bunch, tied on top of the first, is also white and should be about 4 inches. Next is a bunch dyed silvery blue dun, about 4½ inches long. A bunch of pink, the same length as the last, is tied to encircle the wing. Next is another bunch of blue dun (but not tied to encircle the wing). Then tie a bunch of yellow to veil or encircle the wing to give the fly its yellowish cast. Next, tie a bunch of blue (blackface hair dyed with Rit Evening Blue) prominently over the back.

Head: Deer body hair bunched and trimmed to shape (refer to

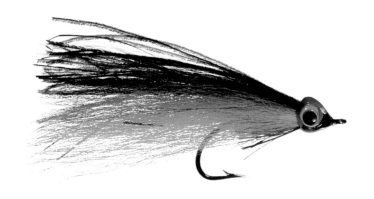

Abel's Anchovy

*Abel's Anchovy
(Wahoo Version)*

*Bay Anchovy
(Carl Richards)*

Cal's Glass Anchovy (C.P. Calhoun)

Green-and-White Glass Minnow

Plate 9

Cusk-Eel

Bay-Delta Eelet

Catherwood's Eel

Plate 10

Janssen's Halfbeak

Janssen's Ballyhoo

Catherwood's Needlefish

Lentz's Needlefish

Steve Bailey's Cuda Fly

Page's Bonito Needlefish

Plate 11

*Alewife
(Dave Whitlock's
Match-the-Minnow Series)*

Catherwood's Herring

*Page's Menemsha Minnow
(Atlantic Herring Version)*

*Page's Menemsha Minnow
(Baby Bunker Version)*

Janssen's Sardine

Plate 12

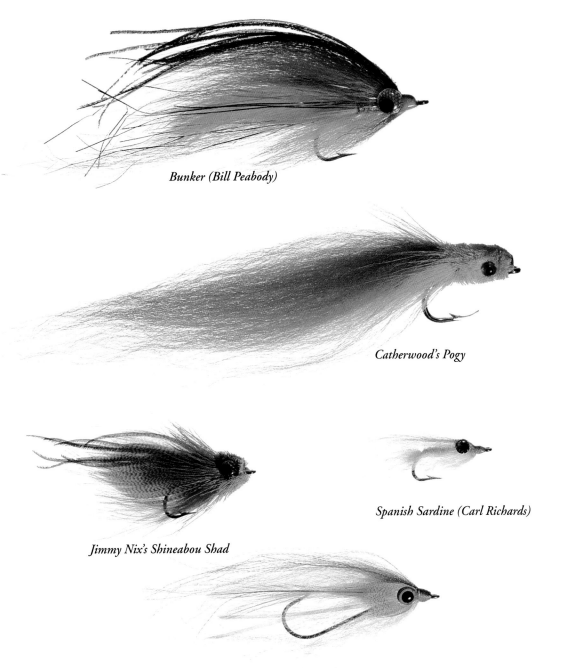

Bunker (Bill Peabody)

Catherwood's Pogy

Jimmy Nix's Shineabou Shad

Spanish Sardine (Carl Richards)

Whitlock's Sheep Streamer

Plate 13

Catherwood's Chub

Catherwood's Tinker Mackerel

Tinker Mackerel
(Bob Popovics' 3-D Series)

Page's Menemsha Minnow
(Tinker Mackerel Version)

Sar-Mul-Mac
(Mackerel Version)

Plate 14

Janssen's Mullet

Jimmy Nix's Shineabou Mullet

Sar-Mul-Mac (Mullet Version)

Siliclone Mullet (Bob Popovics)

Pinfish

Plate 15

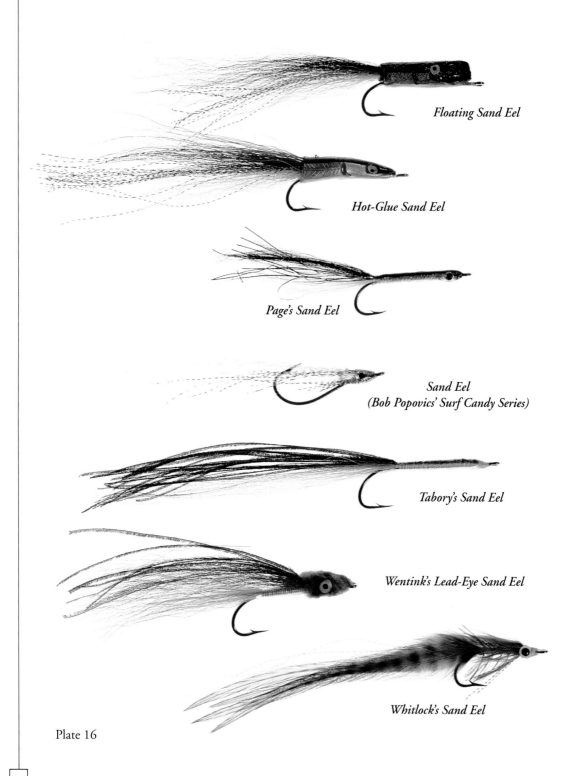

Floating Sand Eel

Hot-Glue Sand Eel

Page's Sand Eel

*Sand Eel
(Bob Popovics' Surf Candy Series)*

Tabory's Sand Eel

Wentink's Lead-Eye Sand Eel

Whitlock's Sand Eel

Plate 16

Troth Bullhead

Whitlock's Salt Sculpin

Whitlock's Matuka Sculpin

Zonker Sculpin

Code Goby (Carl Richards)

Longjaw Goby

Plate 17

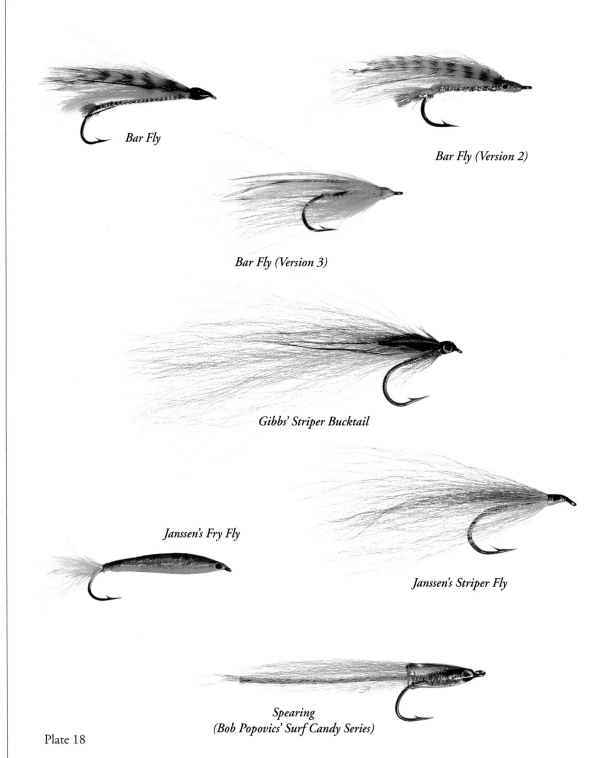

Bar Fly

Bar Fly (Version 2)

Bar Fly (Version 3)

Gibbs' Striper Bucktail

Janssen's Fry Fly

Janssen's Striper Fly

Spearing
(Bob Popovics' Surf Candy Series)

Plate 18

Magog Smelt Bucktail

McNally Smelt

Janssen's Stickleback
(Janssen's Fry Fly Series)

Rolled Muddler

Plate 19

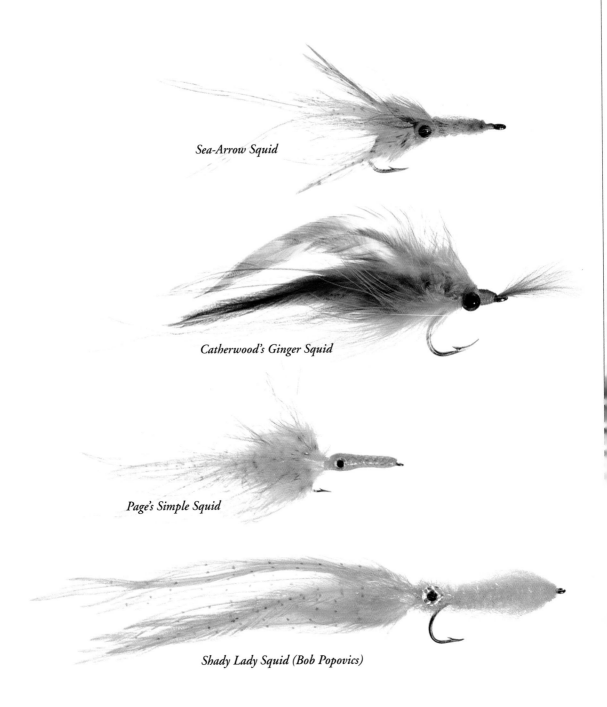

Sea-Arrow Squid

Catherwood's Ginger Squid

Page's Simple Squid

Shady Lady Squid (Bob Popovics)

Plate 20

Dave's Salt Shrimp

Sater's Grass Shrimp

Janssen's Grass Shrimp

Ultra Shrimp (Bob Popovics)

Brown Snapping Shrimp
(Chico Fernandez)

Banded Snapping Shrimp
(Carl Richards)

Plate 21

Whitlock's Near 'Nuff Snapping Shrimp

White Swimming Shrimp
(Carl Richards)

Brown Swimming Shrimp
(Chico Fernandez)

Golden Mantis
(Carl Richards)

Golden Mantis
(Chico Fernandez)

Plate 22

Black-Tipped Mud Crab
(Carl Richards)

Catherwood's Green Crab

Janssen's Floating Blue Crab

McCrab

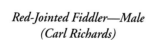

Red-Jointed Fiddler—Male
(Carl Richards)

Olive Swimming Crab

Red-Jointed Fiddler—Female
(Carl Richards)

Sand Flea

Sand Crab

Plate 23

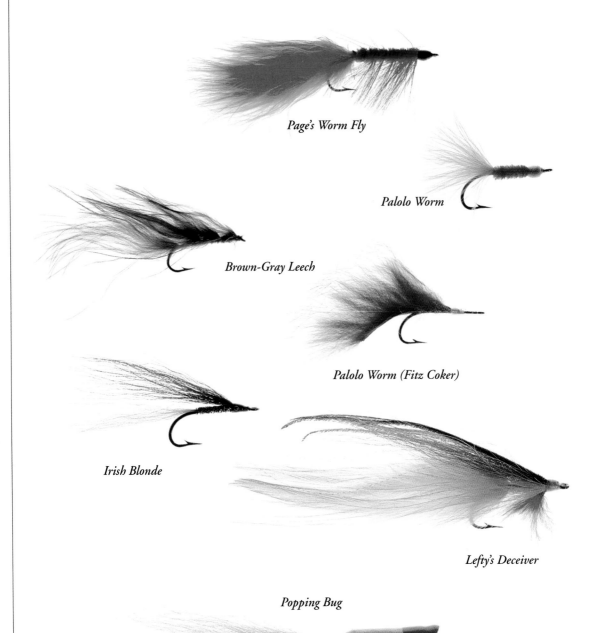

Page's Worm Fly

Palolo Worm

Brown-Gray Leech

Palolo Worm (Fitz Coker)

Irish Blonde

Lefty's Deceiver

Popping Bug

Plate 24

Catherwood's Herring for technique): two bunches of white (the first rather long and flowing back over the wing), one small bunch of yellow, another small bunch of white, and a bunch of blue at the nose.

Eyes: Glass, ¼ inch for the largest flies, attached figure-eight style after the yellow deer body hair.

Menhaden Streamer

Hook: 34007 or equivalent; 1/0 to 3/0.
Thread: Red.
Wing: Bucktail or FisHair tied Thunder Creek style. The bottom part is white, the middle is pink, and the top is blue. The wrappings and head are then coated with epoxy. A painted eye is optional.

This pattern was originated by Morton Ross for striped bass and bluefish. It is also tied as a simple bucktail.

Jimmy Nix's Shineabou Shad

Plate 13

Hook: Mustad 34011 or equivalent; 4 to 1/0.
Underbody: Silver-gray Antron dubbing on rear two-thirds of shank.
Overbody: Fluorescent light-gray marabou surrounding the underbody and extending one shank length beyond the bend. Fasten several strands of pearl and silver Krystal Flash to each side, and six to eight peacock herls on top. To each side of this, fasten one mallard flank feather, extending ½ inch less than the marabou.
Gills: Fluff of red saddle hackle secured to the underside of the shank.
Head: Gray spun deer hair for a floating pattern; gray wool for a sinking pattern.
Eyes: Plastic doll's eyes for a floating pattern; painted lead eyes for a sinking pattern.

(Dressed by Bill Peabody.)

As with his Mullet, Jimmy Nix's Shad began its life in fresh water as a striped-bass fly. It has also proved itself a successful saltwater pattern for a number of gamefishes wherever the natural threadfins occur.

Scaled Sardine (Carl Richards)

Hook: Mustad 3406B Accu-Point; 2 to 1/0.
Thread: Coats & Clark transparent thread.
Tail: Gray hen hackle clipped to shape and fastened to a length of 20-pound mono. Secure the mono to the shank with thread and seal

the wrappings with E-6000 glue that is thinned with Weldwood paint thinner.

Rear Wing: Tie several bunches of white Fish Fuzz to the bottom of the hook shank at the bend so that an equal amount of the mohair is on each side of the hook. Then fasten one bunch to the top of the hook shank at the bend. All bunches should project back to the tail.

Underwing: Several bunches of white Fish Fuzz fastened to the underside of the hook at the head, projecting just beyond the point of the hook. This forms the deep belly of the fly.

Front Wing: One bunch of white Fish Fuzz tied in on top of the hook shank at the head and projecting back to the tail. Over this, fasten a slim bunch of green Fish Fuzz and then a slim bunch of gold Fish Fuzz. Overall, this pattern is deeper than is the Spanish Sardine. Use a marking pen to make two dark spots on the wing—one at the upper edge where the gill cover would be and one just behind that on the shoulder.

Flash: Several strands of silver Flashabou tied in at each side of the wing.

Throat: Bright pink Fish Fuzz to suggest gills.

Head and Eyes: Large Witchcraft press-on eyes. Coat the eyes and head with 5-minute epoxy.

Plate 13

Spanish Sardine (Carl Richards)

Hook: Mustad 3406B Accu-Point; 6 to 1/0.
Thread: Coats & Clark transparent thread.
Belly: Mixture of half raw silk and half lamb's wool.
Body: Pearlescent Larva Lace.
Rear Wing: Polar bear Fish Fuzz tied in at the bend. The entire fly should be 1½ to 4 inches in length.
Topping: Green Fish Fuzz under a slim bunch of gold Fish Fuzz.
Flash: Several strands of pearl Krystal Flash tied in at each side of the wing.
Head and Eyes: Witchcraft press-on eyes. Coat the eyes and head with 5-minute epoxy.

"If I had only one choice of fly to use for big fish," writes Carl Richards, "the Spanish Sardine would be it. It not only catches everything in salt water, but I have taken brown, rainbow, and steelhead trout with it, as well as Atlantic salmon. After all, it is a herring imitation, and there are a plentitude of freshwater herring species it imitates well."

Carl recommends the 1½-inch Sardines for spring and early summer in Florida. Fish these flies the same as you would Richards' Anchovies.

Plate 13

Whitlock's Sheep Streamer

Hook: Tiemco 9394 bent bend-back style so the hook rides point up on the finished fly.

Thread:	Danville's white single-strand unwaxed floss.
Gills:	Several turns of red Antron wool fastened at the forward bend.
Wing:	Wapsi Streamer Hair (Icelandic wool) fastened to the top and bottom of the shank (just forward of the red Antron) to effect the deep-bodied look of the naturals. Pearl or silver Crystal Hair may be worked into the wing as well. Various colors of wool may be used to match specific species, and the wing may be topped with various colors of Crystal Hair or other synthetics. Flank the Streamer Hair with one fairly wide strip of pearl Mylar and one saddle hackle (either splayed or concave sides facing in) to match the side color of the natural (usually pale blue dun).
Cheeks:	Drake mallard breast feathers tied with the concave sides facing out.
Eyes:	Wapsi solid-plastic doll's eyes glued to the cheeks with Goop.

Dave Whitlock is without question the country's most successful fly designer. Commercial ties of his innovative patterns have sold in the millions, and his influence is apparent in fly patterns the world over. Dave developed his Sheep Streamers to imitate the gizzard shad, a primary forage of the freshwater striped bass that inhabit his home waters of Arkansas. These lakes are crystal clear, the stripers frequently selective, and Dave found the usual roster of fly patterns often unproductive. The Sheep Streamers have proved deadly not only on freshwater striped bass, but on a number of saltwater gamefishes as well, including tarpon, snook, redfish, and snappers.

The Icelandic wool is fine, light, and nonabsorbent, making the fly comfortable to cast. The basic dressing may be altered to match virtually any species of herring.

Killifishes

(See also "Mullets," the basic form of which can also suggest mummichogs.)

Catherwood's Chub

Plate 14

Hook:	Mustad 94151; to 7/0.
Thread:	Heavy olive cotton-wrapped polyester.
Marabou:	Olive over pink over yellow. Refer to Catherwood's Herring for construction details.
Wing:	Four or eight saddle hackles (depending on the desired fullness)—equal numbers of olive and grizzly dyed light yellow, the grizzly on the outside. The wing is flanked by one olive-dyed mallard breast feather.
Head:	Deer body hair dyed olive (refer to Catherwood's Herring for construction technique).
Eyes:	Glass, ¼-inch diameter for the largest flies.

Mackerels

Plate 14

Catherwood's Tinker Mackerel

Hook:	Mustad 94151; to 7/0.
Thread:	Heavy blue cotton-wrapped polyester.
Marabou:	White for the belly, one or two feathers tied concave side up on top of the shank at the bend of the hook and over the barb. Over this is a silvery blue dun feather, also concave side up. Over the dun, fasten a pink feather—with the end section cut out to form a V—concave side down. Over this, fasten a green feather and then a blue, both concave side down.
Wing:	Four or eight long saddle hackles—equal numbers of blue and green—tied in alternately (blue, green, blue, green). On each side of this, tie a long grizzly saddle hackle. The wing numbers six to ten feathers total.
Head:	(Refer to Catherwood's Herring for technique.) Deer body hair. First, fasten two thick bunches of blue and one thick bunch of green hair. The first bunch of hair should be exceptionally long and flare out over the wing. Then secure the eyes and fasten a single bunch of blue hair in front of the eyes and tie off. Trim the head to shape.
Eyes:	Glass, ¼-inch diameter for the largest flies, fastened to the shank using figure-eight wraps after the first two bunches of deer hair have been secured. The Tinker Mackerel is also tied without a hair head. To do this, fasten the eyes before you begin to tie the pattern, and secure the marabou farther forward on the shank, laying the stems between the glass eyes.

Bill Catherwood noted early on that although mackerel are blue-green in dorsal coloration, some populations tend toward the green while others tend toward the blue. Bill uses both green and blue in his pattern to offer the predator a color composite.

Although developed primarily for striped bass and bluefish, Catherwood's Tinker Mackerel has proved effective on other species, such as albacore and tarpon. Tom McNally took sixteen tarpon on the pattern in one afternoon on Venezuela's Lake Maracaibo; in three days' fishing there, the Tinker Mackerel accounted for eleven fish exceeding 100 pounds.

Mackerel

Hook:	Stainless, regular or long-shanked; 4 to 6.
Thread:	3/0 black.
Tail:	Green marabou.
Body:	Green Mylar tubing.

Overbody:	Four or five strands of peacock herl fastened at each end of the tubing.
Throat:	White FisHair extending back just beyond the bend of the hook.

This pattern was developed by Don Avondolio for bonito and false albacore around Martha's Vineyard.

Tinker Mackerel (Bob Popovics' 3-D Series)

Hook:	Regular-shanked, noncorrosive.
Thread:	3/0 monocord or fine monofilament thread by Larva Lace.
Wing:	Fasten several bunches of Ultra Hair to encircle the shank. Begin at the bend of the hook and work forward. At the final bunch, trim the excess or fold back the ends and finish the head. Then trim the wing to more closely match the fish's three-dimensional shape. Lite Brite or other flash material may be incorporated into the wing, and various colors of Ultra Hair or other materials may be veiled within the wing to effect subtle hues. Colored Ultra Hair may be used at various stages to create the dorsal coloration, but much of this color will be lost during trimming. Bob Popovics recommends coloring the wing with permanent marking pens.
Eyes:	Witchcraft press-ons or similar eyes glued to the sides near the head of the fly.
Optional Head:	Thin layer of silicone (or epoxy) applied to the Ultra Hair (refer to Popovics' Siliclone Mullet) to increase durability.

Silhouette is one of the most important considerations when choosing a fly for selectively feeding fish, and Bob Popovics' three-dimensional tying style enables the fly-dresser to closely match the specific silhouettes of larger baitfishes not simply in profile, but from all angles. The number of Ultra Hair bunches and their proximity to each other determine bulk. Additional Ultra Hair may be added at various places to effect distinctive body shapes. For instance, you can stack Ultra Hair above and below the shank to create a deeper, more compressed body typical of herrings, or place it at the sides to create a thicker mullet-like body. Careful trimming with serrated-blade scissors adds the finishing touches to the shape.

Page's Menemsha Minnow (Tinker Mackerel Version)   Plate 14

Refer to tying instructions under "Herrings." Use a black Sharpie pen for the top of the dorsal and for the hash marks.

Sar-Mul-Mac (Mackerel Version)   Plate 14

Refer to the Mullet version of the Sar-Mul-Mac for construction details. Dress this pattern in the same way, but omit the multi-colored Krystal Flash flanking and teal cheeks, and substitute a bright-green grizzly hackle for the natural grizzly. Also, top the white saddles with bright-green bucktail and blue Krystal Flash beneath the peacock herl.

Dan Blanton, who originated the Sar-Mul-Mac series, uses a brighter green than is found on the natural mackerel, convinced that gamefishes—particularly billfish—key in to it better.

Mullets

Plate 15

Janssen's Mullet

Hook:	Mustad 79574 cadmium plated, 3X long, 3X strong, down eye; 2/0 to 4/0; Mustad 79573 may be substituted.
Thread:	Heavy white.
Wing:	Combination of saddle hackles and bucktail. Tie four long white saddle hackles—two to each side and concave sides together—on top of the shank about one-third the way back from the eye of the hook. Over these, tie three wide bright-blue grizzly saddles, biplane style; over this, tie three wide olive-green grizzly saddles, also biplane style. All grizzly hackles are nearly as long as the white hackles. The bucktail is tied Thunder Creek style—pulled back and tied off just behind the glass eyes to form a bullet head. The top bucktail wing consists of three parts: olive bucktail over bright-green bucktail over bright-blue bucktail. The top bucktail wing is about two-thirds the length of the grizzly saddles. The bottom bucktail wing is white and is nearly as long as the grizzly saddles.
Eyes:	Glass, painted silver on the back.

Plate 15

Jimmy Nix's Shineabou Mullet

Hook:	Tiemco 800S, or Mustad 3407 or 34007; 2 to 4/0.
Threads:	Silver gray; 3/0 for underbody, and size A monocord for deer-hair head.
Tail:	White bucktail, twice the length of the hook shank, secured at the bend. On top of this, secure eight to ten wide fluorescent-gray saddle hackles, slightly longer than the bucktail, tied splayed. These are flanked by three or four strands each of silver and gold Flashabou that extend back three-quarters the length of the saddles.
Weighting:	0.0025 lead wire wrapped five or six turns just in front of where the tail is tied in (for sinking pattern), overwrapped with tying thread.
Body:	Silver-gray Antron dubbing wrapped forward and tied off just in front of the lead wire.
Collar:	Silver-gray marabou spun on the shank as you would deer hair.
Gills:	Small tuft of red saddle-hackle fluff flanking the collar.

Topping:	Eight or so strands of peacock herl extending back half the length of the saddle hackles.
Head:	Several clumps of deer body hair dyed silver gray, flared (as on Catherwood's Giant Killers) or spun around the hook shank. Trim the head to a mullet shape first with scissors (trimming front to back), and then finish with a razor. Burn an eye socket into each side of the head and clear any charred hair from the sockets with a bodkin.
Eyes:	Hard plastic eyes with the stems removed (doll's eyes pictured) glued into the sockets with 30-minute epoxy.

(Dressed by Bill Peabody.)

As with his Shineabou Shad, Jimmy Nix's Mullet began life in fresh water as a Shiner pattern for black bass. In the salt, it has proved successful on every species that preys on the natural, from redfish to sailfish. (For sailfish, Jimmy uses a large tandem version.) Wildlife artist Bill Elliot's world-record snook taken on a Shineabou Mullet is testament to Jimmy's claim that this is a killer snook pattern. Fish this fly with a floating or uniform-sink line along mangroves, drift lines, logs—wherever mullets and their predators might occur. In some situations, a weedguard (either monofilament or number 5 stainless-steel wire) is desirable.

Jimmy also dresses his Shineabou Mullet in either green or yellow for dolphin, convinced these colors are more effective than those more closely matching the natural.

Sar-Mul-Mac (Mullet Version)   Plate 15

Hook:	Tiemco 811S or Mustad 3407 or 34007.
Thread:	Danville's flat waxed nylon; white.
Tail and Overtail:	Medium bunch of white bucktail (length to determine the overall length of the fly) fastened to the shank at the midpoint. To each side of this, secure six white saddle hackles as long as the bucktail. Flank this with multicolored Krystal Flash and five strips of silver Mylar. The Krystal Flash and Mylar are a little over half the length of the saddles.
Underwing:	After the Mylar and Krystal Flash are secured, turn the fly over in the vise and fasten another bunch of white bucktail, as long as the first, to the underside of the shank.
Overwing:	After the underwing is secured, turn the fly over in the vise again and fasten two natural grizzly saddles, as long as or slightly longer than the white saddles, tent style over the white saddles.
Topping:	Fasten a dozen strands of peacock herl, nearly as long as the white saddles, over the top, the butts left long enough to reach beyond the hook eye.
Cheeks:	One teal flank feather tied to each side after the peacock herl is fastened.
Head:	Add one or two turns of red chenille as a collar in front of the wing to suggest gills (the chenille should go under the butts of peacock herl). In front of the red chenille, secure white chenille to build a

head that tapers to the hook eye (wrap white chenille under the peacock butts as well). Then bring the butts of peacock herl over the top of the head, tie them off, and clip them. Whip finish the head and cement it with Goop thinned with toluene or xylene.

Eyes: Plastic post-type eyes, to 9 millimeters (available from craft shops). Cut the posts off flush and glue the eyes to the sides of the chenille head with Goop.

Optional Weighting: Eight to ten turns of lead wire wrapped between the hook eye and mid-shank, then overwrapped with thread and cemented before the actual tying begins.

The Sar-Mul-Mac was developed in 1971 by Dan Blanton as a series of baitfish simulators. Although the name is an abbreviation of Sardine-Mullet-Mackerel, variations in the basic dressing have allowed Dan to successfully imitate such forage fishes as anchovies, halfbeaks, needlefishes, and jack smelt, to name only a few. The Sar-Mul-Mac series has proved effective on all three coasts, in the Sea of Cortez, and in Central American and Caribbean waters for such gamefishes as bonito, skipjack and other tunas, striped bass, yellowtail, halibut, dolphin, pompano, cabrillo, roosterfish, groupers, and snappers.

Plate 15

Siliclone Mullet (Bob Popovics)

Hook: Partridge Sea Prince; 3/0.

Thread: 3/0 monocord.

Wing: Bucktail tied in near the bend of the hook to encircle the shank. Flank this at each side with two white saddle hackles tied concave sides facing in. Hackles should be slightly longer than the bucktail.

Shoulders: Two clumps of white bucktail tied at each side of the shank. The shoulders should be somewhat shorter than the wing. The construction of the wing and shoulders gives the Mullet its wide, round anterior shape and posterior taper.

Flash: Silver Flashabou or Krystal Flash tied on tip of the bucktail before the hackles are fastened.

Head: Lamb's wool fastened to flare around the shank and clipped to shape. Leave some longer wool at the rear of the head to give a smooth flow to the fly's silhouette.

Eyes: Small Witchcraft decal eyes pressed into the first layer of silicone before it cures.

Coating: Clear silicone rubber (Dow Chemical's DAP, Devcon's Clear Silicone Rubber, and GE's Silicone II Household Glue and Seal are some of the brands that work well) smeared over the head either with your fingers or with a small plastic knife. The silicone must be wet to be worked. Water will not do; Bob prefers Kodak Fotoflo solution (available at camera shops). On the first coat, work the silicone into the material a bit. Add the decal eyes while the silicone is still tacky, and then give the head another, thicker coating of silicone. Smooth it completely and allow it to cure.

Optional Glitter: Sparkle or glitter flakes added to the silicone.

The Siliclone Mullet is Bob Popovics' personal favorite of his many creations. The silicone coating not only adds a soft, squishy feel to the fly, but also prevents the wool head from absorbing excess water, keeping larger flies castable. When used with floating lines, Siliclones run slightly subsurface, pushing water and creating a good wake. Air trapped inside the wool causes the fly to pop back to the surface between strips. Siliclones can withstand considerable abuse, and any tears in the head can be easily repaired with another dab of silicone.

Bob developed the Siliclone Mullet primarily for striped bass and bluefish, though it has proved deadly on a variety of gamefishes in both salt water and fresh.

Any of these flies, appropriately sized and colored, can imitate the mummichog (*Fundulus heteroclitus*) and closely related species fairly well.

Porgies

Pinfish

Plate 15

Hook:	Mustad 34007 or Eagle Claw 254 SS or equivalent; 2/0 to 4/0.
Thread:	Yellow for the rear of the head, black for the front around the eyes.
Body:	Pink braided Mylar (available in craft shops) wound the length of the shank.
Wing:	FisHair, two stacks of white under one stack of gray, tied Hi-Tie style to simulate the deep-bodied natural. Beneath the wing are ten or so strands of pearl Krystal Flash, as long as the wing. The wing should extend about one shank length past the bend. Use a Sharpie pen to mark the wing on each side with two black vertical bars.
Eyes:	Red plastic hemispheric eyes (available in craft shops). The head and eyes are then coated with epoxy.

Bob Stearns, saltwater editor of *Field & Stream*, got the idea for his Pinfish not from the natural, but from a particularly effective balsa pinfish lure he owned. Bob uses the fly over grass beds—home to juvenile forms of the natural—for tarpon and snook, and has taken some very large fish with it. He also likes to use it when the water is less than clear, since he feels the fly's deep-bodied structure makes it more visible to the fish. Red plastic eyes are used to indicate distress.

Sand Lances

(See also the Candlefish Bucktail listed under "Smelts.")

Sand-lance imitations are fished at all levels of the water column along sandy and soft-bottomed shores, and are particularly effective at dusk, when predators such as striped bass move into the shallows to feed. A steady, continuous retrieve is sometimes preferable to individual strips. The easiest way to do this is to hold the rod under the rod arm and retrieve the line hand over hand. Larger sand lances are a thicker-bodied fish than many patterns suggest.

Plate 16

Floating Sand Eel

Hook:	Mustad 34011; 1/0.
Thread:	Monocord; the color is unimportant.
Body:	Lobster-pot buoy, 1 inch long, cut with a ¼-inch plug cutter (available in hardware stores). Trim the front of the foam plug to a V shape to allow the pattern to swim quietly across the surface. Then burn a hole in the rear of the plug with a hot wire to accept the wing. Attach the hook to the plug with hot-melt glue (refer to "Popping Bugs" for precise instructions).
Wing:	Secure the following to a short length of wire (a heavy paper clip works well): brown or black bucktail over sparse olive bucktail over a dozen strands of silver Krystal Flash over white bucktail. Then fit the wire into the plug cavity with hot-melt glue.
Paint:	Coat the plug with an optional base of Liquitex acrylic gesso, and then paint it to suggest the natural either with acrylic paints or Testors paint markers.
Protective Coating:	Two coats of Flex Coat rod-wrapping finish. Allow each coating to drip dry from the eye of the hook.

I based this fly on Lou Tabory's Floating Sand Eel and Surf Board Foam Fly. In general, floating sand eel patterns are most productive on calm waters at night. I've taken some good striped bass on this fly when they were slashing at the naturals on the surface at night. At these times, a slow hand-over-hand retrieve works best. It takes nerves of steel not to set when the water explodes under the fly—but don't. The surface strike of the bass is often tentative, and setting by sight or sound will produce many more misses than hits. Wait until you actually feel the fish before you bury the steel.

Floating sand eels are also used with sinking lines and long leaders and worked to suggest the natural's darting toward the bottom.

Plate 16

Hot-Glue Sand Eel

Hook:	Mustad 34011; 1/0.
Thread:	Monocord; size and color are unimportant.
Wing:	Black or brown bucktail over sparse olive bucktail over a generous amount of silver Krystal Flash over white bucktail. Secure the wing to a short length of stiff wire (a heavy paper clip works well) and insert it into the silicone mold while the glue is hot.
Head:	Hot-melt glue injected into a two-part silicone mold. After cooling, paint the head. Paint the sides with Winsor & Newton iridescent white, the underside with a white Testors paint marker, and

the topside to match the wing. Gills are suggested with a red Testors paint marker or permanent marking pen. Eyes are painted with acrylic enamels—yellow with a black pupil. After the paint dries, use an olive marking pen along the dorsal coloration of the head. Use two coats of Flex Coat rod-wrapping finish for a final protective coating, allowing it to drip dry from the eye of the hook.

Bob Popovics' Surf Candies inspired me to learn how to mold hot glue. I liked the Surf Candies, but found working with epoxy tedious and messy (as did Bob when he first began), and I always ended up with glue-sniffer's headache. Molding hot glue is quick and neat and far less expensive than epoxy, and the results are consistent. The style enables you to mimic nearly any small baitfish well, particularly the head, which is the focal point for predators feeding on baitfish. These flies are fairly durable, they turn over well into a breeze, and they look good in the water. I've taken striped bass and bluefish with these Sand Eels, and have been told they work well on landlocked salmon to imitate smelt.

For dealers of Shin-Etsu Silicones in your area, contact Shin-Etsu Silicones of America, Inc., 431 Amapola Ave., Torrance, California 90501, Tel. 310-533-1101.

Page's Sand Eel Plate 16

Hook:	Extra-long shank, straight eye, noncorrosive.
Thread:	Danville's flat waxed nylon.
Tail:	Black 24-denier FisHair over salt-and-pepper Flashabou over 24-denier pearl-white FisHair. (Mystic Bay Fly Fur in black and polar bear may be substituted for the FisHair.)
Body:	Large pearl Mylar tubing fastened at the hook eye and pushed inside out back over the length of the shank and whip finished near the bend. Any unraveled Mylar may be trimmed or left hanging.
Coloring:	Black marking pen over dorsal. Gill is red Testors paint marker.
Eyes:	2-millimeter Witchcraft prismatic press-on eyes (yellow with a black pupil).
Epoxy:	A thin coating of Devcon 5-Minute Epoxy over the body.

Tied in a variety of sizes and color combinations (though best on hook sizes 6 through 2), this Page Rogers beauty has accounted for stripers up to 35 pounds along Dogfish Bar and Lobsterville Beach on Martha's Vineyard. It can be deadly on finicky late-season bluefish, and is also a good inshore pattern for Vineyard bonito and false albacore.

Sand Eel (Bob Popovics' Surf Candy Series) Plate 16

Refer to the Popovics' Spearing (Popovics' Surf Candy Series) listed under "Silversides" for construction details. Use a long-shanked hook (Mustad 34011 or equivalent) and Ultra Hair colored to match natural sand lances. Pull on the Ultra Hair from the rear as the epoxy sets to obtain the long, slender profile of the natural.

Plate 16

Tabory's Sand Eel

Hook:	Wright & McGill 66SS; size 1/0.
Thread:	White.
Wing:	Peacock herl over white bucktail tied in at the hook eye and extending at least one shank length beyond the bend. Overwrap the wing with a thin strip of Ziploc bag and give it at least one coat of epoxy. Similar patterns use clear monofilament or clear Swannundaze for the overwrap.

(Dressed by Bill Peabody.)

Plate 16

Wentink's Lead-Eye Sand Eel

Hook:	Mustad 34011; 1 to 2/0.
Thread:	White 3/0 monocord or 2/0 nylon.
Tail:	White bucktail or FisHair, one and one-half times the length of the hook. To each side of this, add three or four thin strips of silver or pearlescent Mylar.
Body:	Silver Mylar tinsel overwrapped with clear V-Rib or Swannundaze.
Wing:	Six to eight strands of peacock herl over olive bucktail extending back even with the white bucktail.
Eyes:	Lead eyes, 1/36 or 1/24 ounce, painted yellow with black pupils.
Head:	Olive chenille wrapped figure-eight style over the eyes, or a dubbing of olive lamb's wool clipped to shape.

Frank Wentink, author of *Saltwater Fly Tying*, developed this pattern for striped bass and bluefish in the Hudson River, though it has also taken weakfish, Spanish mackerel, jack crevalle, snappers, snook, and barracuda. The lead eyes cause the fly to dive toward the bottom between strips, suggesting a sand lance attempting to burrow. According to Ed Mitchell, such Clouser Minnow-type flies are particularly effective on striped bass when they are rooting in the sand to uncover buried lances.

Plate 16

Whitlock's Sand Eel

Hook:	Mustad 34007 or Tiemco 800S; to 1/0.
Thread:	Danville's white single-strand unwaxed floss.
Tail:	A half dozen strands of Krystal Flash or Crystal Hair secured at the bend of the hook. To each side of this, tie two olive-dyed grizzly hackles (the tail is composed of four hackles total), concave sides together.
Body:	A length of braided pearl Mylar and one olive-dyed grizzly hackle fastened at the base of the tail. Secure the hackle at the tip and palmer it toward the head. Then wind the Mylar forward as well, but allow the hackle fibers to stick out between the wrappings.

Throat:	Ten or so strands of Krystal Flash or Crystal Hair, mixed red and pearl, long enough to extend down to the barb of the hook.
Eyes:	Wapsi solid-plastic doll's eyes glued to the sides of the head with Goop.
Weedguard:	Heavy monofilament.

Similar to his Eelworm Streamer, Whitlock's Sand Eel is dressed in a variety of colors and has been effective on a number of saltwater gamefishes.

Sculpins and Gobies

Beginning with Don Gapen's Muddler Minnow (an imitation of a freshwater sculpin—and probably the slimy sculpin or slimy muddler [*Cottus cognatus*] native to his home waters of Minnesota and Canada), sculpin imitations have evolved into a multitude of styles and patterns for both fresh and salt water and have gained popularity worldwide.

Sculpin imitations are characterized by a large head of spun deer hair or wool. Often, various feathers are tied in behind the head (concave sides out) to suggest the large pectoral fins of the naturals. As the habits of the naturals suggest, sculpin and goby imitations should be fished on or near the bottom. In some areas, a monofilament weedguard is necessary.

Troth Bullhead

Plate 17

Hook:	To 3/0; usually tied on a salmon hook for fresh water.
Thread:	Black monocord.
Tail:	A small bunch of white bucktail extending one shank length beyond the bend.
Body:	Cream angora yarn.
Wing:	A large bunch of ostrich herl fastened at the forward part of the hook and at the tail, colored to suggest the natural.
Head:	Natural deer body hair, spun and trimmed to shape. (It is left untrimmed at the rear of the head as a collar.) The top of the head is colored with a waterproof marker of the same color as the ostrich herl.
Weighting:	Usually weighted with lead wire wrapped around the bend of the hook and with split shot clamped to the leader just above the knot.
Variation:	To fish deeper waters, Al Troth substituted the spun-deer-hair head for one dubbed of rabbit fur.

(Dressed by George V. Roberts Jr.)

The Troth Bullhead was developed for trout and is also used for freshwater bass, but its shape is suggestive of sculpins in general. It is sometimes tied with a monofilament weedguard.

Plate 17

Whitlock's Salt Sculpin

Hook:	Tiemco 811S; to 1/0; bent down slightly just behind the hook eye to enhance jigging action.
Thread:	Danville's yellow single-strand unwaxed floss.
Underbody:	A loop of Mason monofilament, the same diameter as the hook's wire, fastened to the sides of the hook shank. The technique is similar to the one used for monofilament nymph underbodies. Coat the wrappings with Zap-A-Gap cyanoacrylate.
Pectoral Fins:	Cock pheasant flank feathers, two to each side, tied with the concave sides facing out.
Gills:	Several turns of red hackle in front of the pectoral fins.
Back:	A strip of rabbit skin (*not* a Zonker strip); the fur should be dyed dirty olive or another appropriate color. Cut the skin tapering gradually to a point at the rear. Punch a hole through the skin and put the point of the hook through. Position the skin and tie it to the hook just behind the hook eye and just in front of the dumbbells. Then glue it with Zap-A-Gap to the underbody and also to the belly skin.
Belly:	Tapered rabbit-skin strip (white or another appropriate color) about three-quarters the length of that used for the back. Fasten the skin to the shank just behind the hook eye and just in front of the dumbbells, and then glue it with Zap-A-Gap to the underbody and also to the back skin.
Weighting:	Lead dumbbells secured with tying thread to the top of the hook shank at the forward bend so that the hook rides point up on the finished fly. Put these on when the underbody is attached.

Plate 17

Whitlock's Matuka Sculpin

Hook:	Tiemco 811S or equivalent (salmon hook shown); to 4/0.
Thread:	Danville's yellow single-strand unwaxed floss.
Underbody:	A loop of Mason monofilament, the same diameter as the hook wire, fastened to the sides of the hook shank. The technique is similar to that used for monofilament nymph underbodies. Coat the wrappings with Zap-A-Gap cyanoacrylate. These underbodies help to keep materials from twisting on the hook shank.
Weighting:	Lead wire wrapped over the underbody.
Body:	Fuzzy wool or mohair yarn, cream or colored to match the natural, covering the rear two-thirds of the hook shank. Wrap several turns of red Antron yarn in front of the cream-colored yarn to suggest the red gills.
Wing:	Secure four to eight wide grizzly or cree saddle hackles dyed tan and olive (or colored to match the natural) to the body Matuka style with a rib of fine stainless-steel wire.

Pectoral Fins: Cock pheasant flank feathers secured to the shank just in front of the red Antron, concave sides facing out.

Head: Deer body hair flared to each side of the monofilament underbody and trimmed to a flattened sculpin shape. Use cream deer hair for the underside of the head and a mixture of olive, black, and golden brown for the topside of the head to effect the mottlings of the natural. Cut an eye socket on each side of the head.

Eyes: Wapsi doll's eyes glued into the eye sockets with Goop.

Optional Weedguard: Monofilament.

Zonker Sculpin

Plate 17

Hook: Long-shanked, noncorrosive.
Thread: Black 3/0 monocord.
Body: Black wool.
Wing: Black Zonker strip secured to the body Matuka style with wire or monofilament.
Pectoral Fins: A black hen hackle tied concave side out to each side of the body, as on the naturals.
Head: Black wool spun and trimmed to shape.
Weighting: Heavy lead wire wrapped under the wool body.
(Dressed by George V. Roberts Jr.)

Code Goby (Carl Richards)

Plate 17

Hook: Mustad 34006B Accu-Point; size 4.
Thread: White Dyna Cord; 3/0.
Weighting: Flat lead. The hook should ride point up on the finished fly.
Body and Tail: Rub-R-Mold latex.
Pectoral Fins: Green-dyed partridge.
Head: Green lamb's wool.
Eyes: Witchcraft press-on eyes, secured with 5-minute epoxy.

Carl Richards uses this fly primarily for bonefish, but it also takes flats-cruising sharks and barracuda. Fish the fly close to the bottom, retrieving it in short, hopping strips. Use a wire leader if sharks and barracuda are the intended game.

Loring Wilson simplified goby-pattern selection by creating flies imitating representative species of the East, West, and Gulf coasts. He suggests you allow these patterns to sink, and then retrieve them in short twitches no longer than 6 inches.

Naked Goby

Hook: 3X long; size 4.
Thread: White.

Tail:	Two pale blue hackles one and one-half times the length of the hook.
Body:	Weighted with five turns of solder, over which is wrapped gray chenille.
Pectoral Fins:	Two partridge body feathers tied concave sides out.
Head:	Natural deer body hair, spun and trimmed to shape.

Sharptail Goby

Hook:	3X long; 4 to 1/0.
Thread:	Yellow.
Tail:	Two cream hackles one and one-quarter times the length of the hook.
Body:	Weighted with solder: five turns for size 4, six turns for size 2, eight turns for size 1/0.
Pectoral Fins:	Two partridge body feathers tied concave side out.
Hackle:	Reddish orange, tied in front of the partridge feathers.
Head:	Yellow deer body hair, spun and trimmed to shape.

This fly was reported by Loring Wilson to be especially effective on river tarpon on Florida's Gulf Coast, particularly when they are cruising the shallows.

Plate 17

Longjaw Goby

Hook:	3X long; size 4.
Thread:	Brown.
Tail:	Two dark-olive hackles, one and one-half times the length of the hook.
Body:	Weighted with five wraps of solder over which are two strands of chenille—one olive, one brown—twisted together and wrapped as one.
Pectoral Fins:	Two grouse body feathers.
Hackle:	Reddish orange, tied in front of the grouse feathers.
Head:	Green deer body hair, spun and trimmed to shape.

(Dressed by Bill Peabody.)

Silversides

Plate 18

Bar Fly

Hook:	Long-shanked, stainless steel; 1/0.
Thread:	Black or gray 3/0 monocord.
Tag:	Short tuft of red wool.
Body:	Silver Mylar overwrapped with clear medium Swannundaze.
Wing:	Fine ice-blue or clear nylon hair topped with white polar bear hair

(goat may be substituted). This is flanked by one grizzly hackle, which is in turn flanked by one strand of peacock herl slightly shorter than the grizzly. The wing should extend just beyond the bend of the hook.

Head: Black; painted eyes optional (white with a black pupil).
(Dressed by J. Edson Leonard.)

Flies author J. Edson Leonard, who has been fly-fishing in salt water since the 1930s, considers this creation of the late Charlie Benson the most productive striped-bass fly he has ever used. A lifetime on the water has convinced Mr. Leonard that white should be the predominant color in any striper fly. The color and structure of the Bar Fly is particularly suggestive of silversides, a primary forage of striped bass on both coasts, and Mr. Leonard has used the pattern and its variations successfully whenever bass were feeding on the naturals. Properly tied, the Bar Fly is also extremely durable.

Versions 2 and 3 are Mr. Leonard's variations of the original Bar Fly. Each is tied on a regular-shanked hook, which deprives the fish of the leverage it could use to work the hook free. Version 2 has a body of braided Mylar and a wing of fine nylon—white over thin yellow over white—flanked by a grizzly hackle and a strand of silver tinsel. Version 3 has a body of silver Mylar overwrapped with clear Swannundaze, an underwing of white polar bear, a wing of white polar bear, and several strands of lime Krystal Flash throughout, flanked by a light chinchilla hackle.

Gibbs' Striper Bucktail Plate 18

Hook: Regular shank, noncorrosive; to 3/0.
Thread: Black.
Body: Narrow flat silver tinsel.
Wing: Bucktail, 2½ to 5 inches long, white over thin blue over white.
Cheeks: Jungle cock breast feather (barred teal or guinea hen may be substituted).
Throat: A small bunch of red bucktail or hackle fibers.
Head: Black with painted eyes.
(Dressed by Bill Peabody.)

Originated by Harold Gibbs, this classic saltwater pattern is perhaps the earliest silverside imitation on record. It has outlived its creator and continues to be produced commercially.

Janssen's Fry Fly Plate 18

This pattern is a good imitation of a number of silverside species, particularly the East Coast *Menidia* species and the West Coast topsmelt. See Janssen's Stickleback for tying instructions.

Janssen's Striper Fly Plate 18

Hook: Allcock; 2 to 4/0.
Thread: White.

Underbody:	Padded and tapered with tying thread and waxed dental floss. Leave ¼ inch of the shank behind the hook eye bare.
Overbody:	Size 10 oval silver tinsel.
Wing:	Turn the hook upside down in the vise and tie a small clump of somewhat crinkly bucktail onto the bottom of the shank in the bare space, and spin it along the lower half of the hook. Then turn the hook right side up and do the same thing on top. The hair should flare out over the body, but it should *not* be tied tightly against it. Tie a clump of royal-blue bucktail over the white, and then tie a clump of fluorescent green over the blue. All clumps of bucktail are the same length.
Head:	Wound rather full, continuing the fish taper. Cover the head with clear Pactra Aerogloss enamel, and then paint it with Pactra enamels. For the top of the head, mix green enamel with a bit of yellow. For the blue stripe, mix royal-blue enamel with a bit of white. The painted eye (yellow with a black pupil) is large. Allow at least 20 minutes for the enamel to dry, and then coat the head with 5-minute epoxy for gloss and durability.

A grunion imitation, the Janssen Striper Fly was created by Hal Janssen in 1959 for use in the Richmond/San Rafael area of San Francisco Bay, one of the striped bass' first resting spots on its spawning migration up the Sacramento River. Janssen's technique of flaring the bucktail wing around a floss-padded body of oval tinsel suggests the grunion's translucence, iridescence, and bulk, while keeping the fly comfortably castable. Using bucktail along the underside of the hook shank (rather than stacking the whole wing on top) helps prevent the fly from fouling during casting.

This style of fly has been used to imitate many baitfish species and has taken a variety of gamefishes, including silver (coho) salmon in northern California and dolphin in Baja California.

Plate 18

Spearing (Bob Popovics' Surf Candy Series)

Hook:	Wright & McGill 254SS or Tiemco 800S or 811S; size 1/0.
Thread:	3/0 monocord or fine monofilament thread by Larva Lace.
Optional Tail:	A dark hen body-feather section (or dark saddle-hackle section) tied to a length of stiff 20- or 30-pound monofilament, the wrappings coated with Flexament. Over the monofilament, slip an equal length of slim silver Mylar tubing so that the end of the Mylar covers the thread wrappings. Fasten this tail section to the hook shank and dab the end of the Mylar tubing near the tail with Super Glue, epoxy, or Flexament to keep from it from unravelling.
Body:	Flat or braided silver Mylar fastened just behind the eye of the hook, wrapped back to the bend, and then wrapped forward again and tied off behind the eye.
Wing:	Ultra Hair fastened to both sides of the shank just behind the hook eye—white Ultra Hair for the belly and light green for the back. If

the pattern has a tail, the Ultra Hair should extend back to the base of the tail. A few strands of green Flashabou or Krystal Flash may be added along the dorsal. The butts of Ultra Hair are then trimmed, wrapped, and tied off.

Head: Devcon 5-Minute Epoxy (added glitter flakes optional) worked into the Ultra Hair along the entire shank with a bodkin, dubbing needle, or similar tool as the fly is rotated by hand. Use just enough epoxy to evenly penetrate the materials (this will prevent excessive running or sagging). To obtain the desired fish shape, pull at the Ultra Hair as the epoxy sets (for a silverside shape, squeeze the Ultra Hair just behind the bend; this gives the fly a bit deeper profile). Do this until the epoxy sets sufficiently. Then, apply Witchcraft prismatic eyes or paint the eyes. Draw gill slits with a red marking pen. Give the head a second coat of epoxy, being sure to cover all areas. Use the tip of the bodkin or dubbing needle to skim off the excess and slide any sagging epoxy to the proper position for the desired shape. Continue this until the second coat has set sufficiently.

Bob Popovics began experimenting with epoxy in the mid-1970s to create a longer-lasting fly for bluefish. Although prototypes of the modern "Pop-Fleyes" were winged with natural materials, durability improved remarkably simply because the epoxy protected the area where the materials were fastened. With the advent of Ultra Hair, which is just as strong as epoxy, durability increased tenfold. Bob has taken as many as thirty bluefish with a single Candy.

This style of tying has spawned a multitude of offshoots, including Sea Candies (flies in the 3/0 to 4/0 range for larger gamefishes), Stick Candies (long-shanked versions to imitate the long, slender profile of sand lances), and Keel Eels (bend-back design for bottom-fishing).

Smelts

In the northeastern United States and southeastern Canada, where landlocked populations of rainbow smelt (*Osmerus mordax*) are primary forage for trout and landlocked salmon, smelt flies abound. Each region boasts its own killing patterns, the most famous being Carrie Stevens' Gray Ghost (refer to Bates' *Streamers and Bucktails* for a more comprehensive listing). While many of these trout/salmon flies have undoubtedly been used in salt water, none has become a standard.

Magog Smelt Bucktail   Plate 19

Hook: Regular- or long-shanked.
Thread: Black.
Tail: Teal body feather fibers.
Body: Flat silver tinsel.
Wing: Bucktail, small and equal amounts of violet over yellow over white.

> **Topping:** Six strands of peacock herl.
> **Cheeks:** Body feather of barred teal.
> **Head:** Black, usually with a painted eye (yellow with a black pupil).
> (Dressed by Bill Peabody.)

Originally used for trout and landlocked salmon along the Vermont-Quebec border, the Magog Smelt was popularized as a striped-bass fly by Harold Gibbs, originator of the Gibbs' Striper Bucktail (see "Silversides").

Plate 19

McNally Smelt

> **Hook:** Mustad 34007; 1/0 to 3/0.
> **Thread:** White 3/0 monocord.
> **Tail:** White bucktail, about 3 inches long, secured at the bend of the hook.
> **Wing:** Six white saddle hackles, 4 to 6 inches long, secured to the top of the shank just behind the eye of the hook. On each side of these is one grizzly saddle, about as long as the white saddles. These are flanked by one strip of silver Mylar tinsel (to suggest the silvery stripe of some smelts), nearly as long as the wing.
> **Topping:** Fifteen to twenty strands of peacock herl as long as the wing (to represent the smelt's dark back).
> **Underwing:** A good amount of white bucktail secured to the underside of the shank just behind the eye of the hook and extending back well beyond the bend.

This pattern was developed by Tom McNally for silver (coho) and chinook salmon in the Great Lakes, but it is also used for many saltwater gamefishes. I've found it an effective all-around striped-bass fly.

Despite the number and abundance of Pacific species of the family Osmeridae, the only established West Coast pattern appears to be the Candlefish Bucktail. This is presumably an imitation of the eulachon smelt (but a poor one at that), and is used in estuaries and rivers for silver (coho) and chinook salmon during their spawning runs. Since salmon do not feed once they enter fresh water proper, the flies used to catch them at this time are usually attractor patterns designed, it is believed, to appeal to the fish's curiosity or aggression. A few patterns, however, suggest prey that the salmon fed on at sea, such as shrimps and smelts. Some anglers believe that presenting a specific food form to the salmon triggers a feeding memory, causing it to strike out of habit—a sort of conditioned response.

Candlefish Bucktail

> **Hook:** Extra-long shanked; 1/0 to 3/0.
> **Thread:** Black.
> **Body:** Flat silver tinsel.
> **Wing:** FisHair preferable, but bucktail can also be used. Pale blue over red over a mixture of pale green and pale blue. Finished wing is sparse.
> **Head:** Black, often with a painted eye (white with a black pupil).

In his *Streamers and Bucktails: The Big Fish Flies*, Joseph Bates Jr., confuses the eulachon smelt (*Thaleichthys pacificus*) and the Pacific sand lance (*Ammodytes hexapterus*) and their life histories, calling the Candlefish Bucktail a sand-eel imitation. It is interesting to note, however, that the color scheme and configuration of the Candlefish Bucktail are closer to those of the Pacific sand lance—also a primary forage of West Coast salmon—than to the fish whose name it bears. For an elaboration and variations of this dressing, refer to the aforementioned book.

Sticklebacks

Janssen's Stickleback (Janssen's Fry Fly Series)   Plate 19

Hook:	2XL or 3XL, perfect bend, turned-down eye; to size 1.
Thread:	White Nymo or monocord.
Tail:	Short clump of white marabou, the tips colored with a marking pen.
Underbody:	Grumbacher #7123 Bristol Artist Paper or cardboard the thickness of a matchbook cover. Cut two body forms from the paper and secure them to each side of the shank with thread.
Overbody:	Braided pearlescent Mylar tubing secured at each end.
Paint:	Pactra Aerogloss enamel or Testors dope in white, olive, gray, black, yellow, clear, and thinner.
Sealer:	Rod Builder's Epoxy (drying time 2 hours), manufactured by Epoxy Coatings of Hayward, California.

Developed in the early 1960s by Hal Janssen, the Fry Fly series has been successful the world over in both fresh and salt water. Hal uses the Stickleback version particularly for brackish-water chinook salmon and striped bass. The epoxied Mylar body, in conjunction with the turned-down hook eye (which acts like the lip of a swimming lure), causes the fly to dart side to side and up and down when retrieved in sharp strips—an action suggestive of crippled minnows, but also suggestive of the movements of natural sticklebacks (especially their mating dance).

Rolled Muddler   Plate 19

Hook:	Mustad 9671 or similar; 12 to 3/0.
Thread:	Fluorescent orange; 6/0.
Tail:	Rolled mallard flank folded once.
Body:	Silver Mylar tinsel.
Ribbing:	Fine silver wire or oval tinsel, counter wound.
Wing:	Mallard flank, sparse, folded twice. (Two or three strands of Krystal Flash are optional.)
Throat:	Fluorescent-red thread allowed to show through the rear of the head.
Head:	Spun deer hair clipped to shape.
Eyes:	Originally tied with plastic bead-chain; small plastic doll's eyes shown.

(Dressed by Bill Peabody.)

This pattern was originated by Tom Murray, of British Columbia. It is used for silver (coho) salmon, flounder, sea bass, as well as for freshwater species. Tom recommends a floating line, a 4- to 6-pound tippet, and a fast retrieve.

SQUIDS

Plate 20

Sea-Arrow Squid

Hook:	5XL noncorrosive; to 4/0.
Thread:	White size-A Nymo.
Tag:	Braided gold Mylar wrapped over the shank.
Tail:	(To represent tentacles.) White chenille fastened just behind the tag to form a ball. Directly in front of this, secure ten white saddle hackles, eight of which are 2½ inches long, and the remaining two twice that length. These hackles represent the squid's arms. The ball of chenille keeps the hackles splayed. The tail is flanked by a sparse amount of purple bucktail (to simulate blood veins), which extends back about halfway between the short and long hackles, and by various colors of Krystal Flash about as long as the short hackles.
Body:	Medium to large white chenille.
Eyes:	Plastic post-type eyes, to 9 millimeters (available from craft shops). Cut the posts off flush and glue the eyes to the sides of the chenille (at the base of the tail) with Goop.
Fins:	Originally tied with four pieces of large acrylic yarn, 3 inches long, fastened near the eye of the hook and the fibers of the yarn worked out so they radiate in a complete circle. Clear silicone bathroom sealer was worked into the fibers and allowed to dry. The fin was then cut to shape.
	Dan Blanton has since simplified the fin by securing a tuft of white calf tail at each side of the fly, extending back to just behind the eyes. The entire fly is then mottled with Sharpie pens: black, red, and brown.

Developed by Dan Blanton and Bob Edgley, the Sea-Arrow Squid has proved effective on such gamefishes as striped bass, yellowtail, rockfish, lingcod, spotted sand bass, white seabass, albacore, Pacific bonito (of which it has taken two world records), skipjack tuna, king salmon, pompano, snappers, groupers, cabrillo, and various sharks. Dan has even jumped a couple of tarpon with it on Costa Rica's Colorado River.

Catherwood's Ginger Squid Plate 20

Hook:	Mustad 94151; to 7/0.
Thread:	Heavy pink cotton-wrapped polyester.
Marabou:	Pink, tied concave side up near the bend, the butt of the feather laid between the glass eyes (refer to Catherwood's Herring).
Wing:	Long strand of black bucktail or Scottish blackface hair (to simulate ink) tied in over the marabou. Over this are fastened eight long ginger hackles as on a conventional streamer.
Tentacles:	Eight short ginger hackles tied just behind the eye of the hook to encircle the shank. The hackles will splay when the fly is retrieved.
Eyes:	Glass—¼-inch diameter for the largest flies—secured figure-eight style before any other materials are attached.

Page's Simple Squid Plate 20

Hook:	Long-shanked, straight eye, noncorrosive.
Thread:	Danville's flat waxed nylon.
Tail:	(To represent tentacles.) Four white saddle hackles tied in splayed at the bend of the hook. These are flanked by a mixture of gray-ghost and fluorescent-cerise Krystal Flash. A white marabou feather is then tied in tip first and wrapped around the base of the tail as a skirt and tied off. The tail and skirt are then dotted with a black Sharpie pen.
Body:	Built up with the core from medium or large Everglow tubing. Tie in the tubing at the hook eye so that the length of tubing projects in front of the hook eye. Whip finish, and then push the sock of tubing inside out over the body. Secure the tubing and whip finish just before the hook bend. Unravel the tubing and let the strands encircle the tail hackles and skirt. They should be about half the length of the tail.
Eyes:	3.5- or 4-millimeter Witchcraft press-on eyes.
Sealant:	5-minute epoxy, or Aquaseal thinned with Cotol-240 (available wherever Aquaseal is sold), or silicone thinned with Kodak Fotoflo (available in camera shops), covering the body and eyes.

This fly works well in sheltered waters and can be made to glow in the dark by hitting it with a halogen beam before casting.

Shady Lady Squid (Bob Popovics) Plate 20

Hook:	Noncorrosive.
Thread:	Fine monofilament thread by Larva Lace.
Tail:	(To represent tentacles.) Lay a 1½-inch-long base of monofilament thread over a length of 60-pound monofilament and coat the

wrappings with Hard As Nails. At the front of this thread base, wrap a small ball of purple chenille and tie it off. Directly behind this chenille ball, fasten eight to twelve saddle hackles in pairs around the mono (in larger versions, add two extra-long saddles), concave sides facing in. (The chenille ball opens the feathers up a bit, enhancing the squid's action.) Overwrap the butt ends of the feathers to an even taper, and coat the wrappings with Hard As Nails. Dot the saddles with a marking pen.

Head: A long length of Estaz or cactus chenille tied in at the base of the feathers and wrapped forward to form the shape of the head. Tie off and whip finish.

Body: Lay the bare mono of the head section along the hook shank, threading the tag end of the mono through the hook eye. Wrap the mono on both sides of the shank and cement with Super Glue. Fasten Estaz or cactus chenille at the bend of the hook and wrap forward, tying it off just behind the eye of the hook. There fasten long sheep fleece to encircle the shank and extend back just behind the squid's head.

Eyes: Witchcraft press-on eyes affixed with Super Glue to the headsection. The eyes should be prominent and not covered by any of the materials.

Bob ties this fly in a multitude of variations—short-shanked versions, long-shanked versions, tandems, and silicone versions, to name only a few—and he is forever experimenting with new possibilities. For colors, Bob likes white, black, and chartreuse (one of Bob's friends does well with red Shady Ladies for tuna). These flies have proved deadly on big striped bass around Martha's Vineyard.

CRUSTACEANS

DECAPOD SHRIMPS

Grass Shrimps

Plate 21

Dave's Salt Shrimp

Hook: Regular shank; 1 or 1/0.
Thread: To match the color of the fly, usually gray or olive.
Antennae/Tail: Two stripped hackle stems extending 1½ inches beyond the hook.

Over this, tie a ⅛-inch-thick clump of squirrel tail (natural or dyed to suit) ½ inch long.

Eyes: Burnt mono.

Body: Seal-Ex dubbing (colored to suit), tapering to ⅛ inch of bulk at the hook eye.

Legs: Grizzly hackle (natural or dyed to suit) wound four turns over the front third of the body (the rear third of the hook) and secured.

Shell Back: Strip of Ziploc bag cut so ¼ inch projects over the bend of the hook, secured with a ribbing of heavy thread (color to suit imitation). A small amount of the Ziploc should be folded back to the rear of the hook to suggest the shrimp's tail fan. This pattern usually includes a weedguard of heavy monofilament.

(Dressed by Umpqua.)

This pattern was originated by Dave Whitlock for use on the Gulf Coast, particularly for redfish. I've found it a good striped-bass fly in the Northeast.

Sater's Grass Shrimp
Plate 21

Hook: Mustad 34007; 1 to 4.

Thread: Gray 3/0 monocord.

Tail: Olive saddle hackle tip tied down into the bend.

Shell Back: Polyethylene strip secured at the bend and pulled down after the hackle is trimmed. (The hackle suggests legs.)

Ribbing: 6-pound monofilament wound to secure the shell and to suggest segmentation.

Body: Underbody of dark olive wool, over which is dubbed gray seal fur.

Legs: Palmered olive-gray saddle hackle wound heavily near the eye and clipped close to the body on top of the shank.

Eyes: Burnt 30-pound mono secured at the head before the shell is tied down.

(Dressed by Bill Peabody.)

This pattern was developed by Robert Sater for striped bass and weakfish.

Janssen's Grass Shrimp
Plate 21

Hook: Mustad 9671, 2 XL; 4 to 1/0.

Thread: Olive brown.

Tail: Olive-brown marabou, slightly longer than the gape of the hook.

Body: Golden-olive fur ribbed with olive-brown ostrich herl.

Legs: Olive hackle.

Shell Back: Latex marked with brown and olive Pantone pens and ribbed with tying thread.

Eyes: Melted 40-pound mono, painted pearl white with a brown cornea.

Hal Janssen uses this fly on brackish-water chinook salmon that have just begun their spawning runs and will still feed (particularly the Smith and Eel rivers in California, and the Chetco River in Oregon). Hal uses a floating or slow-sinking line and a long leader. The grass shrimp, he observes, is capable of rapid bursts of 12 to 15 inches, and on several occasions he has witnessed them actually leap from the water in flight from adult chinook salmon.

Hal has also used this fly to take striped bass.

Fernandez's Grass Shrimp

Hook:	Mustad 34007 or equivalent; 2 to 8.
Thread:	Black.
Body:	Light-green synthetic yarn.
Wing:	Light-blue FisHair with a blue grizzly hackle tip tied on each side. The wing is inverted so that the hook rides point up.
Optional Weighting:	Lead wire.

This pattern was developed by Chico Fernandez to represent the arrow shrimp (also known as the grass shrimp [*Tozeuma carolinensis*]).

Plate 21

Ultra Shrimp (Bob Popovics)

Hook:	Mustad 34007 or equivalent; 6 to 1/0.
Thread:	Tan 3/0 monocord or fine monofilament thread by Larva Lace.
Tail:	(To represent the walking legs and head region.) Short stalks of Ultra Hair tied in at the bend to slope downward from the shank (for walking legs), with short butts of copper Krystal Flash on top of the shank at the bend. Above the Krystal Flash, fasten a slightly longer length of Ultra Hair (but not longer than the legs). Tie in the monofilament eyes—30-pound mono burned to a ball and colored with a black marker—to extend past the bend of the hook, and then fasten antennae made from Ultra Hair.
Swimming Legs:	Ginger hackle palmered, widely spaced, to within one-third the shank length from the eye of the hook. All hackles above the shank are clipped; side hackles are left untouched.
Carapace:	A length of Ultra Hair fastened at the eye of the hook to lie along the top of the shank, tapered at the end to approximate the shape of the natural's head. Flare the butts of the fastened end to represent the tail fan.
Epoxy (optional):	Devcon 5-Minute Epoxy applied to the top, sides, and rear of the body, but *not* to the tail fan.

Originally designed for striped bass and weakfish, the realistic and simple-to-tie Ultra Shrimp has also proved effective on such predators as bonefish and permit. Bob dresses this pattern in a number of colors in addition to tan, including olive and clear. He says chartreuse is an excellent color.

Snapping Shrimps

Banded Snapping Shrimp (Chico Fernandez)

Hook: Mustad 34007 or equivalent; 2 to 8.
Thread: Brown or orange 3/0 monocord.
Body: Brown synthetic yarn.
Wing: Orange or brown FisHair marked with five or six black vertical bands (also refer to the color variations of the banded snapping shrimp [*Alpheus armillatus*] in Part Two). The wing is tied inverted so that the hook rides point up.
Optional Weighting: Lead wire.

Brown Snapping Shrimp (Chico Fernandez)   Plate 21

Hook: Mustad 34007 or equivalent; 2 to 8.
Thread: Brown 3/0 Monocord.
Tag: Red floss or similar material.
Body: Tan synthetic yarn.
Wing: Brown FisHair tied inverted.
Optional Weighting: Lead wire.
(Dressed by Bill Peabody.)

Yellow Snapping Shrimp (Chico Fernandez)

Hook: Mustad 34007 or equivalent; 2 to 8.
Thread: Red 3/0 monocord.
Body: Yellow synthetic yarn.
Wing: FisHair, mixed green and yellow, tied inverted.
Optional Weighting: Lead wire.

Banded Snapping Shrimp (Carl Richards)   Plate 21

This fly is tied in much the same way as is Richards' White Swimming Shrimp, except that the body is a little more stocky and, of course, the fly is more brightly colored.
Hook: Mustad 34011.
Thread: White Dynacord.
Claws: Rub-R-Mold liquid latex. Claw sections are secured to the hook shank with tying thread.
Carapace, Abdomen: Fish Fuzz or lamb's wool.
Legs & Swimmerets: Hackle.

Eyes:	Burnt mono.
Coloring:	Marking pens and liquid latex mixed with acrylic paint.
Snapping Noise:	Plastic-worm rattle.

This is Carl Richards' favorite fly for bonefish and permit, and it is deadly on redfish also. The worm rattle really enhances the pattern's effectiveness. Carl has had entire schools of permit turn and attack a rattling fly when they wouldn't look at one without a rattle.

Plate 22

Whitlock's Near 'Nuff Snapping Shrimp

Hook:	Tiemco 811S—to size 4—bent downward slightly near the eye to enhance the fly's jigging action (the hook rides point up on the finished fly).
Thread:	Orange Flymaster.
Antennae:	Two strands of speckled rubber and two strands of tan Crystal Hair fastened at the bend.
Claws:	One rounded rust-colored grizzly feather over one light or mottled hen breast feather fastened on each side of the hook shank to suggest the natural appendages.
Underbody:	A loop of Mason monofilament, the same diameter as the hook wire, fastened to the sides of the hook shank. The technique is similar to that used for monofilament nymph underbodies. Coat the wrappings with Zap-A-Gap cyanoacrylate.
Body:	Dubbed with a 50-50 mixture of Orlon and rabbit fur, all dyed rusty orange.
Legs:	Webby rust-dyed grizzly hackle tied in at the tip just behind the claws and palmered toward the hook eye. The bottom hackles (that is, those that face the sand on the finished fly) are then trimmed off.
Weighting:	Lead dumbbells secured to the top of the shank just behind the hook eye at the same time the monofilament foundation is attached. Use Zap-A-Gap cyanoacrylate or 5-minute epoxy to cement the dumbbells securely to the hook shank.

Swimming Shrimps

Plate 22

White Swimming Shrimp (Carl Richards)

Hook:	Mustad 34011; 6 to 1/0.
Thread:	White monocord.
Carapace, Abdomen:	Small flies: FisHair or Fish Fuzz. Large flies: polar bear or Spectra streamer hair (polar bear color) by Umpqua.
Belly:	White mohair yarn wrapped one-quarter the length of the hook from the bend of the hook toward the eye to form a ball.

Front Legs:	Same as body.
Swimming Legs:	White hen hackle tied in at the base behind the ball of mohair and wrapped forward to the hook eye. A light olive or tan marabou feather is tied in and wrapped forward as well. This gives the shrimp its olive or tan tint.
Antennae:	White boar bristles.
Eyes:	Artificial flower stamen (found in craft shops) or a length of burnt mono, coated with 5-minute epoxy. The stalk is tinged with a gold marker, and the cornea is colored black with a Sharpie pen.
Carapace:	Clipped cock-hackle segment, light gray or tan, tied on top of the shank behind the ball of mohair.
Tail:	Same as body.

Carl Richards ties these shrimps to face either way on the hook (to simulate the leisurely forward swimming or backward darting), and does not weight them or tie them to ride hook point up unless he is using them on bonefish flats. Then he ties them on a size 8 to 4 hook and weights them. Carl fishes these flies at all levels of the water column, and has taken tarpon, ladyfish, snook, redfish, and bonefish.

Brown Swimming Shrimp (Chico Fernandez) Plate 22

Hook:	Mustad 34007, or equivalent; size 2.
Thread:	Brown.
Body:	Beige synthetic yarn.
Wing:	FisHair, reddish brown over pale blue, 2¼ inches long, tied inverted so that the hook rides point up.
Optional Weighting:	Lead wire.

(Dressed by Bill Peabody.)

Pink Swimming Shrimp (Chico Fernandez)

Hook:	Mustad 34007, or equivalent; size 2.
Thread:	Brown.
Body:	Pink.
Wing:	FisHair, dark brown over pink, 2¼ inches long, tied inverted.
Optional Weighting:	Lead wire.

Mantis Shrimps

Green Mantis (Chico Fernandez)

| Hook: | Mustad 34007, or equivalent; 2 to 8. |
| Thread: | Emerald green. |

Body:	Pale-blue chenille.
Wing:	Dark-green FisHair, up to 2 inches long, tied inverted so that the hook rides point up.
Optional Weighting:	Lead wire.

Plate 22

Golden Mantis (Chico Fernandez)

Hook:	Mustad 34007, or equivalent; 2 to 8.
Thread:	Red.
Body:	Fluorescent-green chenille.
Wing:	Golden-yellow FisHair, tied inverted. On each side of this, tie a yellow grizzly hackle tip. The wing should be about twice the length of the shank.
Optional Weighting:	Lead wire.

(Dressed by Bill Peabody.)

Plate 22

Golden Mantis (Carl Richards)

Constructed in much the same manner as are his Snapping Shrimps, Carl Richards' Mantis Shrimps are built on Dai Riki 700 B 3X-long hooks that are weighted with flat lead and lead dumbbells to ride point up. They are fished in short strips along the bottom. Carl has had much success with bonefish and redfish with his Golden Mantis, particularly in the Berry Islands and on Andros Island.

Crabs

Plate 23

Black-Tipped Mud Crab (Carl Richards)

Hook:	Mustad 3406B Accu-Point; 6 to 2/0.
Thread:	White.
Body:	White egg yarn, spun on the hook shank and trimmed to shape. After the fly is finished, spray the yarn carapace with Scotchgard to waterproof it. If this is not done, the fly will not right itself if it lands upside down.
Legs and Underside:	Rub-R-Mold liquid latex. Legs and underside are formed first (cured for 72 hours at 70 degrees F), and then glued to the bottom of the trimmed egg-yarn body with more liquid latex. Then place the weighting on the underside and cover it with liquid latex. Let the latex set for 3 or 4 hours, and then cover it again with liquid latex to suggest abdominal segments. Let it set another 3 or 4 hours.
Weighting:	Lead strips.

Eyes:	Burnt mono, 40- to 80-pound, cemented into the yarn with E-6000 glue thinned with Weldwood paint thinner.
Antennae:	Boar bristles set just inside the eyes with thinned E-6000.
Coloring:	Sharpie or Pantone pens.

This fly is Carl Richards' number-one pattern for redfish and bonefish when fishing around mangroves and oyster bars, where mud crabs abound. Carl usually ties this pattern to ride hook down with a weedguard around weeds or coral rock (he prefers a double-wire guard to mono). When fishing around sand or mud, Carl prefers the hook to dig into the bottom a bit to kick up a puff of mud on the retrieve as might the natural. Bonefish are ever watchful for these telltale smoke signals, conditionally associating them with prey.

Catherwood's Green Crab

Plate 23

Hook:	Mustad 94151; size 1.
Thread:	White cotton-wrapped polyester.
Legs:	Eight grizzly or ginger variant neck hackles dyed Kelly green.
Claws:	Barred mallard dyed Kelly green, slimmed and allowed to stiffen with aircraft nitrate cellulose tautening dope (used for repairing aircraft control surfaces). To do this, put the dope on your thumb and index finger and draw the feather through.
Carapace:	One or two small hen feathers dyed Kelly green and mottled with a dark marking pen.
Abdomen:	One or two white hen feathers.
Eyes:	Waterfowl breast feathers, the quills stripped except for the fibers on the very end, which are cut short and dipped in black enamel.
Weighting:	Copper wire.
Frame:	Single-strand leader wire (.020 to .033 inches in diameter) bent to a U shape with each end left sticking out ³⁄₁₆ inch on each side. Wrap near the top of the U tightly with tying thread to close it off and form a loop or eye at the base. Tie the hackle feathers four to a side on the ³⁄₁₆-inch ends, and then tie in the mallard claws so they are upright and slightly cocked forward. Tie in the eyes so that they are about ¼ inch above the frame. Tie in the feathers for the carapace and belly near the loop, and put a dab of tautening dope between them to hold the crab together. Then tie off the loop as you would the head of a fly. Apply tautening dope to the wrappings as head cement, and dip the wrappings in beach sand.

Before you weight the hook with copper wire, fasten a short length of the single-strand leader wire (with about a 30-degree bend) to the shank to protrude past the hook bend. Wrap the copper wire heavily on the hook, and then overwrap the weighting with thread and tie off. Slip the eye of the frame over the protruding leader wire so that the point of the hook will ride up if the crab is right side up. Lash the tag end of the leader wire to the bend of the hook with the thread and tie off. Apply tautening dope to all wrappings and coat them with beach sand.

Bill Catherwood uses this crab in rocky areas for tautog, and also on flats for striped bass and other species. This fly looks great in the water, automatically assuming a defensive posture when it hits the bottom.

Janssen's Floating Blue Crab

Plate 23

Hook:	Allcock—regular shank, stainless steel, bent eye; 4 to 1/0.
Thread:	White.
Legs:	Four short brown cree saddle hackles tied at each end of the hook shank and splayed slightly.
Body:	Balsa wood, whittled and sanded to shape, fitted with a slot and epoxied onto the hook shank. The cree hackles should also be fit into the slot.
Eyes:	Black plastic pin heads.
Paint:	Pactra Aerogloss enamel. The crab body is olive brown on top, dirty white (mix white with a dash of olive) below. Put a dash of bright blue where the legs originate, and a bit of red at the base of the hackles. Mottle the top with shades of dark olive brown, dirty olive brown, olive brown mixed with a bit of white, and blue. Since you want to maintain a dull finish, do not coat the body with epoxy.

Developed primarily for permit (though it works on any fish that preys on the natural), Hal Janssen's Floating Blue Crab is a departure from most crab patterns. Rather than weighting the fly, Hal uses a sinking line and casts well ahead of cruising fish, allowing the line to sink while the Crab stays afloat. As the fish approaches, Hal begins his retrieve—quick 3- to 4-inch strips—and the fly begins working its way to the bottom as would the natural.

McCrab

Plate 23

Hook:	Mustad 34007; 8 to 1/0.
Thread:	Kevlar, tan or brown.
Tail:	Tan marabou, pearl Flashabou or Krystal Flash, and two short brown hackles tied splayed.
Body:	Deer or elk body hair, tan or brown, spun on the shank in three bunches. Each bunch is packed tightly after spinning and the wrappings secured with Super Glue. The hair is trimmed to a crab shape—from about the diameter of a dime to slightly less than that of a nickel—the carapace convex and the underside flat. The carapace on the finished fly is mottled with a brown marking pen. Secure the legs and eyestalks to the underside with Pliobond. After this sets for 5 minutes or so, secure a small pancake of lead putty over the legs with Super Glue. Then paint white Plasti-Dip (available in hardware stores) over the lead, but not quite out to the edge of the body.

Weighting:	⁵⁄₃₂-inch lead eyes tied to the top of the shank behind the eye of the hook, the wrappings coated with Super Glue; a pancake of lead putty on the bottom of the deer-hair body.
Eyes:	60-pound mono, melted and painted black with marine enamel.
Legs:	Strong, narrow rubber bands, knotted and mottled with marking pens. It is important to have the legs on the finished fly curve slightly upward; this helps the fly kick over and sink hook point up.

(Dressed by Umpqua.)

Developed by George Anderson, John Barr, and Jim Brungardt, the McCrab is reported to be among the first fly patterns to take the spooky permit consistently (though some anglers contend that the real breakthrough in permit fishing came not with a new crab pattern, but with a different approach to the retrieve). George recommends a 10- or 11-weight rod and a tapered leader from 9 to 12 feet long with a 2- to 3-foot tippet of 12-pound mono and a Duncan Loop knot at the fly. (The longer leader and tippet are for calmer conditions, the shorter ones are for when the water has a good chop.) For fly line, George likes the sinking version of Scientific Angler's braided-core Tarpon Taper.

For cruising permit, George casts 10 to 15 feet ahead of the fish; for fish moving more slowly or tailing, he puts the fly 5 or 10 feet to the side. The fly should hit the water with a light splat. George then gives the fly a sharp dart sideways using the rod tip. He takes up the slack, and then gives it another dart, moving the fly quickly to give action to the rubber legs. The permit, George notes, usually rush the fly and then decide quickly whether to take or reject. Strike the instant you feel anything or see any sudden taughtness in the line or leader. Sometimes the permit will follow the fly to the bottom. If this happens, give it another couple of twitches.

Permit in a school present a good opportunity for the angler because the competition among them is often fierce. In such situations, George has had good success by making short strips and speeding up the retrieve to tease the fish into striking.

In its smaller sizes, the McCrab has proved itself a good fly for bonefish.

Olive Swimming Crab   Plate 23

Hook:	Mustad 3407 or TMC 800S; 1 to 6.
Thread:	Olive 6/0 prewaxed.
Legs:	Olive speckled rubber legs, knotted to suggest segmentation. Legs and claws are secured to the underside of the body with white-tinted epoxy or white hot-melt glue.
Claws:	Four olive-dyed grizzly hackle tips.
Antennae:	Pearl Krystal Flash.
Eyes:	Mono nymph eyes.
Body:	Dark olive wool, spun and clipped to shape, mottled with marking pens. Other colors to suit.
Weighting:	Lead eyes secured to the hook just behind the eye. The hook rides point up on the finished fly.

Joe Branham and the staff of Kaufmann's Streamborn, Inc. (P.O. Box 23032, Portland, Oregon 97281-3032, Tel. 503-639-6400) designed this series of bonefish flies to imitate the small swimming crabs of Belize. Other colors in the series are olive green, brown, and tan—all mottled. The intent is to match the color of the fly to that of the bottom against which it will be fished, thereby more closely matching the colors of the crabs found living there. A frightened crab, Randall Kaufmann observes, often makes a quick dart and then remains motionless, relying on its camouflage for protection. Thus, he recommends you give this crab a single strip, and then let it lie motionless for the fish to grab off the bottom.

Plate 23

Red-Jointed Fiddler (Carl Richards)

This fly is constructed in the same way as is Richards' Black-Tipped Mud Crab, and is colored to suit.

Plate 23

Sand Flea

Hook:	Mustad 34007; size 2.
Tail:	(to suggest antennae) Two grizzly hackle tips tied splayed.
Body:	Three wraps of small tan chenille. White-painted bead-chain eyes are secured, and then a natural deer-hair body is spun and clipped to a pear shape.

(Dressed by Bill Peabody.)

Developed by Tom Lentz from a fly of unknown origin tied to suggest East Coast mole crabs, this pattern proved effective (if not widely popular) for a number of surf-dwelling fishes along the Florida coast—pompano in particular.

Plate 23

Sand Crab

Hook:	Mustad 3407, shank bent bend-back style; size 6.
Thread:	Heavy yellow.
Body:	Coral-colored chenille (to suggest eggs) wound into a ball.
Collar:	Natural rabbit Zonker strip wound on as a wet-fly hackle would be.
Weighting:	Lead dumbbells secured near the hook eye. The head is then coated with epoxy.

Few of the major West Coast gamefishes eat significant numbers of crabs; hence, crab imitations are practically nonexistent there. Exceptions to this are the sand or mole crabs of the family Hippidae. The Sand Crab, developed by Nick Curcione, is used primarily for corbina and barred surf perch. Marine biologists speculate that sand crabs might compose as much as 90 percent of the diets of these fishes.

Nick fishes this pattern in pockets and troughs along the surf line. These feeding zones can be as much as 10 feet deep, and because water turbulence is considerable, a fast-sinking line is a must. Nick recommends using a fast-sinking shooting head and shooting basket.

ANNELID WORMS

Clamworms

Because of their skywriting-like movements, most species of spawning nereids are difficult to match closely with a fly. Therefore, Ed Mitchell notes that it is easier to fish in an area where there is some current. There, the worms tend to be less active, generally falling with the tide—and a fly dead-drifted through a current is often close enough to the natural to draw a strike. Also, fish feeding in a current have to be more aggressive and commit to the fly sooner.

There are few established imitations of spawning clamworms, and none produces consistently in all situations—perhaps less because of any shortcomings in the patterns than because of the difficulty in matching the movements of the naturals and of the immense numbers of worms that sometimes appear during a swarming. Ed usually uses a size 1 or 2 black Woolly Bugger-type fly: short marabou tail, buggy body, and a short palmered hackle. Similar patterns have a small Muddler-type head to keep the fly near the surface and perhaps to push a bit of water (even small worms will sometimes leave a wake).

Ed also carries a large black streamer to try if his worm fly fails. Sometimes the larger fish around a swarming are not feeding solely on worms, but also on the smaller fishes and squids that are drawn to the worms. Ed likens this to pulling a streamer fly through an insect hatch: sometimes it will take the biggest trout from the group.

When feeding on spawning nereids, the rise and take of a striped bass are gentle. Often the fish has no more than to open its mouth and draw the worm in. During worm-spawning periods, look for rises that don't break the surface, particularly small whirlpools. Sometimes I've had good luck with a simple worm fly—marabou tail, small muddler head—in calm water during the dark of the moon when neither worms nor rises were to be seen.

Page's Worm Fly   Plate 24

Hook:	Long-shanked, straight eye, noncorrosive.
Thread:	Danville's flat waxed nylon, tobacco brown.
Tail:	A small tuft of fluorescent-pink marabou topped with a small tuft of fluorescent-red marabou.
Body:	Fluorescent-pink chenille.
Ribbing:	Two fluorescent-red hackles palmered the length of the body and trimmed along the top.
Coloring:	The top of the body is colored with a dark-brown marking pen.
Head:	Built up prominently with tying thread.

This pattern is tied in a number of sizes to match various species. A floating variation of this pattern uses a body of closed-cell foam.

Tabory's Snake Fly

Hook: Mustad 34007 or 34011; 6 to 1/0.
Tail: 1½ to 4½ inches of ostrich herl or saddle hackle, tied near the bend.
Wing: Two sections of marabou tied halfway between the bend and eye with room left for the head.
Head: Spun deer body hair, trimmed flat on the bottom and rounded on top, some hair left long for a collar.

Tie this fly with a slim build. Lou Tabory's favorite colors are all black, and black and orange.

Plate 24

Brown-Gray Leech

Hook: Mustad 9671; size 4.
Thread: Tan.
Wing: Brown mottled marabou by Umpqua fastened to the top of the hook shank in four evenly spaced clumps from the bend to the head (Hi-Tie style).

Despite the number of West Coast nereid species, few anglers there attend to their swarmings. Among those who do is Hal Janssen. Hal fishes this leech pattern at night, particularly in May and June, in the man-made brackish-water fingered lakes surrounding and to the south of San Francisco Airport. These lakes are fed by water pumped from the tidal rivers that flow into San Francisco Bay and are connected to the Bay by a system of locks. Every fifteen days the lake water is replenished, bringing nereid worms, as well as shrimps, sculpins, gobies, and striped-bass eggs. These lakes are in effect artificial nurseries for striped bass. Because the lakes are lined with homes, however, access is limited, though other areas around San Francisco Bay should present good opportunities for interested anglers to fish the worm swarmings.

Plate 24

Palolo Worm

Hook: Regular shank; 2/0 or 3/0.
Tail: 1 inch of bright-orange marabou or calf tail tied at the bend.
Body: Rear three-quarters of the shank is wrapped with small bright-orange chenille; the front is wrapped to the hook eye with small tan chenille.

Plate 24

Palolo Worm (Fitz Coker)

Hook: Tiemco 800S or Mustad 7766; 1/0 or 2/0.
Thread: Gray or tan monocord.
Wing: Rust, red, or orange-red rabbit-fur strip, 1½ inches long and ⅛ inch wide, tapered to a point at the tail and secured to the shank nearly halfway back from the hook eye and also at the bend.

Head: Built up with tying thread and lacquered.
(Dressed by Tom Kokenge.)

Developed by Fitz Coker, this simple pattern is Tom Kokenge's favorite palolo imitation. Tom reports that this is a killer tarpon fly not just during the palolo swarmings, but for the rest of the year as well. A 100-pound tarpon, he affirms, will readily jump on a fly only 1½ inches long. Tied on a number 4 hook with an undyed strip of rabbit fur, this fly is also an excellent bonefish pattern.

OTHER FLY PATTERNS

Blonde Series

The Blonde was developed in the late 1940s by Homer Rhode Jr., and was popularized by Joe Brooks. Originally used for tarpon, the Blonde has taken many species of freshwater and saltwater fish the world over. Its form is the basis for other, more complex patterns (such as Cal's Glass Anchovy and Wentink's Lead-Eye Sand Eel). Colors of the original Blonde series, which are more attractive than imitative, interest me less than the pattern's basic form, which, depending on the dressing, can effectively suggest a multitude of forage fishes. This is a simple, effective fly, and no angler should overlook its potential for general imitation.

Irish Blonde

Plate 24

Hook: Regular- or long-shanked; 4 to 5/0.
Thread: Black, or to match overwing.
Tail: White bucktail is laid along the shank to the point where the overwing will be tied in, and then overwrapped back to the bend with thread. Head cement worked into the fibers along the shank adds to the fly's durability.
Body: Flat silver Mylar tinsel.
Overwing: Green bucktail the length of the underwing.
Head: Black or green, painted eye optional.
(Dressed by George V. Roberts Jr.)

In terms of imitation, this pattern has perhaps the broadest application of any Blonde in the series.

Lefty's Deceiver

Plate 24

No roster of saltwater fly patterns would be complete without the Deceiver, the most popular saltwater pattern to date. While its design was motivated by functional concerns—the fly casts well, sinks readily, and seldom fouls—there are few forage fishes that this fly, appropriately dressed, does not imitate well. I have even used a Deceiver with its wing clipped to ½ inch and retrieved in 2-inch strips to catch striped bass feeding selectively on grass shrimp.

The Deceiver in all its variations and progeny could make up a book by itself (refer to Kreh's *Salt Water Fly Patterns*). Listed below is the bare-bones dressing with some suggestions for variations.

Hook:	Regular- or long-shanked. Bend-back hooks have also been used.
Thread:	Monocord.
Wing:	Tied at the bend are two (for very small sizes) to twelve saddle hackles. Overall length of the fly ranges from 2 to 14 inches.
Body:	Sometimes wrapped with silver Mylar tinsel or other materials, but often wrapped only with thread.
Collar:	Bucktail or equivalent, fastened to encircle the hook shank. The collar should extend well beyond the bend of the hook.
Variations and Embellishments:	Tied in a variety of colors and color combinations. Also tied with a variety of natural and synthetic materials. Marabou and FisHair have been used to collar the fly on some patterns, and FisHair has also been used for the wing. Flash material usually flanks the wing, but is often added to the collar as well. Toppings are either of bucktail or peacock herl, and throats can be red calf tail, rabbit, or Krystal Flash. Eyes are sometimes painted on the head, but are also painted on various breast feathers (such as mallard or teal), which are then tied in as cheeks. Plastic doll's eyes can be fastened to the collar easily with hot-melt glue. Deceivers used for large offshore species such as sailfish sometimes have a foam popping head slipped over the eye of the hook.

(Dressed by Bill Peabody.)

Plate 24

Popping Bugs

The adult size of some prey species exceeds the limits of practical imitation for average fly tackle. The largest forage fishes are perhaps better imitated with popping bugs, the disturbance created by which can suggest a creature much larger than itself. Popping bugs can be particularly effective when foraging schools are breaking the surface in pursuit of prey; however, anyone who has used large popping bugs knows what a miserable experience casting them can be. Unsatisfied with all established and commercially produced patterns, I set out to create one that was durable, easy to cast, had good action, and was foul-free—in short, I wanted a popping bug that overcame all the things I disliked about popping bugs. What I arrived at is similar to Gallasch's Skipping Bug (refer to Kreh's *Salt Water Fly Patterns*), but with alterations in composition and structure that improve the bug's overall performance significantly.

The body is made from lobster-pot-buoy foam, which is lighter than cork, balsa, or the denser closed-cell foams. Its resiliency allows it to stand up respectably even to bluefish. The hook is attached with hot-melt glue, which creates a hook-body bond superior to that attainable with epoxy or any of the cyanoacrylates. For a hook I prefer a nickel-plated spinnerbait trailer. It's about a third lighter than the extra-long-shanked stainless-steel hook used in most commercially made poppers. The trailer hook sacrifices nothing in gap, hooks well, and the shorter shank deprives the fish of the leverage it could use to work the hook loose. Also, carbon steel sharpens to a better point than does stainless. The tail is fastened directly into the body with hot glue, and its position is such that it rarely fouls. Most skipping bugs, I've found, don't skip very well; hence, the face of this bug is cut to a sharper angle. This not only allows for a wider range of action, but it also cuts wind resistance, making the bug easier to cast.

Hook: Wright & McGill 261 or equivalent; to 2/0.

Tail: 3½ inches of bucktail. Prepare the tail ahead of time by cutting a length, picking out the undesired hairs, and trimming the butts even. Dab the butts with hot glue and, with wet fingers, mold them into a point. The tail can also be made out of a number (six or more) of saddle hackles, or combinations of hackles and marabou and embellished with flash material.

Body: Lobster-pot-buoy foam, ⅜-inch diameter, 1½ inches long (for the largest flies). The foam can be cut with a plug cutter (available in hardware stores). Push a nail lengthwise through the center of the plug and spin it with a power drill, using a medium-grained sandpaper to taper one end. Remove the nail from the plug and, with a hot dubbing needle, burn a hole for the tail in the tapered end and also a shallow slot for the hook. The angled face can be cut freehand with a razor, but for consistency I suggest you build a wooden jig. The face should be angled such that the top extends ⅜ inch beyond the bottom.

To fasten the hook to the plug, squirt hot glue the length of the slot (Stanley Formula II is the strongest I've found) and press the shank into it. Holding the hook in the proper position, smooth the seam with a wet finger. The glue will set in moments. Then squirt hot glue into the hole and insert the pointed butt of the tail.

The popper is now ready to be painted. Brush the popper head with a thin coat of Liquitex acrylic gesso. (This priming coat isn't critical, but makes for a better-looking popper, and the additional weight is insignificant.) When the gesso dries, brush on a thin coat of Liquitex acrylic color. Paint on eyes, if desired.

Finally, brush the popper head with a protective coating of Flex Coat rod-wrapping finish. To prevent the Flex Coat from sagging while it cures, make sure that the eye of the hook is the lowest point of the popper, allowing any excess to drip from it. When dry, apply a second coat for increased durability.

The popper can be painted in any color or color combinations desired. My favorites for general use are all white or all yellow, or white with the front third painted red. It can also be dressed and painted to suggest the color schemes of various forage fishes.

This basic style can be used to construct a variety of poppers, sliders, divers, and floating sand eels.

BIBLIOGRAPHY

Ali, M.A. 1974. *Vision in fishes: New approaches in research*. New York and London: Plenum Press.

Bassler, Ray S., and C.E. Resser, W.L. Schmitt, and P. Bartsch. 1931. *Shelled invertebrates of the past and present*. (Smithsonian Scientific Series, Volume Ten.)

Bates, Joseph D., Jr. 1979. *Streamers and bucktails: The big fish flies*. New York: Knopf.

Bateson, P.P.G., and R.A. Hinde, editors. 1976. *Growing points in ethology*. Cambridge: Cambridge University Press.

Bigelow, Henry B., and William C. Schroeder. 1953. *Fishes of the Gulf of Maine*. Fishery Bulletin of the Fish and Wildlife Service. 74: 577 pages.

Bliss, Eugene L., editor. 1968. *Roots of behavior: Genetics, instinct, and socialization in animal behavior*. New York: Hafner Publishing Company.

Bohlke, James E., and Charles C.G. Chaplin. 1968. *Fishes of the Bahamas and adjacent tropical waters*. Wynnewood, Pennsylvania: Livingston Publishing Company.

Bone, Q., and N.B. Marshall. 1982. *Biology of fishes*. Glasgow and London: Blackie & Sons, Ltd.

Boschung, Herbert T., Jr., et al. 1983. *The Audubon Society field guide to North American fishes, whales, and dolphins*. New York: Knopf.

Brethes, J.C.F., R. Saint-Pierre, and G. Desrosiers. "Growth and sexual maturation of the American sand lance (*Ammodytes americanus*) off the north shore of the Gulf of St. Lawrence." *Journal of Northwest Atlantic Fishery Science* 12 (0) (1992): 41-8.

Brown, Frank A., Jr., editor. 1950. *Selected invertebrate types*. New York: John Wiley & Sons, Inc.

Brown, Margaret E., editor. 1957. *The physiology of fishes*. New York: Academic Press, Inc.

Burghardt, Gordon M., editor. 1985. *Foundations of comparative ethology*. New York: Van Nostrand Reinhold Company.

Butler, T.H. 1980. *Shrimps of the Pacific Coast of Canada*. Canadian Bulletin of Fisheries and Aquatic Sciences. 202: 280 pages.

Collins, M.R. 1985. *Species profiles: Life histories and environmental requirements of coastal fishes and invertebrates (south Florida)—striped mullet*. U.S. Fish and Wildlife Service Biological Report 82(11.34). U.S. Army Corps of Engineers, TR EL-82-4. 11 pages.

Cornsweet, Tom N. 1970. *Visual perception*. New York and London: Academic Press.

Cousteau, Jacques-Yves. 1973. *Octopus and squid: The soft intelligence*. Garden City, New York: Doubleday & Company, Inc.

———. 1973. *Quest for food*. New York: World Publishing.

Crowder, William. 1928. *A naturalist at the seashore*. New York and London: The Century Company.

Curio, Eberhard. 1976. *The ethology of predation*. Berlin, Heidelberg, New York: Springer-Verlag.

Daiber, Franklin C. 1982. *Animals of the tidal marsh*. New York: Van Nostrand Reinhold Company.

Davey, Graham. 1989. *Ecological learning theory*. London and New York: Routledge.

Dewsbury, Donald A. 1978. *Comparative animal behavior*. New York: McGraw-Hill.

Drickamer, Lee C., and Stephen H. Vessey. 1986. *Animal behavior: Concepts, processes, and methods*. Belmont, California: Wadsworth Publishing Company.

Emmett, R.L., S.L. Stone, S.A. Hinton, and M.E. Monaco. 1991. *Distribution and abundance of fishes and invertebrates in West Coast estuaries, Volume II: Species life history summaries*, ELMR Rep No. 8. NOAA/NOS, Strategic Environmental Assessments Division, Rockville, Maryland. 329 pages.

Engemann, Joseph G., and Robert W. Hegner. 1981. *Invertebrate zoology*. 3d edition. New York: Macmillan Publishing Co., Inc.

Eschmeyer, William N. 1983. *A field guide to Pacific Coast fishes of North America*. Boston: Houghton Mifflin. (Peterson Field Guide Series.)

Funderburk, Steven L., et al., editors. 1991. *Habitat requirements for Chesapeake Bay living resources*. Solomans, Maryland: Chesapeake Research Consortium, Inc.

Gosner, Kenneth L. 1971. *Guide to identification of marine and estuarine invertebrates*. New York: Wiley-Interscience.

Gould, James L. 1982. *Ethology: The mechanisms and evolution of behavior*. New York: W. W. Norton & Company.

Green, James. 1961. *A biology of crustacea*. Chicago: Quadrangle Books.

Grzimek, Bernhard, editor-in-chief. 1973. *Grzimek's animal life encyclopedia*. New York: Van Nostrand Reinhold Company.

———. 1977. *Grzimek's encyclopedia of ethology*. New York: Van Nostrand Reinhold Company.

Haefner, Paul A., Jr. 1979. "Comparative review of the biology of North Atlantic caridean shrimps (Crangon), with emphasis on *C. septemspinosa*." Bulletin of the Biological Society of Washington. No. 3, pages 1-40.

Hinde, Robert A. 1970. *Animal behaviour: A synthesis of ethology and comparative psychology*. 2d edition. New York: McGraw-Hill.

Hoar, W.S., and D.J. Randall, editors. 1969. *Fish physiology*. New York and London: Academic Press.

Hoese, H. Dickson, and Richard H. Moore. 1977. *Fishes of the Gulf of Mexico: Texas, Louisiana, and adjacent waters*. College Station and London: Texas A&M University Press.

Immelmann, Klaus. 1980. *Introduction to ethology*. New York and London: Plenum Press.

Johnson, Myrtle E., and Harry J. Snook. 1927. *Seashore animals of the Pacific Coast*. New York: Macmillan.

Kamil, Alan C., and Theodore D. Sargent, editors. 1981. *Foraging behavior: Ecological, ethological, and psychological approaches*. New York and London: Garland STPM Press.

Kaplan, Eugene H. 1982. *A field guide to coral reefs of the Caribbean and Florida*. Boston: Houghton Mifflin. (Peterson Field Guide Series.)

Killam, Kristie A., Randall J. Hochberg, and Emily C. Rzemien. 1992. *Synthesis of basic life histories of Tampa Bay species*. Columbia, Maryland: Versar, Inc.

Kreh, Bernard "Lefty." *Salt water fly patterns*. Fullerton, California: Maral, Inc.

Lamb, Andrew, and Philip Edgell. 1986. *Coastal fishes of the Pacific Northwest*. Madeira Park, British Columbia: Harbour Publishing.

Leiser, Eric. 1987. *The book of fly patterns*. New York: Knopf.

———. 1989. *The complete book of fly tying*. New York: Knopf.

Leonard, J. Edson. 1950. *Flies*. New York: A.S. Barnes and Company (now published by Lyons & Burford).

Love, Robin M. 1991. *Probably more than you want to know about the fishes of the Pacific Coast*. Santa Barbara: Really Big Press.

Love, Robin M., and Gregor M. Cailliet, editors. 1979. *Readings in ichthyology*. Santa Monica: Goodyear Publishing Company, Inc.

Manning, Raymond B. 1969. *Stomatopod crustacea of the Western Atlantic*. Coral Gables, Florida: University of Miami Press.

McClane, Albert J. 1988. *The compleat McClane*. New York: E. P. Dutton.

McDowall, Robert M. 1988. *Diadromy in fishes: Migrations between freshwater and marine environments*. Portland, Oregon: Timber Press.

McFarland, David, editor. 1981. *The Oxford companion to animal behavior*. Oxford and New York: Oxford University Press.

MacGinitie, G.E., and Nettie MacGinitie. 1968. *Natural history of marine animals*. New York: McGraw-Hill.

Mitchell, Ed. 1991. "Sand eels." *Fly Fisherman* 23 (1): 38-41, 58-59.

Morse, Douglas H. 1980. *Behavioral mechanisms in ecology*. Cambridge: Harvard University Press.

Morton, T. 1989. *Species profiles: Life histories and environmental requirements of coastal fishes and invertebrates (mid-Atlantic)—bay anchovy*. U.S. Fish and Wildlife Service Biological Report 82(11.97). 13 pages.

Nelson, D.M., E.A. Irlandi, L.R. Settle, M.E. Monaco, and L.C. Coston-Clements. 1991. *Distribution and abundance of fishes and invertebrates in southeast estuaries*. ELMR Rept. No. 9. NOAA/NOS Strategic Environmental Assessments Division, Rockville, Maryland. 177 pages.

Nelson, Joseph S. 1984. *Fishes of the world*. New York: John Wiley & Sons, Inc.

Ohguchi, Osamu. 1981. *Prey density and selection against oddity by three-spined sticklebacks*. Berlin and Hamburg: Verlag Paul Parey.

Pattilli, M.E., T.E. Czapla, D.M. Nelson, and M.E. Monaco. In preparation. *Distribution and abundance of fishes and invertebrates in Gulf of Mexico estuaries, Vol. II: Species life history summaries*. NOAA/NOS Strategic Environment Assessments Division, Silver Spring, Maryland.

Pettibone, Marian H. 1963. *Marine polychaete worms of the New England region*, Bull. U.S. Natn. Mus. 227 (1): 356 pages.

Pitcher, Tony J., editor. 1986. *The behavior of teleost fishes*. Baltimore: The Johns Hopkins University Press.

Pratt, Henry S. 1935. *A manual of the common invertebrate animals exclusive of insects*. Philadelphia: P. Blakiston's Son & Co.

Radakov, D.V. 1973. *Schooling in the ecology of fish*. New York: Halsted Press.

Ricketts, Edward F., Jack Calvin, and Joel W. Hedgpeth. 1985. *Between Pacific tides*. 5th edition revised by David W. Phillips. Stanford, California: Stanford University Press.

Robinette, H. 1983. *Species profiles: Life histories and environmental requirements of coastal fishes and invertebrates (Gulf of Mexico)—bay anchovy and striped anchovy.* U.S. Fish and Wildlife Service, Division of Biological Services, FWS/OBS-82/11.14. U.S. Army Corps of Engineers, TR EL-82-4. 15 pages.

Robins, C. Richard. 1986. *A field guide to Atlantic Coast fishes of North America.* Boston: Houghton Mifflin (Peterson Field Guide Series).

Roper, Clyde F.E., and Richard E. Young. 1975. *Vertical distribution of pelagic cephalopods.* Smithsonian Contributions to Zoology, Number 209.

Russel-Hunter, W.D. 1979. *A life of invertebrates.* New York: Macmillan.

Scott, W.B. and M.G. Scott. 1988. *Atlantic fishes of Canada.* Canadian Bulletin of Fisheries and Aquatic Sciences. 219: 713 pages.

Sosin, Mark, and John Clark. 1973. *Through the fish's eye.* New York: Harper & Row.

Stewart, Richard B. 1989. *Bass flies.* Intervale, New Hampshire: Northland Press.

Stratham, Megumi F. 1987. *Reproduction and development of marine invertebrates of the northern Pacific Coast.* Seattle: University of Washington Press.

Sweeney, Michael J., et al. 1992. *"Larval" and juvenile cephalopods: A manual for their identification.* Smithsonian Contributions to Zoology, Number 513.

Tabory, Lou. 1992. *Inshore fly fishing.* New York: Lyons & Burford.

Thorpe, W.H., and O.L. Zangwill, editors. 1961. *Current problems in animal behaviour.* Cambridge: Cambridge University Press.

Tinbergen, Nikolaas. 1965. *Animal behavior.* New York: Time, Inc.

———. 1951. *The study of instinct.* Oxford: Clarendon Press.

Voss, Gilbert L., and Robert F. Sisson. 1967. "Squids: Jet-powered torpedoes of the deep." *National Geographic* 131 (3): 386-411.

Wentink, Frank. 1992. *Saltwater fly tying.* New York: Lyons & Burford.

Williams, Austin B. 1984. *Shrimps, lobsters, and crabs of the Atlantic Coast of the eastern United States, Maine to Florida.* Washington, D.C.; Smithsonian Institution Press.

Wootton, R.J. 1976. *The biology of the sticklebacks.* New York: Academic Press.

Wulff, Lee. 1980. *Lee Wulff on flies.* Harrisburg, Pennsylvania: Stackpole Books.

Zeiller, Warren. 1974. *Tropical marine invertebrates of southern Florida and the Bahama Islands.* New York: John Wiley & Sons.

INDEX